Despair to Deliverance

A True Story of Triumph Over Severe
Mental Illness

Sharon DeVinney, Ph.D.
Robin Personette

ISBN: 1537687727
ISBN 13: 9781537687728
Library of Congress Control Number: 2016916041
CreateSpace Independent Publishing Platform
North Charleston, South Carolina

This book is dedicated to Jim and Charlene Personette

Introduction

I SPENT THE first decade of my career as a psychologist doing full-time clinical work at a large community mental health center. I was an outpatient psychotherapist working primarily with adults, couples and families. Being a therapist is very rewarding but also very stressful. Spending hour after hour, day after day, immersed in the pain of others is not an easy job.

In early 2002 one of my long-term clients, Robin, became intractably depressed. In this book Robin and I detail the events surrounding what she calls her "meltdown," its aftermath and her recovery. It is quite unusual for a psychologist to collaborate on a book with a former therapy client, and warrants a brief discussion about therapeutic "boundaries."

Without clear, appropriate boundaries defining the therapy relationship, clients are left confused about what to expect and are vulnerable to therapists knowingly or unknowingly taking advantage of them or making things worse for them. Clients should be able to count on sessions being on time and lasting a certain length of time, having the focus of the sessions be on their issues, and the therapist always keeping their best interests and well-being as the top priority.

Therapy should generally take place in an office. Phone contact between sessions should be limited or at least well defined.

Therapists should not be in a role with their clients other than that of therapist. All of these guidelines provide a predictable framework that creates a sense of safety for clients and a way for therapists to maintain their objectivity to the best of their ability.

I was very rigid about therapeutic boundaries until the experience with Robin helped me understand that, while boundaries are crucial, it is equally important to know when those boundaries need to be extended for the sake of the client. My hope is that reading this story will help both therapists and therapy clients understand and get clearer about boundary issues. This is an important topic that does not get discussed nearly enough by mental health professionals, with each other or with their clients. We therapists don't ever want to be judged negatively by our peers. And, we don't do nearly enough processing with our clients about the impact of the therapy relationship on them.

Boundary issues following the ending of therapy represents a whole other issue that is rarely discussed. The events that led Robin and I to feel okay about writing a book together were unimaginable at the time when we were working together in therapy. It is an amazing story which can only be told from the perspective that it seemed meant to happen.

For readers who are unfamiliar with the whole process of psychotherapy, there are a few things to know while reading this book. Most people with severe mental illness require both medication and psychotherapy in order to heal and maintain stability. Psychologists, social workers or mental health counselors perform the psychotherapy, while psychiatrists (who have medical degrees) typically prescribe the medication. It is ideal if treatment providers communicate and collaborate with each other in order to coordinate their interventions, although too often this does not happen.

The field of mental health treatment is not an exact science. There are no definitive tests that tell what someone's exact mental illness is, or what medication or therapy interventions he or she needs. The process of finding the right medications, and often the right psychotherapy techniques, can be a lengthy process of trial and error if a person's symptoms are complex. This was certainly the case for Robin.

This book is likely to be helpful for anyone who has experienced the stigma of mental illness or has struggled with finding an identity that is not impacted by that stigma. This book will be helpful for family members of people with mental illness to gain a better understanding of what their loved one may be experiencing. For anyone who has been in psychotherapy and wondered what their therapist experiences when things get rough, this memoir will offer perspective about how one therapist, at least, was impacted. And, for mental health professionals or people considering entering the field, this book offers a glimpse into the private world of psychotherapy that is rarely discussed in detail. Our hope is that all readers can gain a better perspective on mental illness and its impacts, and on the process of treatment. The ultimate goal in writing this book, for both Robin and I, is to help people.

It must be noted that, with the exception of our names and the names of my friend Giselle and Robin's friend Christi, the names of all other people included in this book have been changed and any identifying details have been purposely changed or excluded.

Finally, it is important to say that Robin's story is ultimately a story of triumph. But along the way there was significant despair. For people who have experienced trauma or mental illness, reading this book could activate painful memories of past experiences. Our hope is that readers will pace themselves, use their coping skills and keep reading all the way to the ending. We promise, it is a happy one.

Sharon DeVinney, Ph.D., December 2015

Part One:

Despair

1
The Meltdown

THE STORY BEGINS with a phone call from Robin. She and I had been working together in therapy for almost ten years. She usually didn't call between sessions, partly because she was very aware of and careful about boundaries, but also because severe anxiety about making phone calls was one of her symptoms. If she ever called it was only to reschedule an appointment, which was a rare occurrence.

"I'm not doing well. Can I see you sometime today or tomorrow?" Robin asked. I was stunned. This was huge. She had never been this blunt about feeling bad, or this direct about asking to see me.

"What's going on?" I asked, trying to hide my surprise.

"I don't want to talk about it right now. I'll explain when I see you," she said. Her voice sounded flat, like she was depressed, which was typical for her at that time. She did not sound overly distressed.

"I'm booked today, but have an opening tomorrow at noon," I said. "Is that soon enough? Are you okay?"

"That'll be fine. I'll be okay," she replied with her voice continuing to sound flat. In retrospect I should have canceled my other clients and squeezed her in that day, knowing how significant it was for her to make this request. But, she said she would be okay. I knew her well and trusted her to be honest with me.

At that time Robin was a 36-year-old, single woman who lived alone and worked as a case manager at a mental health agency in a neighboring county. I was a busy psychologist in the prime of my career, working at a large community mental health center with a full caseload of adult therapy clients. When I walked toward the waiting room at noon the day after her unusual phone call, I knew Robin would be there. She was always on time for her appointments. Always.

When I saw her I immediately knew something was very wrong. Robin was sitting with her head in her hands, looking exhausted. After she got into my office and started talking, I immediately noticed her speech was slurred. She looked very anxious with her leg vigorously bouncing, a sign of her significant anxiety I had seen many times before. I asked what had happened that led to her call the previous day.

"I went to work Monday morning and got a voice mail from my boss," she said. "She had left it on Friday afternoon. She was saying what a good job I do and how valuable a team member I am, and how important my contributions are. It made me start crying and I couldn't stop." Robin said she told a co-worker she wasn't feeling well and then just went home.

Robin had been depressed for the previous year. I knew she had not been sleeping well, and I knew she had been having suicidal thoughts. Her psychiatrist and I had been trying different medication options to get her significant depression under control, without much success. It had been frustrating for all of us, since medication is usually an effective form of treatment for depression, and Robin had always responded well to antidepressant medications in the past.

I knew Robin had been struggling at work, but her boss' voice mail confirmed my belief that she had been faking it well. It did not surprise me that she had been able to hide her depression and do well at her job, as she had developed this ability after years of practice. The voice mail from her boss, however, apparently was the last straw for her already fragile defenses. Being so highly complemented by a person she respected, when she was feeling so bad and just trying to get through each day, touched her and overwhelmed her to the point of tears. For Robin, crying in front of other people was humiliating.

"So what did you do next?" I asked. "What have you been doing since Monday? What about yesterday?"

"I went home on Monday and started drinking." Robin reluctantly said. She did not usually drink at all, but when her depression got worse she would drink to numb herself. It had been a frequent pattern for her in the past, but she had made significant progress in treatment and had not drank for years. She went on to say, "I've been thinking more about suicide. I've been researching methods. I have Tylenol, but I don't want to take too little and ruin my liver, or go into a coma and just make things worse. I went to Barnes and Noble to try to find a book that would tell me how much I need to take."

I was astonished to hear this. In all the years I had known her, Robin had never talked so seriously about killing herself. She had talked about suicide attempts in high school and college, prior to starting therapy. But this was completely out of character for the Robin I had come to know. I knew something was very, very wrong. Thankfully, she said she was not able to find any resources that would definitively tell her the amount of Tylenol that would be lethal. I took a deep breath to relax myself, and continued asking questions.

"Why does your speech sound slurred, Robin?" I tentatively asked. I was not prepared to hear her answer.

"I guess I've been taking too much medication along with the alcohol. This morning, I went to Eddie's grave." Eddie was her older brother who had died of cancer when he was four years old. Robin and her twin brother had been younger, so she did not remember Eddie. But he had been a significant topic of discussion in her family, and she frequently connected his memory to her suicidal thoughts. I was distressed already, but her report of visiting Eddie's grave that morning was a particularly bad sign in terms of her level of suicidal risk.

It did not take long for me to determine that Robin needed to be in the hospital. She had never been hospitalized before, and would have never previously considered it an option. She had been working in the mental health field for years and had always been horrified to imagine herself being on the other side of the treatment relationship any more than she already was. On this day, however, when I suggested the hospital she did not argue at all.

I had hospitalized many clients over the years and they often asked lots of questions before they agreed to go. They usually wanted to go home and pack clothes and personal items, or talk to someone else about doing so. Robin was so depressed and so unable to think clearly, she did not do any of these things. She agreed to follow me over to the agency's inpatient unit which, thankfully, was attached to the outpatient building where we were.

Before we made the trip over to the hospital, I asked if she had any concerns about being there. She said, "I don't want my parents or my brother to know." This was not surprising to me as I was aware of Robin's pattern of hiding the extent of her symptoms from everyone, including her family. But I also knew her family was very supportive and she would benefit from having them know. I tried to convince her, but she was persistent. "No," she said emphatically. "I won't go if they have to know." I was not about to argue with her, figuring I could try to change her mind later. At that point I just needed her to be safe.

Robin and I were waiting together in the waiting room of the hospital for her insurance company to approve the admission. I will never forget the big fish tank sitting next to us...I guess it was there to help people feel more calm. But, there was not a fish tank in the world that could make either of us feel calm at that point. I was worried about what I had just heard from a person I had known for so long. I was concerned that she did not want her family to know what was happening. It was there, with us both looking at the fish, where Robin asked me a simple question that stunned me.

"Are you older than I am?" she questioned sheepishly. I was shocked. With that one question I became acutely aware of the degree to which I had kept myself detached from Robin for almost ten years.

In typical therapist fashion, I answered her question with a question. "Why do you ask?"

"Because I've always wondered, but never wanted to ask," she replied. I don't know if it was the intensity of the moment, or her impulse control being impaired that made her finally ask what she had apparently most wanted to know.

"Yes, I am four years older than you," I answered.

"I'm glad. I didn't like the idea that you would be younger than me," she said with no emotion in her voice.

Self-disclosure is a topic of some debate among therapists. Those who follow more of a psychoanalytic or psychodynamic model tend to shy away from all self-disclosure. They believe therapists should be a "blank slate," not revealing anything personal, keeping offices free of family pictures, etc. The theory is that if a client has feelings about us, being a blank slate means those feelings must be "projected" onto us and are actually feelings about people from the client's past. I disagree with this theory, as do many other therapists these days.

My approach to self-disclosure was to limit it to only those times when it was beneficial to the client. I did not usually talk about myself during sessions. I did so only if it was completely relevant to what we were discussing and was relatively benign. I'd answer questions my clients asked about me as long as they were not inappropriate or too personal. Clients would often ask about my age, marital status, or whether I had children. I thought it was important for them to know a little about who I was, and I very willingly answered these questions...if they asked.

The problem for Robin, as I realized all at once sitting in the waiting room of the hospital in January 2003, was that she had never felt comfortable asking me anything. My policy about only answering questions when asked and her policy about never asking, had led to the situation in which, after ten years Robin "had always wanted to know" how old I was. I certainly understood that many clients would not usually ask their therapist's age. But, Robin and I had known each other for a decade. I had just assumed, for years, she was completely comfortable. It surprised me to suddenly realize she had never asked anything about me. What did that say about how distant I had been? The reality of this and everything she must have wondered through the years without asking, as I said, stunned me. But, I had to stay focused in the moment. I needed to make sure she got to our inpatient unit safely.

Early the next day I received a phone call from Robin's psychiatrist, Dr. Greene. He had been treating Robin on an outpatient basis for about seven years. Although we had a good working relationship, it was uncommon for him to call me directly about a client.

"It's been a long time since I've seen someone this depressed," he said. "I've talked to Robin about ECTs but she won't agree to them without talking to you first. Can you go and talk to her?" Coming from an experienced psychiatrist who treated hundreds of people, I knew what a significant statement this was. I also knew Dr. Greene did not rush to recommend electroconvulsive therapy ("shock treatments"), and in fact, used it very sparingly. Therefore, I knew how momentous it was that he was ready to have Robin undergo a course of ECT immediately.

Most people are scared by the idea of ECT. Of course, the images from the well-known movie *One Flew Over the Cuckoo's Nest* come to mind for many people. But, the latest techniques for performing ECT treatments, with anesthesia and medications to soften the muscle contractions caused by the seizure that is produced, are completely different from the portrayal in that movie. Patients are asleep during the procedure, and generally have few side effects afterward.

ECTs do tend to cause some memory loss for the time period before and during the treatments. Otherwise, they are a safe and very effective way to alleviate depression, especially when the symptoms are severe and medications have not worked. I went to see Robin, talked with her about all of this, and convinced her to give ECTs a try. She was desperate to feel better and ready to try anything.

Later that day I received a panicked phone call. "I can't do it," Robin cried. "I'm not ready to have ECTs." She explained that Dr. Greene had set her up with his colleague who would be performing the treatments, for a consultation about whether she would be an appropriate candidate. This person had asked many detailed questions about her childhood sexual abuse history, which had triggered painful memories and emotions for her. He planned to start the treatments the next morning. "He told me I can't take any medication for anxiety or sleep tonight," Robin anxiously explained to me. "I can't do this!"

I calmed her down, and assured her I would call Dr. Greene and let him know she needed some time to prepare herself to start the ECTs. When I got ahold of him, I let Dr. Greene know about Robin's distress. "It doesn't matter," he said. "I just got off the phone after talking to her insurance company. They won't approve the ECTs. Tell Robin she can take her meds tonight and we'll talk tomorrow about the next step."

Dr. Greene and I talked briefly about the insensitivity of his colleague who had done the consultation, and we commiserated about the complete short-sightedness of her managed care insurance company in not approving the ECTs. We hung up, both feeling frustrated. I called Robin and reassured her she did not need to start the ECTs the next day (Friday) and I would visit her before leaving for the weekend.

• • •

As a therapist to adult outpatients, often with significant and chronic symptoms, I did not make it a practice to visit clients in the hospital. I always wanted them to know I was not the only person who could help them. I tried very hard not to foster too much dependence within the therapy relationship, especially with people who I had treated for a long time. But Robin's hospitalization in 2003 felt very different. Dr. Greene calling and asking me to go talk to her about ECTs set a different precedent with Robin than usual. After the confusion about the ECTs, I felt I needed to check in with her before the weekend.

I found Robin sitting on her bed in her room of the inpatient unit. She was wearing sweat pants and a sweatshirt, and was fidgeting with the "sculpie" she had been bringing with her to our therapy sessions. It was a multi-colored material similar to Silly Putty, which she was able to play with and keep her hands busy during times when she felt especially anxious.

Robin was very angry, which was unusual for her. "They're trying to make me go to groups. I don't want to," she said. Because she had significant social anxiety and had run many therapy groups during the course of her career, she felt both terrified about being open with other people and embarrassed to find herself on the other side of the group therapy process. As we were talking she suddenly asked another question, out of the blue, that rocked me to the core.

"So, are you going to ditch me now?" She asked anxiously.

"Of course not! What would make you think that?" I asked, even more baffled and shocked than I had been two days earlier when she asked me about my age.

"I thought you told me a long time ago that if I was too suicidal you wouldn't work with me anymore," she said. I was unable to hide my surprise and confusion, and spent some time reassuring her that I had absolutely no intention of "ditching" her. I was unable to figure out what led her to that mistaken belief. She said she couldn't remember.

I tried to reason with Robin about the therapy groups, suggesting she go and fake it. I hoped she might actually get something out of being open with people. It didn't work...she remained adamant about her refusal to attend group therapy or any activities with other clients. I decided not to push it. At that point, I was just happy she was safe while Dr. Greene and I tried to figure out what to do to help.

I went home and thought a lot about Robin that weekend. Why she thought I would stop working with her if she was "too suicidal," whatever that meant, was a mystery to me. By that point in my career I was very used to working with suicidal clients. There was no question in my mind that I would keep visiting Robin in the hospital. From the very beginning of that hospital stay I sensed that my standard concern about fostering too much dependence was less of an issue than Robin feeling comfortable being open with someone. And, I knew it needed to be me. She had always been more open with me than anyone else in her life. What she had to say would have completely freaked out her family and friends.

The following Monday we had another discussion that disturbed me even further than our conversations from the previous week. I found Robin sitting on her bed in the sterile room of the inpatient unit. The rooms had most of the comforts of home absent, in order to make sure people could not access any items that might be used to hurt themselves or others. I stood while I talked to her, as I did not want to be too informal and sit on her bed, and there were no extra chairs in the room. Too many chairs, I knew, had been thrown at people in anger during the course of inpatient stays.

"I've always just wanted you to like and respect me," Robin explained when I asked why she had not let me know how suicidal she had been feeling. "I didn't want you to think I was crazy."

"So, what made you think I would ditch you if you were too suicidal?" I asked.

"I don't remember. It was a long time ago. You said something that made me believe that."

And then, out of nowhere, Robin blurted out the words, "I made a suicide attempt a few years ago that I never told you about." I was again surprised, but had heard many people talk about suicide attempts. I wanted her to feel comfortable talking to me about what had happened so I remained calm. She kept playing with her "scul-pie" and would not make eye contact. I sat down on the bed across from her, letting her know I was prepared to listen. But I was not even remotely prepared for what I was about to hear.

"It was about the time I left my job when that kid hit me in the face," Robin said. I remembered the approximate time frame. She had been working at a residential treatment facility for children and adolescents and it had been getting more and more stressful for several months. She had been having difficulty managing the stress and was more depressed. I remembered her feeling pressure to quit her job, and we had been meeting more frequently in therapy than usual during that time. But I did not know she had been acutely suicidal. I was gradually realizing how much she had been keeping from me over the years.

"So tell me about the suicide attempt," I said, trying to prepare myself to hear anything.

"I was still living in that house with my roommates...the one that had a garage," Robin explained. "I waited until everyone left for work, and went into the garage and ran a hose from the tailpipe to the driver's window. I turned on my Jeep and let it run." I was blown away! People did not often describe suicide attempts to me that were this lethal. But I knew Robin well enough to know she would have obsessively thought it out very thoroughly, and she would have chosen a plan relatively certain to succeed. I was trying to process what she was telling me. I had not known any of this at the time. She reminded me it had been almost four years earlier.

My brain was reeling as I was trying to imagine how awful it must have been for Robin to feel so desperate, so hopeless and so unable to share this with anyone. Part of me was already wondering what else she had never felt comfortable telling me. The rest of my brain stayed focused in the present. I asked her what stopped her from killing herself that day.

"Well," Robin explained, appearing slightly embarrassed, "it was taking longer than I thought it would. I think I sat there for about forty-five minutes. I didn't know why it was taking so long. Finally, I looked at my watch and realized that if I didn't get going I was going to be late for work. I put everything away, and I went to work. I had a bad headache for the rest of the day."

Wow! Inside, I was dumbfounded. Robin had revealed over the years that she had a number of obsessive-compulsive habits. But, at that time I was just trying to process what she was telling me. One of these obsessive-compulsive habits ended up saving her life that day...her compulsive need to be on time. Thank God! She was apparently not able to recognize that if she killed herself it wouldn't matter if she was on time for work. I was very grateful as I realized, all at once, that her OCD symptoms were more severe than I had ever realized and that her inability to be open with me had almost killed her.

I had always received good feedback about my ability as a therapist from clients, colleagues and supervisors. I generally felt good about myself in terms of my career and my ability to help people. But I found myself in a complete crisis along with Robin during that hospital stay. I found myself thinking, "How could I have been so oblivious? Why had I not been able to recognize that Robin was still dealing with so many more symptoms and painful emotions than she was saying?" I had realized early on in our work together that there were things she wasn't comfortable telling me, but I had thought this was no longer an issue.

I found myself doing my own obsessing. Why didn't it occur to me that she might want to know something about me but was afraid to ask? Why didn't I make sure to talk about our relationship, and make sure she was comfortable with it and being honest?

As I grasped the reality of the number of years we had worked together and everything she must have felt unable to say to me, I began to comprehend how completely alone Robin must have felt and how much that must have contributed to her symptoms of depression through the years. I felt like I had let her down.

Robin's "meltdown" led to a three-week hospitalization. I continued to be involved in her treatment even though this was not standard protocol at the agency. Outpatient therapists usually turned the treatment over to the inpatient staff, while the psychiatrists continued to follow their patients in both arenas. Dr. Greene knew Robin would be more open with me than anyone else (including him) and he needed to know what she was really thinking in order to make appropriate treatment decisions. He not only encouraged me to keep seeing her, but we consulted each other frequently in order to make sure we were on the same page.

Robin continued to be open with me once she was reassured I would not "ditch" her. Depression causes people to think less rationally than usual and severe depression can cause people to completely lose perspective. Robin was so depressed she became someone I barely recognized. "I hate myself, I hate my life and I want to die" was her automatic declaration when I asked how she was feeling. I felt completely helpless as I continued to hear the details of what was going through her mind. She seemed to suddenly feel driven to share all her feelings and thoughts with me, like she was making up for all the years when she kept many things to herself. I felt honored that she was finally willing to really let me in, but also disturbed about what I was hearing.

Robin's Thoughts About Her Meltdown

I was depressed for about a year prior to the Meltdown, but I was able to function at a fairly high level. I was living on my own in an apartment and I worked full time at a challenging job as a child and adolescent case manager. I managed to hide my depressed mood from the people in my life and went about my business despite suffering from intermittent insomnia and suicidal thoughts. Sharon and I were talking about a lot of things that were causing stress for me, and Dr.

Greene was working hard to find the right medications to decrease my depression. It is important for people to understand that treating mental health issues with medication is a trial and error process. There is no way to know what each person's brain needs. I trusted Sharon and Dr. Greene, who had been treating me for years. I knew they were doing their best to find a combination of treatments that worked.

My life at that time mostly revolved around work. I spent much of my time there during the week, and brought paperwork home to be completed on the weekends. I was doing well at my job and enjoyed the respect of my coworkers. I performed a variety of tasks such as transporting clients to appointments, teaching parenting skills, and helping people return their houses to a livable condition in order for them to attempt to be reunited with their kids. I liked my work and felt like I was making a difference in the world, which gave me a positive sense of self. I was proud of the fact that I was doing something meaningful with my career.

Many of my social needs were met through my coworkers. Most of the members of my case management team were around my age, in the 25 to 35-year-old range. They were an intelligent, witty bunch who made work fun, despite the sometimes depressing experiences encountered in working with children from abusive, neglectful families. We were a close-knit group, as we at times had to rely on each other to have one another's backs in scary situations. We were a home-based case management team, so we often had to go into some uncomfortable environments. We carried pagers and cell phones and used each other as backup when the need arose. For instance, I had to make visits to the home of an angry father, who was known to own a gun. It was common for me to ask a coworker to accompany me to visits at this home, if I wasn't able to meet the family in a neutral location.

Working with abused and neglected children can obviously be stressful and depressing, and we supported each other through

rough times. We were still a little idealistic (or we'd have moved on already), but we had seen enough to develop the gallows sense of humor common to police, firemen, soldiers, and health care workers. We cared deeply about our clients, but used humor to cope with situations that would have otherwise led to tears at times. We would often play practical jokes in the office to lighten the mood. We had a wall that was used to post some of the more tragic and outrageous comments we heard from clients and Welfare Department caseworkers. When I decided I wanted to get a tattoo I held a contest, taking suggestions from my colleagues for the design. The prize for the best idea was a hula dancer dashboard figurine. We did stupid stuff like that to cope with the stressors we encountered.

A main outlet of support from each other was our weekly staffing meeting. It was a ninety-minute meeting held every Friday. The whole team was included along with our immediate supervisor, her boss who was the manager of the child and adolescent department, and our staff psychiatrist. It was the time for us to staff our clinical cases with the psychiatrist and get the required signatures on treatment plans. We discussed issues that came up and received feedback from each other. The gallows humor often was heard in staffing, as we talked about the various unbelievable situations that we encountered.

My Meltdown in 2003 was precipitated by a voice mail I received from my supervisor's boss, the manager of the child and adolescent department. I really liked and respected her, and her opinion was important to me. I did not expect to walk in that Monday morning to a voice mail from her, referring to the staffing meeting the previous Friday. In her message she was complimenting me and telling me what a valuable team member I was. She went on and on saying nice things about me. Because I was struggling with increased depression at the time, I was unable to contain the feelings I experienced when I heard the voice mail. I was very touched, but also unable to reconcile how bad I felt with what she was saying. In my depressed state I was not feeling very competent, let alone "valuable" to my co-workers. I started crying uncontrollably, told a co-worker I wasn't feeling well, went home, and got drunk. On Tuesday I knew I was not okay, and called Sharon to schedule an appointment for noon on Wednesday.

I slept very little that night and woke up exhausted. I started drinking as soon as I got up. I was drinking vodka and lemonade, my drink of choice, and listening to a CD of depressing music. I have always connected to my emotions through music. When I was a freshman at the University of Arizona in 1985, I made cassette tapes of songs with melancholy themes and depressing sounds. By the time of the Meltdown, I had upgraded to CDs. Some of the songs on the CD I was fixated on that day were "Torn" by Toad the Wet Sprocket, "Leave Me Alone" by New Order, "Start of the Breakdown" by Tears for Fears, and "Blasphemous Rumours" by Depeche Mode. These are some of the songs I used to connect with when I was especially depressed. Anyway, that morning I decided to visit my brother's grave, despite the fact that it was winter and very cold at the cemetery. I sat at Eddie's graveside and talked to him. The gist of it was that I wanted to die so that I could be with him.

By the time I met with Sharon for our appointment, I was in a really bad place. I was feeling hopeless despair and dissociating on and off. It's difficult to describe what dissociating feels like. It's like I'm there but not really there, like I'm watching from inside my head what is going on around me. I don't feel real. When I used to dissociate a lot, I would often self-mutilate by cutting myself with a knife. It was as if feeling pain counteracted the dissociation. I think the reason I didn't resist when Sharon suggested the hospital is because I was so zoned out. Had I been myself, I would never have gone.

I have a Bachelor's degree in psychology, and in 2003 I had worked in the mental health field for twelve years in various positions. My first job was as a houseparent in a group home for emotionally and behaviorally disturbed adolescent girls. I had also worked as a psychiatric technician in a residential treatment facility for emotionally and behaviorally disturbed adolescents, and as a group facilitator in a partial hospital program for chronically mentally ill adults. The adult patients in this program were severely mentally ill with diagnoses such as schizophrenia and bipolar disorder.

Having had all these work experiences, the idea of being a patient in a psychiatric hospital was unacceptable to me, despite knowing that I was deeply depressed and suicidal. When I got to the hospital, had I been myself, I would have been terribly anxious about the new situation and being around people I didn't know. But I wasn't myself.

In an Advanced Placement class during high school, one of the great works of world literature we read was *The Inferno*, by Dante. It's an epic poem written in the 1300's. The Inferno is the tale of Dante's journey through the nine Circles of Hell, accompanied by the Roman poet Virgil. Dante and Virgil travel down through Hell and back out again. In each level of Hell, sinners suffer according to the type and extremity of their sin. The deeper the level, the greater the suffering. Dante's writing had a huge impact on me, probably because of an ongoing sense of deserving to be punished, which always accompanied my depression. At one time I actually though about writing a modern day version of *The Inferno*, putting modern day sinners in the appropriate levels with appropriate punishments.

My life during the Meltdown year felt like something straight out of Dante's *Inferno*, right from the beginning. For instance, when Dante and Virgil reach the entrance to Hell, the gates are inscribed with the quote "Abandon all hope ye who enter here." This pretty much sums up my experience and feelings upon being admitted to the hospital. I was in utter despair and it felt like my life was over. After spending my adult life periodically thinking about and making reference to Dante's *Inferno*, I felt like I had actually entered hell. I didn't know what circle I had entered, but I was pretty sure I was there somewhere.

2
The Hospital

EACH INPATIENT ROOM in the hospital had a window overlooking a river with an alcove large enough to sit in. It was a beautiful setting, with a peaceful view. It was late January and the view was often filled with falling snow. If Robin had a roommate who was in the room I would take her to a small, sterile office off of the main hallway that was used for consultations so we could talk privately. If not, we would talk in her room. Often I would walk into the room to find Robin sitting in the window alcove, staring out the window at the river. Early in the hospital stay she rarely came out of her room. Robin remained very anxious and agitated. She said she could not sleep, and presented with "flat affect" which is a physical sign of severe depression where people do not smile or laugh and show virtually no emotional expression. She continued to play with her "sculpie" whenever we talked, as this helped her to calm herself.

During the first few days in the hospital Robin remained very angry that she was being pushed to attend groups and other hospital programming activities. Her anger, however, was mostly directed at herself. "I'm mad at myself for drinking so much last week. If I hadn't been so out of it when I came to see you, I'd never have agreed to come to the hospital," she said. "I never planned to come in that day.

I must have dissociated and just ended up in your office. I don't know why I did that when I just wanted to die."

"I don't know why either, Robin, but I'm so thankful you did. We'll figure out what you need and you'll feel better now that you are finally letting me know what's going on," I said. Even though I was very concerned about some of the things she was saying, I wanted to try to provide some sense of hope.

Dissociation means to numb oneself emotionally, sometimes to the point of being consciously unaware of what is going on in the moment. This was a defense Robin had apparently developed as a result of the trauma she experienced as a child. It is quite common for people who have been traumatized at a young age to develop this unconscious defense mechanism to protect themselves from feeling pain. Robin had dissociated frequently when she began therapy, but this had not been an issue for years. It became an issue again surrounding the severe depression she was experiencing during her "meltdown." The fact that she was dissociating on the day I hospitalized her explained why she did not argue at all about going there. It also seemed to explain her sudden lack of impulse control about saying things she would not normally say. This pattern continued.

"Adults should be able to make the decision to kill themselves. It seems like natural selection to me," Robin said several times during the beginning of her hospital stay. "The people who are weak and unable to cope get weeded out of the population that way. Killing myself just makes sense." She revealed that she had chosen the specific date when she was planning to commit suicide.

"I know my family will be upset if I kill myself. That's why I picked February 9th to do it. That's the day Eddie (her brother) died," she said. "I figure that's a good day, because my family will already be sad about Eddie and it'll make it easier for them to just grieve all at once."

What? In what Universe would this make it easier for her family? I couldn't believe how little sense she was making and how irrational she was. Obviously she was not thinking clearly enough to understand that committing suicide would devastate her family members, no matter what day she picked. I remained calm and reassuring on the outside, as therapists somehow manage to do. I don't even know how I developed that skill. I suppose it just happens automatically as we listen day after day, and hour after hour to the horrific pain people reveal. All I knew was that Robin, who was normally extremely sensitive to the feelings and needs of other people, somehow believed her family would grieve less if she killed herself on the day her brother died! Wow.

Severe depression can sometimes cause psychotic symptoms including hallucinations and delusions, in which people lose complete touch with reality. Although Robin never became psychotic, her thinking just seemed so illogical. Dr. Greene and I were grasping in terms of what to do to help her feel better. We had been collaborating closely about Robin for over a year at that point, talking about and trying different medication options in an attempt to get her intractable depression stabilized. We mutually decided to try an antipsychotic medication, partly to help her think more rationally and partly because it was something different in terms of augmenting the antidepressants she was already taking.

As I expected, Robin was upset when I suggested it. But, she understood we had been doing everything we could think of for a long time, and she was just getting worse. She reluctantly agreed to try Geodon, an antipsychotic medication.

I had never seen someone so depressed. Day after day she was verbalizing consistent suicidal thoughts. Even though she hated being in the hospital, she said she was "a danger" to herself and agreed to stay. She talked, over and over, about her fear about what her co-workers would think, her fear that her brother and sister-in-law would not trust her to babysit her young nephew anymore, and other fears related to her new status as someone who had been psychiatrically hospitalized.

Her three-week hospitalization was much longer than most inpatient stays, especially for people with "managed care" insurance companies who closely monitored whether the care being provided was "medically necessary." She obsessed about whether her insurance company would cover the cost and how much she would have to pay for the hospital bill. Our conversations revolved around me trying to help her regain perspective...the first priority was to get her feeling better, and everything else could be sorted out after that. My efforts were unsuccessful. She remained very obsessive and unable to shift her thinking but, thankfully, still willing to share her thoughts with me.

"Do you know how I could get life insurance?" she asked me one day. "I wonder if I have life insurance through my job?" She was willing to admit she had a lot of debt and was worried about her family having to deal with a "financial mess" if she killed herself. I told her what I knew about life insurance, not wanting to dismiss her concerns. Without knowing whether it was true or not, I told her I thought most life insurance policies would not pay if someone died by suicide.

Another frequent discussion topic was her cat, Epiphany, who she worried about abandoning. As I continued to learn more and more about the degree to which Robin had been isolated in her severe depression, I realized her attachment to her cat had probably been keeping her alive. "I want to find someone who will take Epiphany if something happens to me," she said. "It's the only thing that keeps me from doing it. I know everyone else will grieve and move on. But I need to know Epiphany will be okay." Everyone else will grieve and move on? Seriously?

These statements were a reflection of Robin's depression, not her personality. She was simply just not herself. Severe depression had taken over her thinking completely, and caused her to be unable to maintain any kind of realistic perspective. I continued, day after day, to try to integrate the reality of how ill she was and how completely hopeless she felt.

• • •

The inpatient unit consisted of ten rooms with two beds per room, in a long hallway with a nurses' station in the middle of the unit. The nurses' station was a room enclosed in shatterproof glass which extended from the top of the encircling counter to the ceiling, serving to protect the staff from people who might become violent. A half door (which could quickly be closed in a dangerous situation) allowed staff to enter the hallway and clients to talk to the staff without the separation of the glass.

Shatterproof glass was a common phenomenon among inpatient units built several decades ago, but it perpetuated the stigma felt by people with mental illness. The glass contributed to a dynamic of "us" and "them" between clients and staff. As an outpatient therapist I did not often spend time in the inpatient units, but during my visits with Robin it did not take long for me to grasp the sense of separation. Staff members were usually behind the glass talking about the clients rather than on the unit interacting with them. I believe most psychiatric hospitals built more recently have removed the glass in all but the units that house the most dangerous patients, in an effort to remove this dynamic.

As her hospital stay entered its second week, Robin continued to be very depressed, suicidal, irritable, anxious and obsessive. Her interaction with other clients and staff members was minimal and superficial. She was alone and isolated other than sessions with me and Dr. Greene or short visits during very sporadic visiting hours from two trusted friends.

Robin finally reached out to her twin brother. "I called Bob," she told me one day. "He was supportive, but he was asking so many questions. It was overwhelming. I didn't know what to say." I had met Bob once when Robin had first started treatment years earlier. She had always described their relationship as close, and I was relieved to hear she had finally told him what was happening. I immediately offered, with her permission, to call him and answer his questions to the best of my ability. It had only been a week since Robin's meltdown, but part of me was already feeling isolated and overwhelmed. As the only person she trusted within her world of crushing despair, I was very ready for her to let another person in.

When we talked, I did my best to explain to a surprised and concerned Bob, why Robin was doing so poorly. "I think her job has a lot to do with it," Bob replied. "I've always thought it's too stressful for her to be working with all those people who have so many problems." I didn't disagree with him, but I tried to help him understand that her choice of careers was not the most immediate problem.

"Robin has two separate issues that interact with each other. She's very depressed, which causes her to feel hopeless and bad about herself. And, she has severe obsessive-compulsive symptoms which cause her thoughts to get very stuck. Right now she's so depressed, her thinking is stuck on killing herself. I've never seen her like this. We're adjusting her medications to try to decrease her depression."

"We're twins," Bob said. "We had mostly the same experiences growing up. I've never been able to understand why Robin has so much more difficulty coping with things than I do."

I tried to explain my belief that Robin's obsessive-compulsive symptoms, in addition to a biological tendency toward depression, were a big part of the reason she had such trouble at times. But, on some level I knew Bob didn't really need all the explanations. He was just trying to integrate the same reality I was...that Robin was not okay. She was a smart, funny, competent and kind person who many people deeply loved. But, she wanted to die. I did not know how to help Bob understand this reality. I knew it was unfathomable to him. He just wanted Robin to be okay. After all my experience with many other people who had been depressed, it was also unfathomable to me that Robin had gotten to such a bad place, seemingly so quickly.

Bob and I talked about Robin's refusal to tell her parents where she was. He said he had promised her he would honor this. He told me he understood. I was glad he did, because fully understanding this was hard for me under the circumstances. After the startling disclosures I had heard from Robin in the previous few days, I was just beginning to understand the degree to which she had never felt comfortable telling anyone about her internal torture. Her incredible ability to mask her symptoms and present herself to the world as "normal" had extended to her family. Intellectually I understood that being vulnerable in any way caused anxiety for Robin. But I was also beginning to understand that her complete sense of aloneness had to be contributing to her depression. I already knew she needed to let the people who loved her also support her, if she was going to get better and stay alive.

It took almost two weeks for Robin to finally feel compelled to let her parents know where she was. I walked onto the unit one day and found her pacing back and forth in the hall, wringing her hands and looking very distressed.

"My friend can't take care of Epiphany any longer," Robin anxiously announced. "The only other person I can ask is my mom. Bob is too busy. I have to call my mom to let her know where I am." I was relieved she was finally ready to talk to her parents, but also aware of how nervous this made her feel. I offered to sit with her while she made the call. We went to the small office off of the main hallway so she could have privacy.

"Hi, Mom. I have something big to tell you," Robin said, her voice cracking with the tension. "I'm so sorry. I haven't been honest with you and Dad about what's going on, but I'm in the hospital. Sharon and Dr. Greene are trying to get my medication adjusted. I'm sure it will be okay, but I need you to take care of Epiphany for me while I'm here."

I was not able to hear Robin's mother's reaction on the phone. I had never met her mom. I had always heard from Robin that her mom was supportive. But Robin never wanted her mom to know how much she struggled. She cried as she painfully revealed that she had been dishonest about being in the hospital. "I didn't want to worry you," she said to her mom. "I'm so sorry." She repeated this over and over during the conversation. "I didn't want to worry you. I'm so sorry. I'm so sorry." When she hung up she was still tearful, but obviously relieved. "That went better than I expected," she said.

Even after this conversation, Robin did not initially want her parents to visit. She wanted to protect them from the reality of where she was. But she eventually allowed her mother to bring clothes and other items, and her parents started to visit regularly. I was extremely relieved to have her family involved, even though Robin was rallying all of her energy during their phone calls and visits and still presenting herself as if she was much better than she really was.

What was becoming apparent as I was beginning to integrate all the new information Robin was sharing, was that her life-long pattern of hiding her severe symptoms was not something she had done consciously or purposely. I was beginning to understand her in a whole new way. It made her extremely anxious to be open with people...with anyone. Whether those people cared about her or were trustworthy was irrelevant. I finally got it. Robin's incredible ability to mask her symptoms was all about avoiding anxiety! Avoiding anxiety was a driving force in her life. I knew that. But, in January 2003 I finally, finally understood that one of the things that made Robin most anxious, was being open about herself and the reality of her mental illness.

Two weeks into what would become almost a year-long crisis, I was already beginning to think about drastic changes I needed to make in my approach to her treatment. I needed to help Robin get past the anxiety she felt about being open with people, and she needed to stop feeling so completely alone!

It was partly Bob's suggestion and partly me encouraging it, but Robin reluctantly agreed to a family session with her brother and parents so we could explain what was going on. As expected, she had enormous anxiety leading up to this session. When the session finally happened, she had gotten herself so worked up that she actually dissociated through most of it.

Robin's parents could not have been more caring, understanding and kind to her. I was thrilled to meet them, and felt honored and touched to witness them genuinely loving and supporting her. We talked about how they could be helpful. We talked about how hard it was for Robin to be open with them, and why. I assured them I was going to keep doing whatever I could to help. Afterward, I was relieved to have her family involved. But Robin was not relieved.

"I feel more depressed and suicidal," Robin said the day after the meeting. She had given up her familiar, unconscious defense of keeping everything inside. It made her feel vulnerable on a level way beyond her comfort zone to be open with her family. She was worried about their reactions and the extent to which they would view her differently after knowing some of the truth about her symptoms.

Overall, Robin was still not improving. She remained obsessed about the insurance coverage for her hospital stay. Her insurance company was monitoring things closely and only approving a few days at a time. They required detailed updates about what was happening in treatment so they could decide whether they would continue to cover the costs. Finally, they threatened to stop covering treatment unless Robin began to attend group therapy.

Reluctantly, she complied. She began to feel a bit better, as the groups distracted her somewhat from her depressed thinking. Things worsened for her, though, in terms of the dynamics with the staff on the unit. While they were used to seeing people ruminate in hopelessness and depressed thinking, they did not understand the impact of Robin's severe obsessive-compulsive symptoms.

• • •

Because the names are similar people often confuse OCD and OCPD, but they are two different things. Robin actually had both. Obsessive-compulsive disorder (OCD) is a biological illness that causes people to experience intrusive, unwanted, anxiety-provoking thoughts and often to develop compulsive rituals to decrease the anxiety caused by those intrusive thoughts. People who experience these symptoms are usually completely aware they are irrational, but their significant anxiety compels them to do what they know will help them feel better.

An obsessive-compulsive personality pattern is a tendency toward perfectionism, rigidity, preoccupation with details and anxiety about change or uncertainty. A mild version of this pattern can be very adaptive and can lead to high levels of conscientiousness and achievement at school or work. The pattern becomes a problem when it is severe enough to get in the way of relationships or impairs functioning, which then qualifies the person for an Obsessive-Compulsive Personality Disorder (OCPD) diagnosis. I have obsessive-compulsive personality traits which tend to be genetic and have run in my family for generations. Whether these traits in me are severe enough to interfere with my relationships and thus impair my functioning, probably depends on whom within my circle of friends and family is asked. As a high-achieving person, I have always referred to my obsessive-compulsiveness as "functional."

What had become apparent over the years as I got to know Robin was that she had specific symptoms of both OCD and OCPD. She had a double dose of anxiety and rigidity in her thinking. When she was biologically depressed her brain would automatically get stuck in self-destructive thinking and she would have extreme difficulty shifting out of those thoughts. Obsessing about suicide, without being able to stop thinking about it, was a frequent occurrence for Robin during periods of depression.

I was introduced to the severity and dangerousness of Robin's obsessive-compulsive symptoms relatively early in our work together. It was 1995 and I was a somewhat inexperienced psychologist, having earned my Ph.D. three years earlier. Robin had been in therapy for two and a half years and had made significant progress in terms of resolving trauma issues. But she was living with her parents after having quit a job impulsively due to overwhelming stress. She had found a new job, but was trying to recover financially from a period of unemployment by living with her parents and saving money.

Robin was depressed about living with her parents, and was pushing herself to find an apartment and move out. She admitted she was having some suicidal thoughts but always assured me she did not want to kill herself. Discussions about "passive" suicidal thoughts (no plan or intention of acting on them) are a common occurrence in therapy. Imagine my surprise one day, though, when Robin came into my office and revealed that she had "almost done it."

"I had set a deadline of December 1st to move out of my parents' house," she reluctantly told me. "I figured that would motivate me." I knew taking the steps to find an apartment was overwhelming to Robin, especially in her depressed state. But she was putting a lot of pressure on herself because having to live with her parents, after previously living on her own, caused her to feel inadequate. She worried a lot about what other people thought about her and how living with her parents would worsen their opinions.

"I told myself if I didn't meet my deadline I would have to kill myself," Robin revealed. "I didn't want to, but as the deadline got closer I got more and more anxious."

"So what did you do?" I asked, starting to get anxious myself as I was trying to process what she was telling me. I couldn't believe she had not told me she was so seriously suicidal!

"I was getting so freaked out I finally decided on the day of the deadline that it would be okay to extend it," Robin said. "Then I felt guilty about not telling you."

I remember being stunned by this revelation at the time. Robin had struggled with self-destructive thinking and behavior in the midst of depression for years. Medication adjustments always seemed to return her to "baseline" where self-destructive thinking and behavior was not as much of an issue. Robin and I had developed a good therapeutic relationship and she frequently referred to me as her "accountability." If she was ever self-destructive she felt compelled to tell me. As her therapist I had learned to count on this honesty and to feel relieved that this was one of her self-imposed rules. I learned over the years that any hint of increased self-destructive behavior was a signal that her depression required a medication adjustment. It was clearly a biological pattern.

When Robin told me in December 1995, though, that she had gone through the suicidal crisis surrounding her self-imposed deadline without anyone else knowing about it, I was very surprised and scared. I was young and inexperienced and didn't really know what to make of this. I suddenly didn't know if I could trust her to tell me the truth about her suicidal thoughts. It shook me and made me very nervous. The worst fear of every outpatient therapist is that one of their clients, who they are entrusted to help, will kill themselves. Unlike in 2003, I wasn't focusing back then on how alone Robin must have felt. I was too busy thinking about myself, my fear, and how it would affect me if she committed suicide.

At that time there was a semi-retired psychiatrist, Dr. Rios, whose office was two doors down from mine. He was extremely helpful to me as a young, inexperienced psychologist. I was very interested in learning about medications and he enjoyed teaching me about them. When Robin entered treatment I had referred her to see him because of the severity of her symptoms. They had developed a good working relationship, although it always made her anxious to talk to him. After Robin told me about feeling compelled to kill herself even though she didn't want to, I immediately scheduled her to see Dr. Rios. I needed help. I didn't understand. After meeting with her, Dr. Rios said something to me that I never forgot.

"Robin is at extremely high risk for suicide at some point," he said. I think he probably tried to explain why he said this, but I didn't really process it. I was too stunned and scared by his statement. At that point in my career I had never seen anyone in therapy with Robin's level of cognitive rigidity and self-destructiveness. I didn't understand the dangerousness of this combination. Dr. Rios, with his many years of experience did understand, and was apparently trying to tell me something. I should have asked him what he meant. The fact that I did not, would become one of my biggest regrets as Robin's therapist.

• • •

When Robin entered the hospital in 2003, she was caught up in her life-long pattern of imposing rules in her own head which she then felt unable to break. Being depressed meant those rules were self-destructive, or at least self-defeating. One of her rules at that time became her refusal to attend groups. Another was that she could not eat anything other than apples and peanut butter. Robin was not making conscious choices about her rules. Her own intrusive thoughts were driving her, and she had very little ability to control this. She was overwhelmed with anxiety in addition to profound despair. Robin was always, on some level, driven by her anxiety. Her internal rules were always about what caused the least anxiety for her.

Unfortunately, because the inpatient staff did not understand Robin, in the context of the "us" and "them" dynamic on the unit they almost immediately began to label her as "manipulative." They thought she was purposely being difficult. In addition to refusing groups and all meals, she refused medication at times if she was concerned about the side effects. I tried to explain Robin's cognitive rigidity to them but it didn't matter. They continued to think of her as "uncooperative."

I couldn't fault the inpatient staff members too much, because Robin's behavior was difficult to understand. It had taken me years to begin to understand it myself. It was easy for them to mistakenly believe Robin was purposely refusing to participate in programming because, as a mental health professional herself, she felt she did not need what they had to offer. Robin even made statements consistent with this belief, in order to explain herself in a way that made sense.

"I've run groups like this," she would say to the staff. "I know all about them. I am not a group person." Unfortunately, the staff members would interpret this as Robin being condescending.

Robin started to attend groups after almost two weeks in the hospital, only because her insurance company threatened to stop covering the costs of her treatment. Her anxiety about the prospect of having a large bill to pay overrode her anxiety about coming out of her room and interacting with people. It was that simple. Her brain changed the rules based on what made her least anxious. That was how Robin's brain worked.

No staff members behaved rudely to Robin. Nobody did or said anything wrong. But there was that palpable dynamic of separation and distance, made worse by the shatterproof glass of the nurse's station. Staff members were distant and Robin was hypersensitive. She was able to sense that some of them did not like her, without them doing anything overt to indicate it. This, in turn, caused an increased level of anxiety for her.

Robin was still not sleeping well and remained quite depressed. She was responding slightly to the antipsychotic medication, though, and had begun to think a bit more rationally. Her suicidal thoughts had decreased somewhat. Although she was still not stable, when the dynamics with the staff worsened, her psychiatrist Dr. Greene and I became concerned that being in the hospital was actually making things worse for Robin rather than better. I began to believe she might do better if she could get back to somewhat of a normal routine. After meeting with her family and being able to explain to them what was going on, I hoped she would feel more comfortable relying on them a bit for support. Dr. Greene and I talked, almost three weeks after she entered the hospital, about discharging her.

Dr. Greene had told Robin in no uncertain terms that he would not be releasing her from the hospital until after February 9, 2003. This was the day she had originally planned to kill herself. It was the day her brother Eddie died...the brother she never knew because he had died of cancer when she was two years old. Dr. Greene under-stood Robin's cognitive rigidity well enough to know how important it was to keep her safe until that date passed. He agreed that being in the hospital seemed to be making things worse for Robin in terms of anxiety and insomnia, but also that her depression symptoms had improved enough that we would be able to continue her treatment on an outpatient basis.

Meanwhile, Robin was campaigning to go home. She was insist-ing she had fewer suicidal thoughts and no intention of acting on whatever thoughts she had. She was showing signs of improvement including better mood and clearer thinking. She had been able to relax her rule about food and was eating about one meal a day.

I went to talk to Robin and found her in her room. I suggested we go to the private office. "Dr. Greene and I have talked about get-ting you ready to go home. I need to tell you something, though," I reluctantly explained. "I have a conference out-of-town next week. I know how hard that will be for you and I'm really sorry about the timing."

Robin could tell how bad I felt. "Of course you need to go," she said. "I'll be okay. I won't kill myself while you're gone. I promise. I owe you that much."

"Thank you...I'm really happy to hear that. But before you go home, especially since I will be gone, you need to put together a safety plan." I went on to emphasize that some things were not nego-tiable. "You can't just go home and sit in your apartment by yourself. It'll just make you feel more depressed." We talked about the specif-ics of what her safety plan needed to involve.

Robin agreed to all of the conditions, but it wasn't like she had much choice. She wanted to go home. She immediately directed her obsessive-compulsive personality characteristics into organizing a very detailed safety plan involving her friends and family, who she referred to as her "angel network." When I went back the next day I was surprised, pleasantly this time.

"I talked to my brother, my parents and three friends," said Robin. She showed me a written schedule of plans she had made with everyone. She promised not to drink and agreed to call one of her angel network members if she felt unable to manage her symptoms. I was impressed by her ability to organize her safety plan. She was definitely better than when she had entered the hospital. I was thrilled she was being open with her friends and family about needing their support. I talked to each of them to make sure they knew to initiate contact and not just wait for Robin to call them. They were all very supportive and reassured me they would "take good care of her."

Robin's angel network helped me feel okay about leaving for the week-long conference I had planned to attend in Florida. Even though I knew it would be hard for Robin, I also hoped she would be more likely to rely on and continue to be open with her friends and family if I was not there. I still did not want to foster too much dependence. I wanted her to keep working on being honest with people other than me, as I knew this would be crucial to her recovery.

I also knew it would help for me to get some distance from Robin and her difficult situation, as I had been putting a lot of time and energy into being there for her for three weeks. I knew I desperately needed some time to process what we had been through, to regroup emotionally, to think about what I needed to do differently in terms of her treatment and to prepare myself for whatever was going to happen when I returned. To ensure she made a smooth transition after leaving the hospital Robin and I made plans to meet in my outpatient office two days after she was discharged...the day before I was scheduled to leave town.

Robin was discharged from the hospital on Wednesday, exactly three weeks after her admission. Two days later she arrived at my office for our appointment, on time as always. She showed her usual indication of severe anxiety...her leg was bouncing up and down rapidly and she looked exhausted. "I'm not as depressed as I was before the hospital," Robin said. "But I'm still depressed and I only slept five hours last night. I know I'm still not always rational."

"Are you eating?" I asked, trying to get a sense of how bad things were. I had been surprised that not eating had become one of her self-imposed rules, as this had never been an issue in the past. Her sudden focus on refusing food during her hospitalization was one of many things that had surprised and confused me about the previous few weeks.

"I'm not hungry," Robin replied.

"Robin, if you don't start eating, you will sabotage all of our efforts to help you feel better," I said, trying to confront this issue somewhat gently. "Are you trying to kill yourself slowly? What's the whole issue about eating? Help me understand."

"No, it has nothing to do with killing myself," she explained. "Eating is the only thing I have control over." Wow! This was unexpected. It was a statement people with eating disorders often make to explain their need to restrict calories. This was not the Robin I knew. We debated a bit about it, but I did not want to get into a power struggle. The last thing I wanted to do was leave for a week with her worrying about whether I was angry. Any sense of distance on my part might make it easier for her to go against her promise to stay alive until I got back. It worried me that she was still thinking so irrationally.

Two days earlier when she was still in the hospital I had been okay about leaving Robin in the hands of her angel network. But suddenly, with Robin feeling so overwhelmed and still thinking so irrationally, I was no longer completely okay. I knew at a deep level that Robin was still not remotely herself. I also knew, however, I had done everything I could to ensure her safety and I needed to let go for the time being. As a therapist it is not unusual to feel uneasy about someone's safety. In fact, this was a common occurrence for me as a full-time outpatient therapist with many severely mentally ill clients. Making judgment calls about safety issues was a routine part of my job. I often had to remind myself that there is a limit to what anyone can do if someone is determined to commit suicide.

Before ending our session I tried to instill some hope by talking about how huge it was that Robin had finally been open with me and that she no longer had to worry about me "ditching" her. I told her my new understanding would help us approach treatment differently and make more progress. I wasn't very clear yet myself about what this meant, but I tried to be positive for her sake.

Robin walked out of my office that day and I was suddenly over-whelmed with emotions. I sat in my office, looking out the window and processing it all. I felt so many different things. I think it was partly the intensity of the emotions of the previous three weeks catching up. It was partly the realization of the implications of everything Robin had never told me before, the severity of her symptoms, and the suddenness with which she had become so dangerously unstable. I had a new awareness of how much pain she must have been hiding from me for many years, partly out of her fear that I would ditch her.

I felt very bad about leaving so soon after her discharge from the hospital, knowing how unlikely it was that she would talk to anyone about what she was feeling...no matter how bad it got. That day, knowing how irrational and depressed she was, I felt like I was aban-doning her. Whether I had done my job as a therapist to cover all the bases with her safety plan was not the issue. I knew I had. I needed to go to the conference and trust that she would honor her promise to stay alive. But, at the same time I was finally beginning to understand the words of Dr. Rios so many years earlier...Robin was "at extremely high risk for suicide at some point."

In those private moments in my office that day, I was beginning to get a sense of how much Robin would need me to be the one per-son she could continue to be open with about the depth of her pain. I sensed that what was happening was bigger than me, and bigger than my job. My gut told me...Robin needed to stop feeling so alone or she was going to end up dead.

Robin's Thoughts on the Hospital

The first thing I remember about being in the hospital was the body check. A body check requires you to strip down to your undergarments so the staff can make sure you aren't hiding any contraband that could be used to hurt anyone (things like sharp objects, drugs, etc.). They also document any scars or marks on your body. I had been on the checking side of the body check at times in my career. Now I was forced to feel the embarrassment of being on the other side.

The Transitions Unit of the hospital held depressed patients and patients who had addictions issues, and was where I should have gone. But the first night I was hospitalized, I was placed on the Geriatric Unit because there was no room on Transitions. By the time I got to the Geriatric Unit, the numbness was wearing off and I was starting to face my new reality. I was soon horribly anxious and even more depressed because I realized I had hit bottom. It was one thing to be in therapy and on medication, but to be in a psychiatric hospital? How would people react to that? And would I ever work in mental health again? Worrying about what people would think was one of the issues that I became focused on during this period. I remember crying a lot. I hadn't been able to cry for so long, but now it seemed I couldn't stop.

My roommate on the Geriatric Unit was an elderly woman who informed me that she was in the hospital because she tried to kill her husband. Nice, I remember thinking...my first night in a psychiatric hospital and I had to try to sleep in the same room with a homicidal old woman. At least she seemed harmless. I probably wouldn't have slept that first night anyway, but my insomnia was not helped by the loud moaning that went on during that night on the unit. Someone, maybe more than one person, moaned "Help me" over and over during the night. I thought "For God's sake, someone help him!" It was not conducive to a good night's sleep.

The next morning, a bed opened up on the Transitions Unit so I was moved. I had a roommate on this unit also. I don't know why she was in the hospital. All I know is that she had sleep apnea and was on a breathing machine at night. This ensured that I would not get any sleep on my second night in the hospital either. Fortunately, they moved me into a different room the next day.

Early every morning, usually between seven and eight a.m., Dr. Greene came to see me. We talked about how I slept and the status of my anxiety, depression and suicidal thoughts. He adjusted my medication as needed. Normally I wouldn't want to see anyone at that time of day, but I wasn't sleeping anyway, so it didn't matter.

The main programming in the hospital was the groups, which started at 9 a.m. and went until lunch. They started again after lunch and continued until about 2 p.m. For most people, groups perform very important functions in a hospital stay. For one, they provide structure to the day, giving something positive to do instead of watching TV or sleeping all day. They get patients out of their rooms, interacting with others. They also provide useful information as well as a forum to discuss issues with others who can relate.

The first group of the day was always Wrap-up, during which goals were set for the day. Wrap-up was also held in the evening, so everyone could report on how they did on their goals that day. I wasn't sure what we were wrapping up in the morning. I didn't care about living, let alone setting goals for the day, so I didn't want to attend.

There was also Nursing group, during which a nurse usually did a general educational session on topics like coping with stress or anxiety, or the symptoms of depression. If I were myself I could have led these groups so I didn't see the point in attending.

Another group was Occupational Therapy, held in the craft room which was on a different floor of the building, and was full of scissors and other sharp items. I couldn't attend due to being on suicide precautions. It was fine with me, as I had no desire to make collages out of pictures cut out of magazines or to make key chains out of beads.

Participation in groups was important on the Transitions Unit, to the point where your privileges depended on it. This meant that your ability to go outside to smoke, go to the gym, go to the cafeteria, and go to the craft room were dependent partly on your participation. But, being on suicide precautions I couldn't have any of these privileges anyway, so the incentive was irrelevant.

Another issue with the groups was the fact that all patients on the unit were included in every group. This meant up to twenty people who had very different problems were there. It was overwhelming for me to be in a small room with that many people. The rooms were not big enough and were really hot. Some of the people with drug and alcohol problems were scary and I didn't want to leave the safety of my room. I was anxious already, and leaving my safe place to sit with a bunch of strangers and discuss my issues (which I wouldn't even talk about with loved ones) was just not going to happen.

So I stayed in my room most of the time. I laid on my bed and did word searches or sat in the window alcove and stared out at the river. Needless to say, I wasn't very popular with the staff when I refused to attend the groups. From my former work experience I remembered how annoying it was when residents didn't comply with some part of the program. It disrupted the routine for the staff. I am usually a compliant person and concerned that people like me. However, my normal personality went out the window during my Meltdown. I was irritable, which is also unlike me and I just really didn't care whether the staff liked me or not. I was in a whole different mode and being a people person wasn't part of it.

Despite how I felt, my group attendance dramatically improved once I was told that my insurance company was talking about not approving the hospitalization if I didn't comply with the program. The thought of having to pay out of pocket for the expenses was enough to motivate me to at least attend some of the groups. I can only imagine the tens of thousands of dollars it would have cost had my insurance not covered it. Mostly, the groups were a positive thing once I started attending because they got me out of the isolation of my room, got me out of my own head, which was an ugly place to be, and forced some interaction with my peers.

However, sometimes the groups were downright offensive. I was appalled by one in which the leader brought in a guitar. There were maybe seven of us there, all women this time. One of the women was obviously deeply despondent and depressed, as she cried non-stop every day. So the group leader was playing upbeat, encouraging songs, which seemed to make this woman cry harder. It just felt mean to be singing "I Can See Clearly Now" in front of this sobbing woman. Next, she played "If You're Happy and You Know It," which seemed a little condescending with a group of adults, since I used to sing that song with my daycare class, for God's sake. Needless to say, I didn't participate in the clapping or stomping.

Another aspect of being in the hospital that I had an issue with was the nursing students who came for their psychiatric rotation. They walked around in a gaggle of five or six, dressed in their bright scrubs, chattering and giggling. They were upbeat and happy and as a severely depressed patient, I found them extremely annoying. Their chipper moods were an insult, and seemed disrespectful on a depression ward. I didn't expect them to mope around like we did, but neutral professionalism would have seemed more appropriate. I am sure if I was not so depressed I would not have reacted to them so negatively. But I was irritable, and they irritated me.

The best part of the day was visiting hours, because it was a brief distraction from the fact that I felt "crazy" and was in a mental hospital. It was also one of the hardest parts of the day. I say this because I felt like I needed to present myself as normally as possible to my visitors, not like someone who wanted to kill herself and needed to be locked up. I'm sure my visitors were anxious too, but it was still difficult. I was lucky to always get visitors. Initially it was Christi, my friend who took care of my cat, Epiphany, and a friend from work. Once I told my brother what was going on, he visited and my mom came every night once I told her where I was. I was lucky to have very supportive family and friends. It's unfortunate that I wasn't able to share with them what was really going on for me and utilize this support system more, but I was just so used to hiding my symptoms from everyone. I was used to putting on a normal face to the world so nobody would realize that I was actually "crazy."

It may seem contradictory that I talk about how close my family is, given that I chose not to reveal my hospitalization to my parents until I had been there for a couple of weeks. It was easier to tell my friends than to tell my family. A strong dynamic in my family is that we protect each other from upsetting information. Nobody wants to bother anybody. We even apologize when giving each other gifts. We say, "I have the receipt, you can take it back" before the person even opens the gift. When my dad was first diagnosed with oral cancer, I was a student at Indiana University in Bloomington. My parents didn't tell me about the diagnosis for at least a week, until I came home for Spring Break, so as not to upset me at school. Throughout his several recurrences of cancer my dad minimized his symptoms with us, not wanting to worry anybody. He had appendicitis one year at Thanksgiving. He insisted that the rest of us go visit family as planned, and he stayed home alone. When he eventually went to the hospital, we found out that his appendix had ruptured and he could have died. I learned by example to minimize anything that might upset my family. Having grown up in this dynamic, it was just natural for me to keep my Meltdown from them.

It amazes me now that I was so irrational during my hospital stay. For example, I was surprised by things Sharon revealed to me that I said concerning suicide being part of natural selection, as well as other statements I made. I have no memory of saying these things. I was probably dissociating. I had never had psychotic symptoms, and I'm usually a very rational person. I guess it's an indication of how depressed I was that I could convince myself my family would be less affected by my suicide if I killed myself on the anniversary of my brother's death. In reality, they would have been devastated regardless of when I killed myself, and would have felt enormous guilt.

It's the irrational thinking that made my cat, Epiphany, a bigger focus than my family during this time. It really was thoughts of Epiphany's fate if I killed myself that kept me alive. I obsessed about what would happen to her. I couldn't stand the thought of Epiphany living the rest of her life in a cage at the Humane Society, or getting euthanized. It was not irrational of me to be concerned about Epiphany's well-being, but I am astonished now about how disconnected I felt from my family and everyone else back then. All I knew was, even though I couldn't stop obsessing about killing myself, I needed to try to stay alive to take care of Epiphany. She needed me and that kept me alive.

3
The Aftermath of the Meltdown

I RETURNED FROM Florida feeling rested and re-energized. The conference had been about new developments in psychopharmacology, presented by a leading expert in the field. I had learned a lot of helpful information that I could immediately apply to many of my clients. While I was away and distracted I was also able to get some emotional distance from the intensity of the previous few weeks with Robin.

As an outpatient therapist, returning to work after a week away was always a challenge. Many clients needed to be seen regularly, and would get squeezed into my schedule before and after my time away. Those weeks were always busier than usual. On my way to work the day of my return, I was trying to prepare myself for the week ahead. I thought about Robin and had no idea what I was going to hear when we met later that day. I tried to prepare myself for anything.

At the time, I worked in a renovated old factory building in the middle of a big campus at the mental health agency. I loved my office, which was large and had two windows, built-in cupboards and lots of character. The wall with two windows was brick, painted off-white to match the rest of the walls. The office contained a desk, my chair, a bookcase and three light green, relatively uncomfortable old chairs in which my clients sat. One of the green chairs was next to a table with a lamp on it, along with various items I provided for anxious, fidgety people to play with while they talked (a Slinky, a Koosh ball, etc.).

When clients came into my office, session after session, they would almost always sit in the same chair. Whichever chair they picked during their first session, is where they would sit each time we met. Any therapist or client can confirm that this is what usually happens. There are few exceptions. Robin happened to pick one of the chairs away from the table. She didn't have easy access to the Koosh ball or other items to distract her fidgety hands. If she needed something to play with, she would bring her own "sculpie."

Before I left for Florida my gut told me that Robin's inability to be open with anyone, including me, had been contributing to her severe depression. I realized how disconnected she felt from everyone. Deep down I was hoping Robin had been more open with her family and friends while I was gone and that she was feeling more comfortable about this. But knowing her, I doubted it.

Robin arrived for our scheduled appointment on time as always, and looked about the same as when I had last seen her. Her affect was still flat, her leg was still bouncing up and down rapidly, and she immediately started to play with the sculpie she had brought with her.

"So, how did it go while I was gone?" I asked, sounding less tentative and anxious than I felt.

"At the beginning of last week it got worse," Robin said. "When I saw Dr. Greene on Wednesday he put me back on the same meds I was on in the hospital."

Before being discharged from the hospital, Robin had gotten stuck on not wanting to take an antipsychotic medication, mostly because of the stigma involved, but also because it was causing the side effect of dry mouth and could possibly cause weight gain over time. Robin had been willing to try it when she was in the hospital, but not to stay on it long term. Because Dr. Greene knew her rigidity would lead her to just stop taking it anyway, he had discontinued it. Apparently while I was gone he insisted on restarting it since she was doing worse without it. Robin did admit she was feeling a bit better since restarting it, and was sleeping better with the addition of anti-anxiety medication at night.

"How are the suicidal thoughts?" I asked, somewhat afraid of her answer.

"I still think about it," Robin said. "Whenever I'm not busy, that's what I think about. I've been trying to stay busy. I've been hanging out with my friends, going shopping with my mom and going to the library."

"So, how much are you eating?" I asked, knowing this would be a tell-tale sign of progress. Robin said she had begun to eat a small amount. Thank God. She was still focused on food as one of her internal rules. But I was encouraged that she was at least eating something.

"Are you talking to your people about how you are really doing?" I had already guessed what she was going to say.

"No, I don't want people worrying about me. I don't want to freak them out or have them think they have to tiptoe around me." Apparently, Robin was doing just better enough to be able to get back into her lifelong pattern of minimizing her symptoms. "Bob and his wife are going on a cruise together next week," she said. "I'm sup-posed to watch my nephew while they're gone. If I tell them how I'm really doing, I'm afraid they won't go. I'm sure they won't be able to find anyone else to watch him at the last minute. I'd feel terrible if they have to stay home because of me."

This was somewhat reassuring to me, because this was more typi-cal of the Robin I knew. She was always thinking about other people's feelings, not wanting to bother anyone, and worrying about what other people thought of her. It was actually a sign of improvement that she was back to being able to fake it with her friends and family. I figured watching her nephew would give her something positive and distracting to focus on, although we talked about having her mom or her friends help if it got too stressful.

Then we discussed her return to work. She said Dr. Greene had extended her medical leave until the week her brother and sister-in-law returned from vacation and that she would go back half time at first. Robin felt good about this plan. We made plans to meet again later that week.

The next day I received a voice mail message from Robin saying she was going to Chicago to visit a friend. "I wanted you to know where I am in case anybody is looking for me, gets worried, and calls you," she explained. I was happy to hear she was getting out of town and doing something fun and distracting. But, it was completely out of character for her to leave me a voice mail. She had only promised to stay alive until after I returned from my conference, and I did not completely trust her after learning about how much she had hidden from me for so long. Part of me was afraid she was using the story about going to Chicago in order to buy herself time for a suicide attempt. It made me uneasy. I was relieved to get a phone call from her the next day...until I heard why she was calling.

"On my way back from Chicago yesterday, I started having car problems. I took Chuck (her name for her Jeep) to the shop this morning and just found out the engine needs to be replaced." Robin sounded distressed. "I got a call when I was waiting to see Dr. Greene this morning saying it will be around $2,500. I started crying in the waiting room and couldn't stop. I sobbed through my appointment with him. It was humiliating." She hated to cry in front of other people. She was very upset and went on to say, "I know this is just depression, but it just seems like a sign that things aren't ever going to get any better."

I was somewhat relieved to hear her acknowledge it was depression causing her to feel this way. This made me believe she was starting to think more rationally than she had been prior to my week off. In the next sentence, I learned I was wrong.

"I'm done eating," she declared emphatically. She talked about Dr. Greene clarifying that he wanted her taking the antipsychotic medication twice a day and she had only been taking it once. Although she said she would take her medications, she declared, "It will be a race to see if the medications work before I starve to death." I immediately suggested she come in for appointment that day. I needed to determine how suicidal she was.

I learned Robin was still not doing well at all. Her new willingness to be open with me following her meltdown was helpful, but I continued to be mortified by her state of mind. "The whole thing with Chuck just makes me feel more sure I'm supposed to kill myself," she said. "I was on the Internet last week and learned that if you die from overdosing on Tylenol it's painful. I've been thinking about buying a gun, but I know there's a waiting period. Besides, I don't have the money." What? What the hell? Robin was thinking about buying a gun? For God's sake, what next? I stayed calm on the outside, but inside I was back to wondering what happened to the Robin I knew? And more importantly, did I ever really know Robin?

After some discussion, she admitted her rule about not eating had become both punishment for herself and a way to kill herself slowly. I started wondering about the hospital. But two weeks after feeling like we needed to get Robin out of the hospital because it was making things worse, I did not want to go that route unless absolutely necessary. What a nightmare! Whatever rest and relaxation I had felt earlier that week was gone. We were right back to the same place we had been before I left.

I wish I could say I was a brilliant therapist who came back from Florida with a well thought out new treatment plan, knowing exactly what I needed to do for Robin. But that was hardly the case. I was a human being who knew another human being was in tremendous pain and looking to me for help. I didn't have a step-by-step guidebook on how to help a smart, insightful but very depressed client get past her anxiety about being open with people, and I didn't really know why she was still so depressed. I just knew I was reeling from everything I had learned while she was in the hospital and the fact that she was still not remotely okay.

When I learned how suicidal and irrational she continued to be, and with the hospital not being a good option, all I knew to do was trust my gut. In that moment, with Robin sitting across from me in the crappy green chair, leg bouncing, playing with her sculpie and talking about buying a gun, I knew, on the same deep level I had known before I went to Florida...if I didn't do something different, Robin was going to die.

My gut made a decision. If I was going to expect honesty from Robin, I needed to be honest back. I knew what my gut was telling me to do was risky. But, I decided I needed to trust that Robin was strong enough and our ten-year connection was solid enough for me to take this risk.

I told her, more openly than ever before, how I felt.

"Robin, I know you are really depressed and most of you just wants to die," I said. "But to not eat anything just sabotages everything we are doing to get your brain chemistry back to normal. If you don't start eating more, everything is going to get worse." I was familiar with the literature on the effects of starvation on the brain. I had learned a lot about treating eating disorders when I was in graduate school. If she was not getting enough basic nutrition it would counteract all of our efforts. I took my honesty with Robin a step further.

"I care about you and have no intention of ditching you. But, I need you to know that when you act self-destructively it puts me in a huge bind as your therapist," I explained, not knowing how she would react. "I understand you have been unable to tell anyone, including me, how you really feel. I think I need to continue to be more available to you than in the past. We need to stay connected until you feel better. But at the same time I cannot, as your therapist, in any way support or reinforce self-destructive behavior. I don't know what to do about the bind you are putting me in. I want to keep being supportive to you. But, it won't work very well if we are battling about your eating."

Robin did not have much to say in response. I asked her to take her medication as prescribed, to eat two meals a day, and to continue to be open with me about how she was feeling. She said she would think about it and we planned to meet two days later. She walked out the door, and I had no idea what would happen. I had to trust that my gut had been right about me being honest and direct.

Thank God, my intervention seemed to work. In our next session later that week, Robin revealed that she had begun to eat in order to keep from making me mad. "I feel like a hypocrite, though," she said. "Eating and coming to treatment are inconsistent with just wanting to die, which is how I feel."

"Robin, it's okay to be inconsistent. You're battling with yourself. There must be part of you that doesn't want to kill yourself, but you are very depressed and your brain is stuck. It's okay to be inconsistent when you are having this battle."

"I know part of me must want to live or I wouldn't worry about you being mad. But whenever I'm not busy, I still can only think about killing myself." She was able to acknowledge that the increase in the antipsychotic medication, along with the other meds she was taking, was helping her to feel a little less depressed. She assured me she would keep taking her medications as prescribed.

During our conversation I was relieved when Robin said, "I'm not going to kill myself before my brother and sister-in-law come back from their cruise on March 12. I promised I would watch my nephew." This promise, I believed completely. I knew she would never kill herself while taking care of her nephew, whom she loved deeply. It bought me some time during which I would hopefully not have to hospitalize her, and could figure out what on earth to do to help her get to a better place.

I was baffled by what was happening. I couldn't understand why Robin kept feeling so awful and thinking so irrationally. There was no clear explanation. It did not make sense that her depression had been resistant to so many different medications for over a year and seemed to be getting worse and not better. I still couldn't believe her fear that I would "ditch" her had kept her from telling me how hopeless she had felt before her suicide attempt in 1999. How did that happen? My tendency to keep my boundaries very rigid had probably contributed. Although I was reassured about Robin's new willingness to be open and to eat more, I was confused about why she wasn't getting much better. In an attempt to figure it out, I went back and re-read her whole clinical chart...all the progress notes I had written over the previous decade.

· · ·

I first met Robin in 1993, a few days after her roommate had found her sitting under a blanket, dissociating and cutting her arm with a knife. Obviously, this alarmed her roommate who had no idea what to make of this disturbing behavior. She convinced Robin to come to the agency's emergency department, where Robin insisted she was not suicidal and promised to attend outpatient therapy. She had never had treatment of any kind. I was a bit nervous about seeing her since I did not have much experience treating self-mutilation. After I met Robin, though, I instantly liked her. And it was clear she needed help. I consulted with my supervisor a lot, began to gradually dig into the details of her history, and worked to help her verbalize her experiences and her emotions.

In addition to her obvious depression, Robin revealed a trauma history including sexual abuse as a child by someone outside her immediate family. She had significant social anxiety and described herself as a person who had always been very timid and shy. Despite this, she worked in the mental health field and knew a lot about mental illness.

She was able to talk intelligently and insightfully about her issues. But, she had never talked openly with anyone about the extent of her painful symptoms or her sexual abuse.

As Robin and I began to work together, she showed symptoms consistent with her trauma history. She met the criteria for a diagnosis of Posttraumatic Stress Disorder (PTSD) including nightmares, intrusive memories of past trauma, significant anxiety accompanying those memories, avoiding reminders of the trauma, dissociation, insomnia, a negative self-image, detachment from others and self-destructive behavior. The depression she experienced was very common among trauma survivors. The anxiety she felt seemed to be genetic, life-long, and magnified by the trauma.

We spent much time during the first two years of treatment processing her sexual abuse experiences and helping her tolerate painful emotions without needing to dissociate or self-mutilate. Self-mutilation is a common behavior pattern for trauma survivors. It is not about wanting to commit suicide. It serves different purposes for different people, but is generally described by those who do it as a method of coping with emotional pain. For Robin, cutting herself usually accompanied dissociating and drinking too much alcohol, which she readily admitted she did to numb herself when depressed. When we began treatment she immediately agreed to try antidepressant medication, which significantly helped to decrease both her depression and her PTSD symptoms and allowed her to tolerate the painful emotions evoked by discussing her issues.

Robin quickly made progress. I really liked working with her, as her sarcastic sense of humor always made me laugh and was balanced by an overwhelming sense of kindness toward others. These qualities combined with her intelligence, knowledge and insight made our sessions especially rewarding for me. As we worked together, Robin became more able to feel and express her emotions. She felt better about herself, and her tendency to dissociate and cut herself virtually stopped. Sometimes she would stop taking her medication, usually to test whether she still needed it...a common pattern for people coming to terms with chronic mental health issues. For Robin, going off the medication would always lead to more depression. Getting back on it or adjusting it when appropriate always helped, and she was always able to get back on track quickly.

As I was re-reading Robin's chart I came across the incident in which she had set a deadline for herself to move out of her parents' house in 1995, and then felt compelled to kill herself if she didn't meet the deadline. I remembered how scared I felt after she revealed this to me. I had always remembered Dr. Rios' comment about her high suicide risk. In reviewing this incident in her chart, though, I was reminded about what I did in response.

I had learned a lot about cognitive techniques as a therapist-in-training during graduate school. Back then cognitive therapy was starting to become widely used to treat many different issues. Cognitive therapy focuses on identifying irrational or self-defeating thought patterns and helping people shift their thinking to being more realistic and healthy. After I learned about her suicidal crisis in 1995, I suggested Robin try a specific cognitive strategy.

I figured that as long as she was always seeing suicide as an "out," she was not putting as much energy as possible into healing and moving forward with her life. I was focused on trauma as her main issue and I assumed that if she could put her energy into processing her emotions effectively, she would eventually heal. I suggested she work on shifting her thinking to incorporate the belief that suicide is just not an option. In hindsight, I imagine this intervention was partly unconsciously motivated by my own fear. I was scared at the time by what had just happened surrounding her deadline, and by what Dr. Rios had said. Whether Robin was ready to do this or not, I desperately wanted her to stop believing suicide was an option.

This cognitive intervention did make a significant difference. Shortly after we had this discussion I felt very gratified to hear Robin say she was going to try harder to focus on living and not dying. She began to talk more openly about her significant OCD symptoms and the rigid routines she felt compelled to follow. She was able to move out of her parents' house and in with some friends. She returned to a previous job, which worked well because she was surrounded by people her age and had a built-in social network. This job eventually became too stressful for her, which is what prompted the suicide attempt by carbon monoxide I never knew about. Instead of killing herself at that time she ended up quitting this job, finding a new one, and fairly quickly getting back to a place of stability.

Robin's severe OCD symptoms have always revolved around sun tanning. She had an irrational need to be as tan as possible and would lay in the sun for many hours at a time without sunscreen. If it was sunny and warm outside and she was not able to lay in the sun, she would become anxious and obsessively preoccupied with the need to do so. Although she enjoyed tanning, this was not the main reason Robin did it. She felt compelled to lay in the sun to avoid feeling unbearable anxiety. She spent a great deal of time and energy obsessing about the weather and focusing on getting "fresh color." She knew how irrational this pattern was and did not want to "lose my respect," so Robin did not reveal to me that tanning was an obsessive-compulsive symptom until we had been working together for several years. I obviously noticed her deep tan, but she would just say she liked laying in the sun. She eventually revealed the truth about these symptoms and we tried to address them in treatment.

Robin remained mostly stable for many years. She socialized with friends, generally enjoyed her work, and continued to feel better about herself. She was proud to move into her own apartment and to finally feel completely independent. We stopped meeting as regularly, but Robin continued to see a psychiatrist for medication management and expressed a desire to check-in with me because I represented "accountability" to her. Meeting with me once every month or two helped her stay on track.

Through the years when she was stable, we made attempts to work on decreasing her severe OCD symptoms with both medication and therapy, consistent with the latest research. Medication did not decrease these symptoms at all. With therapy, Robin was able to decrease her tanning time slightly, but this was one issue she remained completely unable to overcome. Her life continued to revolve around laying in the sun during "tanning season" from May to September.

Robin and I started meeting more regularly again in 2002 when her depression worsened, and Dr. Greene and I worked closely together to find the right medication combination to alleviate these symptoms. Her depression had always responded to antidepressant medications in the past. We kept trying different antidepressant medications, alone and in combination...right up to the time of her meltdown.

• • •

In March 2003, after I had re-read Robin's whole chart and reviewed her history without any light bulb ideas coming forward, I decided to tell her about it when she came for her next session. I wanted to help her look at the big picture of her treatment, to recognize how much progress she had made, and to know I had a better understanding about how isolated she had been. At that point, the only explanation for her continuing severe depression that made sense to me was her complete disconnection from people. I wanted her to know this was something we could work on. I wanted to try to instill some hope that things were going to improve.

"I read your chart from the beginning," I explained to Robin. "I wanted to see if I missed something that might explain why you are having so much trouble. Basically the notes show we talked about your sexual abuse for the first couple of years, and then there was a turning point in 1995." I talked about the episode with the deadline (minus Dr. Rios' statement about her suicide risk). I reminded her about my cognitive intervention and that she said she was going to focus more on living. I was surprised by her response.

"That's why I thought you would ditch me if I was too suicidal," she said.

"What? Really? Why?" I asked.

"I don't know," she said. "I don't remember. I just know that was the conversation that made me think it."

The surprises just kept coming! All of a sudden, it made complete sense. Later in our treatment when we had tried to address her OCD symptoms I became painfully aware of the degree to which Robin's severe cognitive rigidity made it very difficult for her to shift her thinking. She was never able to impact these symptoms significantly. In hindsight, I realized that to tell Robin to eliminate suicide as an option had been ridiculous. To suggest she could somehow stop her brain from focusing on suicidal thoughts when she was depressed was a terrible thing to say. I was, in essence, unknowingly suggesting that she should just be able to control her severe OCD symptoms.

I realized that if I had talked to Dr. Rios in more detail about his statement that Robin was "at significant risk for suicide," I might have gained a better understanding of her cognitive rigidity at that time. He seemed to understand what I did not. Had I talked to him I might have understood that I could not just suggest Robin change her thinking and have it work that quickly. I would have talked much more about my cognitive intervention with her over time, to make sure we were on the same page. But I didn't. She had said at the time she was going to focus on living, and she then started to make significant progress. I didn't question it. I had no idea she was actually motivated by the fear that I would ditch her, and that this fear kept her from being able to tell me when she was seriously suicidal. My lack of experience in 1995 had caused a big misunderstanding over many years and had contributed to her feeling completely alone. Obviously there were many reasons she felt alone, but I felt bad about having contributed to it in any way.

Robin and I talked at length about the misunderstanding. I explained what I had been trying to say at the time, and why I said it. We talked about how easy it was for her to misinterpret it, given the impossibility of what I was asking her to do. I admitted I did not fully understand at that time how hard it was for her to shift her thinking, and I apologized for putting her in an impossible position. Robin was very forgiving, and we talked about how good it was that we "cleared that up."

At the time of this discussion in March 2003, Robin was staying at her brother's house and caring for her nephew. She said she did not think about suicide when she was with him, but when she was alone after putting him to bed she would get very depressed. She was sleeping, but not well, and said she was exhausted. She was continuing to spend time with friends and family to help decrease her sense of isolation. In our twice a week sessions we were talking about ways to prepare herself to return to work. And, we started to talk more about our relationship, which had obviously been affected by the misunderstanding about me ditching her.

"Robin, you've been much more open with me since you were hospitalized. How are you feeling about that?" I asked her one day.

"I feel more vulnerable," she said. "It makes me anxious sometimes. I'm afraid I'll become too dependent." She was not able to say what it meant to be too dependent, just that she would know it if she felt it.

"I know it makes you nervous to be vulnerable," I said. "But I would never do anything intentionally to hurt you. Please tell me if you ever feel hurt by something I say or do, or if you feel too dependent and we will talk through it." We talked about the need to have consistent contact as she transitioned back to work, which would be a stressful time for her. "I want you to know I think it is not only fine, but also a good idea for us to stay connected until you are feeling better. We'll figure out the right balance in terms of contact once that happens." We made plans to continue meeting twice a week, and to touch base by phone as needed. Because of the enormous anxiety she felt about calling me, we scheduled times to talk briefly on the phone in between our sessions.

As we talked about her impending return to work, Robin seemed to be starting to think more rationally. She talked to her boss about returning to work as soon as her brother and sister-in-law got home. Although she seemed better, she continued to report thoughts of suicide when she wasn't distracted by something else. When I asked if she would commit to staying alive beyond the time she was responsible for her nephew, she was not ready to make any promises. But, she said she thought it would take "something bad happening" to cause her to become unable to manage her ongoing suicidal thoughts. I was encouraged. I began to relax slightly and to think maybe, just maybe, we were on the right track. This was, however, short lived.

"I'm exhausted," Robin said in a session during the time she was watching her nephew. I asked questions, as usual.

"Why do you think you are so exhausted?" I asked. "I know taking care of a toddler is tiring, but how are you sleeping?" Robin had told me earlier in the week that she skipped her nighttime dose of Geodon out of fear that she wouldn't wake up if her nephew needed her. She said she had slept so badly without it she immediately began taking it again.

"I skipped Geodon again last night," Robin reluctantly confessed. "And I didn't take any of my meds this morning. My friend from Chicago is visiting tonight and I don't want to be on too many meds in case we drink."

In case you drink? Seriously? Just when I thought we were making progress. "Robin, you can't do this! You are just starting to feel better. If you start sabotaging treatment it will just get worse and you won't be able to function when you go back to work. What are you doing?"

"It isn't going to hurt to miss one day of my meds," Robin rationalized.

"But you skipped Geodon earlier this week, and last night and this morning. It isn't just one dose." She could tell I was upset. "You need to get back on your meds as prescribed and for God's sake, don't drink!"

Robin's affect was still flat. Her knee was bouncing. She knew I was not happy. "I don't think I'll kill myself any time soon," she said, trying to reassure me. "I just don't want to keep living the way I've been living."

"I know you feel awful," I replied. "And I know how alone and isolated you've been for a long time. But we can work on that, and your life will get better. You need to be open with all the friends who have been so helpful over the last month. You need to keep working on being more open with your family. It would help if you can let all your people know how hard it is for you to keep reaching out to them. They'll understand."

I had been feeling the relief of knowing Robin's support network had been mobilized and were continuing to regularly spend time with her. I guess I just assumed (or maybe hoped) she was also at least letting them know she was still depressed. I was wrong. With my new awareness of the degree to which being open with people caused severe anxiety for Robin, I should have expected her response.

"Now that the crisis has passed, I've told everyone I'm fine," Robin said. "They believe me."

I always knew Robin had anxiety in social situations. She acknowledged it in our first session. What became apparent after her meltdown, however, was that she actually fit the criteria for what is known as Avoidant Personality Disorder. People with this diagnosis have a lot of social anxiety and trouble being open with anyone due to their fear of being rejected or evaluated negatively. When Robin began to tell me things she had never told anyone before, it became clear this pattern fit. Her statement several weeks after she got out of the hospital that she was back to "faking it" with her friends and family and had them convinced she was "fine," confirmed it for me. Being vulnerable in any way caused anxiety for her. She was more comfortable faking it, even though this caused her to feel alone and isolated. This was all consistent with avoidant personality traits. Realizing this helped me to re-think what I was doing in therapy. It became even more clear that I needed to help Robin feel less alone.

Robin's Thoughts About the Aftermath

I've been naming my vehicles since I owned my first car, Crombie, a gray Mustang. Crombie was named after a friend's cat, Abercrombie, who liked to hang out on top of the bird feeder, which I thought was pretty clever, so I christened my first car after him. In 1995, when it was time to replace Crombie, I purchased a two-year-old white Jeep 4×4 with manual transmission and a black soft top. Being such a fan of the Peanuts comic strip, my Jeep became known as Chuck, for Charlie Brown, from the comic. I loved this vehicle! It had four-wheel drive for the snowy winters but, most importantly, I could take the top off in the good weather and have a convertible. I loved to feel the sun on my skin and wind in my hair all summer.

My love for Chuck is part of the reason I was so devastated when his engine blew shortly after I got out of the hospital. I had gone to visit my roommate from IU in Chicago for a couple of days and was returning home. I was on the Indiana Toll Road going about 65 miles per hour, when it happened. I don't remember the details (what it sounded like, if there was smoke, etc.) just the fact that I lost speed quickly. I wasn't sure what had happened, I just knew I was going more slowly all of a sudden. It was dark outside and I was about ten minutes from my exit on the Toll Road. From there, it was about a fifteen-minute drive to my apartment. I was freaking out, trying to figure out what to do. I really didn't want to pull over in the dark on the Toll Road. I just wanted to be home. So I decided to just nurse Chuck home, rather than figure out who to call to help me. I probably did more damage to the vehicle by choosing to do this, but I have never responded well to car emergencies. A flat tire or dead battery is more than I can handle.

I made it home safely and dropped Chuck off the following day at the car repair shop. I had an appointment with Dr. Greene that day, so I borrowed my dad's truck and went to the appointment. While I was sitting in the waiting room, I received a phone call on my cell phone from the mechanic telling me that I had blown the engine. He gave an estimate of the cost to replace it, which was much more than I had expected and more than I could come up with. When I hung up, I immediately started to cry uncontrollably. I cried all through the appointment with Dr. Greene, alarming him I'm sure. I was already so depressed and suicidal, and this was a catastrophe I just wasn't equipped to handle at this point. Plus, my irrational mind viewed this crisis as another indicator that I should kill myself.

Fortunately for me, my family took over. My dad made the arrangements with the car repair shop to replace Chuck's engine, and my brother and sister-in-law offered to loan me the money to pay for it (knowing that it was unlikely that I'd be able to pay them back such a large sum of money). While I felt guilty about taking the money, I was mostly relieved to have the crisis averted. I was more than happy to let my family help me out since I was incapable at the time of handling it. I am forever grateful to my family for helping me with this situation. I continued to drive Chuck for another five years, when it became time to trade him in for something newer. I still miss Chuck, especially in harsh winters and on sunny summer days...

• • •

After my hospital stay, I resumed my old pattern of faking it to convince my family and friends that I was okay. I was still very depressed and suicidal and having difficulty sleeping, but I wanted everyone to believe that I was back to "normal." This required a lot of effort and energy on my part. My hospitalization came out of the blue for all of them. I think my friends and family were still concerned about me after I got home, but they also wanted to believe that I was okay. They didn't want to upset me with constant hovering, as they knew from past experience that I hated this. Meanwhile, I was telling everyone I was fine and minimizing my continued symptoms (or lying about them, if necessary).

Soon after my release from the hospital, I was supposed to babysit my eighteen-month old nephew for a week while my brother and sister-in-law went on vacation. Some people may question the safety of this for my nephew considering I had just spent three weeks in a psychiatric hospital. However, his safety was never an issue. My nieces and nephew are my favorite people in the world, and I would do anything for them. My brother and sister-in-law knew I loved him and that he'd get the best possible care while I was watching him. Being responsible for him was probably the best thing that could have happened for me right out of the hospital. Even though I was still deeply depressed and ruminating on suicide, caring for him took my focus off of my own issues. Suicide wasn't even an option. As many people know, taking care of an eighteen-month old is a full-time job. I was determined to get it right.

We stayed busy during that week. I stayed at my brother's home, as it was easier to care for my nephew in his home environment than at my apartment. So every day we made the twenty-minute trip to my apartment to take care of my cat, Epiphany. We visited with my parents and went to the store in between naps and meal times. I took him to my office to meet my coworkers one day. One night, one of my coworkers visited us with her young son, and the boys played together. My nephew and I had a good but stressful week together. I slept poorly, partly due to my continued insomnia and partly because I wanted to easily wake up in case my nephew needed me.

I returned to work immediately after my brother and sister-in-law returned home. I worked only half days for the first couple of weeks, and then I went back to full time. My memories are a little hazy of this time, partly because I was still freaking out and partly because it was so long ago. My return to work wasn't as awkward as it could've been, since I had gone to lunch with several coworkers during my time off work (while I babysat my nephew). This helped break the ice a bit. I had to address my co-workers in a team staffing meeting shortly after I returned to work, telling everyone what had happened and reassuring them that I was okay. I joked around a lot about my circumstances to make them more comfortable, trying to lighten the mood for both them and myself.

The truth is I was still depressed and ruminating about death, and feeling very anxious. I continued to have insomnia and felt stressed about being back at work. I did what I did with my friends and family...I faked it. Being a case manager was a stressful job under the best of circumstances, between the expectations of the work and the paperwork that accompanied it. Obviously I was not working under the best of circumstances. I'm not sure how I managed to function as well as I did, convincing others I was okay and taking care of my responsibilities at work. I think it must have been all my years of practice. It had always been automatic for me to go to work, do my job and act "normal" no matter how I felt.

●   ●   ●

Sharon talking to me about the history of our work together made me think back over that time as well. Between the time I started therapy with Sharon in 1993 and the year prior to the Meltdown in 2003, I was generally stable. I worked for four and a half years as a mental health tech at a residential treatment facility for emotionally and behaviorally disturbed adolescents. This was a stressful job, as the kids were prone to verbal and physical aggression. However, I enjoyed the work mainly because of the people I worked with. Most of the mental health techs at this facility were young and recently out of college, so we had a lot in common. Plus, the nature of the work required that we function really well as a team in order to best deal with the acting out of the residents. We frequently had to physically restrain residents and respond as a team to crises, which brought us all together. I made friends with several of my coworkers (this is where I met Christi, the friend who took care of Epiphany while I was in the hospital). Once a week, we had a treatment team meeting to discuss the treatment of the residents. Prior to this meeting on Thursday afternoons, several of us went to lunch together. We also socialized in the evenings, going out after work to local bars. It was a stressful job, and drinking together after a stressful day further solidified our bond. During this period, I applied for an MSW program at the local IU campus. I was accepted, but put on the waiting list. Unfortunately, not enough applicants turned down their acceptances, so I didn't end up in the program. This was a blow to me, as I wanted the chance to move up in the mental health field.

After this disappointment and after about four years of that very stressful job, I was beginning to get burned out. I had always said that if I ever got hit in the face by a resident, I would quit the job. Well, it eventually happened. I was helping a couple of staff members from another unit escort one of their residents from the gym back to their unit. The girl began to struggle, and punched me in the face. That was the last straw and I quit the next day.

I was burned out and stressed, and suddenly without a job. I decided I didn't want anything to do with mental health anymore, and that I needed to find a new career. A large insurance company was looking for new employees, so I applied and was hired. Coincidentally, one of my former coworkers was hired there at the same time, which made the transition to a new job in a different field of work much easier. The Job I was hired to do was telephone insurance sales in a call center. I took classes for about six weeks on insurance law, and then passed an exam to become licensed to sell property and liability insurance for around forty-five states. It was a Monday through

Friday, nine to five job, which was great. Unfortunately, it was a phone sales job which did not work well for me. I hate talking on the phone, and definitely don't have the right personality for sales. I don't know what made me think I would be happy doing this. I think I was just so desperate to get out of mental health that I convinced myself I could do it. I did okay, but not great at the job. After about eight months of getting increasingly stressed by this work, I heard about another job prospect that sounded interesting. I quit selling insurance and returned to mental health.

This is when I got the case management position at the community mental health center, where I was working at the time of the Meltdown. After one and a half years as a case manager there, I had an opportunity to move to the county Office of Family and Children to become a caseworker for the state. I saw this as an opportunity to advance my career, and I took it. I liked this position and would have stayed there, if it weren't for the on-call situation. For one week of each month my caseworker team was on-call for Child Protective Services duties, after hours and on weekends. I didn't mind being on-call, but I didn't feel like I received enough training for this important duty. I shadowed another CPS worker for one week of on-call duty and that was the only training I received. The responsibilities of this job included making determinations such as whether a child needed to be removed from his parents due to abuse or neglect. I felt inadequate about making this decision, based on limited training. I was scared to death when I was on-call, dreading the beeper going off. I managed to do it without any problems, but felt totally stressed. After four months, when I heard of an opening at my former position as case manager I jumped at the chance to return to it. I was re-hired at the community mental health center, and even received a raise!

4
The Diagnosis

TO BE ASSIGNED a diagnosis, people must meet the criteria outlined by the most current version of the *Diagnostic and Statistical Manual of Mental Disorders (DSM)*, published by the American Psychiatric Association. All mental health providers, at least those in the United States, are familiar with this book and the "personality disorders" described within it. In my opinion "personality disorder" is a terrible label. It just sounds bad. I hate the notion of having to label people at all, but diagnostic labels do act as a form of shorthand to communicate quickly among providers of mental health services what is going on for a particular client. Personality disorders indicate a combination of personality traits that interfere with someone's functioning in a significant way. The label informs the provider about the most helpful approach to treatment.

Borderline Personality Disorder describes a pattern of intense and unstable relationships, impulsive behavior and difficulty managing strong emotions. People with this pattern tend to get angry easily, self-mutilate, experience suicidal thoughts and worry excessively about being abandoned by the people they care about. They often quickly become very dependent within their relationships.

I never believed Robin had borderline personality disorder, despite her difficulty managing strong emotions and her tendency to self-mutilate. It just didn't fit. Her relationships were neither intense nor unstable. Her self-mutilation and suicidal thoughts were isolated to times when she was biologically depressed, and getting her on the right medication always stopped her self-destructiveness. She did not usually do anything impulsively except when she was drinking alcohol. In fact, she usually obsessed for a long time before doing anything outside of her usual routine. And, she was rarely angry.

The whole question of which personality disorder diagnoses fit for Robin became very relevant after her meltdown. The staff in the hospital believed she had borderline personality disorder. I did not. Dr. Greene, who had been treating Robin for years, even put "borderline personality traits" on the discharge summary after her hospitalization.

Why did it matter? Because the effective approach to treatment is very different for clients who fit the pattern of borderline personality disorder than for those who do not. I had treated many people with this diagnosis. It is crucial in therapy to maintain clear, fairly strict interpersonal boundaries and to process the dynamics between therapist and client in order for people with borderline personality disorder to learn how to have healthy relationships.

When Robin had her meltdown and her behavior began to resemble that of someone with this diagnosis, I was confused. This was not the Robin I knew. I had a huge dilemma on my hands. My gut was telling me Robin's emotional isolation, consistent with avoidant personality disorder, was contributing to her severe, suicidal depression. I felt like I needed to extend my boundaries and be more available in order to help Robin feel connected to another person, and that this was likely the only thing that would keep her alive until we could get the biology of her brain stabilized.

If I was wrong and she really had borderline personality disorder, to extend the boundaries could be disastrous. Because people with this pattern have usually not experienced healthy relationships, if therapists extend the boundaries (which they often do with these clients because their needs are so great) it can lead to terrible situations in which clients get too attached, too dependent and emotionally destabilized. Therapists then end up needing to set firmer limits to regain a healthy balance in the relationship, which causes the client to feel shamed and abandoned. I had made this mistake while I was a therapist-in-training and had subsequently seen colleagues do so, with painful consequences all the way around. These experiences contributed to my general tendency to keep such firm, rigid boundaries in my role as a therapist.

In March 2003 I needed to make a crucial decision about Robin's treatment. Her life was at stake. Dr. Greene and the hospital staff thinking she had borderline personality traits caused me to question myself. I did not want to do the wrong thing and make things worse for Robin. So I did what all therapists should do when they are unsure and the stakes are high. I consulted my professional support network.

One of my closest friends, Giselle, was a fellow psychologist with much more experience than me. I trusted her to tell me if she thought I was making a mistake. She said something that made all the difference. I will be forever grateful for her wise and reassuring words.

"I hate that I'm so unsure about what to do," I said to Giselle. I filled her in on Robin's history and my dilemma. "I've known this person for ten years. She's never before acted like she's borderline. I really think it's all about severe depression and social isolation, and her obsessive-compulsive symptoms are causing her to be stuck in self-destructiveness. I think she needs me to be very available until she is stabilized. But I don't want to disregard what everyone else thinks and make things worse if I'm wrong!" We went on to talk a bit about my past experiences with clients who had borderline personality disorder, and some of my biggest fears about how making an incorrect therapeutic decision about Robin could make things worse for her.

Giselle then said what I needed to hear. "Sharon," she calmly said, "You've known her for ten years. If she had borderline personality disorder, you'd have known it by now."

Of course! Giselle was right. Personality disorders are pervasive and do not easily change. I had enough experience that I would have sensed it a long time earlier if this was an issue for Robin. Giselle's matter of fact, validating statement allowed me to take a huge leap of faith and trust my gut. Robin was skipping doses of her medication, drinking alcohol, and "faking it" with her friends and family. If something didn't change, she would likely destabilize. It felt like I needed to do something new and drastic to make it harder for Robin to seriously consider suicide.

What was the huge intervention my gut told me to do? I told Robin how much I cared about her. It was as simple as that. It was not something I previously would have done...with any client. But, I thought Robin needed to know, for sure, that at least one person in the world would be very upset if she killed herself. She had rationalized that her family members would "grieve and move on." They did not have an opportunity to correct this mistaken belief because she was not even letting them know she was still depressed, let alone suicidal. So, as the only person Robin was being open with about what she was feeling and thinking, I needed to help her understand the impact her suicide would have.

I took a deep breath, and said what I need to say. "Robin, I'm guessing you would never expect me to say this, but I'm probably just as worried about you ditching me as you were about me ditching you."

"What do you mean?" she asked, appearing confused.

"I don't usually tell my clients how much I care about them. But I want you to know I care about you very much. I've always liked working with you, and I believe we connected ten years ago for a reason. I believe there's a reason you ended up in my office the day you were hospitalized, instead of killing yourself. I think we're supposed to keep working together. I'll be really upset if you kill yourself. I feel bad about our misunderstanding that made you think I would ditch you. I feel somewhat responsible because I should have been talking to you about our relationship all along and I should have helped you to be more open with me. I'm so glad you're now telling me how you really feel. It doesn't make me respect or like you less. In fact, it makes me respect you more because I have a much better under-standing about how strong a person you are. I'm amazed you were able to do your job so well, even though you were so depressed."

Robin said nothing. She listened and stared at the floor. Her leg was bouncing, as usual. I continued talking.

"I intend to be much more available than I was in the past. I know you need to feel connected to someone right now, and that you can't be honest with your friends or family. Because I care about you and don't want to lose you, I'm happy to be that person. I know you're worried about becoming too dependent. We'll keep talking about that. It'll become clear once you are feeling better how much contact is right. You'll need to eventually work on being open with the other people who care about you. I'll help with that."

Robin seemed to be paying close attention to what I was saying, although it seemed to make her uncomfortable. "I have a hard time letting people know how I feel," she said.

"It's okay." I reassured her. "I know you care about me and what I think. I just want you to know what I think, so you don't have to wonder. What I think is that you are an amazing, smart, funny person who has a lot to give to other people. I'm really sorry you're feeling so depressed right now." I told Robin the best way she could show me she cared was to commit to continuing to work with me in therapy, and give it a chance to make a difference.

"Knowing how you feel puts me in a bind. It makes it harder for me to think about killing myself," she reluctantly said. Good, I thought. Thank God. She went on, "I can't promise anything, but I have no plans to kill myself at this point. I'm going to try to get back to work. I think it would take something bad happening for me to kill myself."

Robin was scheduled to start work a couple days later. We made plans to meet after she finished her first day. Something told me, though, to call her before I left work on the day I had told her I cared about her. I was concerned about how she might be reacting to my intervention of being honest.

"I'm glad you called," she said. "I've been trying to decide all afternoon whether to call you. I'm more anxious. I don't know if it's because of our conversation earlier or whether it's because I'm think-ing about going back to work."

"Probably both," I said. I was not surprised to hear she was more anxious.

"I'm not used to people talking about strong feelings. It makes me uncomfortable. And I feel pressured to do things I don't feel able to do." She was referring to me asking her to eat more and commit to not killing herself.

"I am pressuring you about those things. I'm sorry, but I'm still concerned that being self-destructive in any way...not eating, skip-ping medications and drinking will just get in the way of you feeling better. And I don't want you to kill yourself." I told Robin I was sorry about throwing so much at her, especially just before she was sup-posed to go back to work. But, I also told her I had felt strongly I needed to say what I said. We talked a few minutes longer and she assured me of her intention to refrain from drinking and take her medication as prescribed.

I went home that night and worried. I wasn't surprised that being open with Robin had caused an increase in her anxiety. I was relieved she immediately said it was harder for her to think about killing herself, but that was certainly no guarantee of anything. I was just hoping I had not made things worse for her. I imagined how awful it would be and how bad I would feel if she destabilized as a result of my intervention.

• • •

Robin returned to work half-time on March 13, 2003, the day after her brother and sister-in-law returned from their cruise. We met later on that day. She said she had more trouble sleeping the night before and had been very anxious upon returning to work, but that the reactions from her co-workers were positive. We talked on the phone after she finished work the second day.

"I'm just tired," Robin said. "Work was okay, but exhausting. I had to go to two court hearings this morning. It was stressful." She said she had talked to her co-workers about her absence from work, and that this had gone okay but made her very nervous. She sounded more depressed than I had heard her sound for a while, and I commented on it.

"I don't have any plans for the weekend," Robin replied, "I'm worried I'll have too much time to think." I got into typical therapist mode, and started problem-solving how Robin could get through the weekend. In hindsight, I wish I would have reacted differently. But, in some ways I was having as hard a time as Robin was in terms of changing my rigid patterns.

"Why don't you call your friends or family members and make plans to get together this weekend?" I suggested.

"I've already spent too much time this week faking it," Robin said. "I don't really want to be around people." Oh no! This was not good. I did not like what I was hearing. I kept making suggestions. Robin humored me and talked about some things she could do to keep herself busy and distracted.

"How are your suicidal thoughts?" I asked, somewhat afraid of what I would hear.

"They're still there," she said. "But I'm not planning to do anything. I think it would take something catastrophic happening to push me to that point."

"Will you call me if that happens?" I asked.

"Of course I'm not going to call you at home," said the Robin who, for a moment, sounded familiar.

I was concerned enough about how depressed Robin sounded, that I talked to her about a medication adjustment. The antipsychotic medication, Geodon, was definitely helping her sleep. But she was still so depressed. I paged Dr. Greene and he agreed she should increase one of the two antidepressant medications she was taking. She agreed to do so, and we confirmed our two planned appointment times for the following week.

At 4:00 pm that day after I finished seeing my last client for the week, I checked my voice mail. There was a message from Robin: *"I found out it's going to cost much more than I thought to fix Chuck's engine. When I heard that I just started crying and couldn't stop. I'm going to drink until I pass out!"*

After six weeks of medical leave, Robin had been back to work for only two half-days following her meltdown and was stressed about getting through a weekend with no social plans. When I got the voice mail at 4:00 pm that Friday saying she was upset about her Jeep and was going to get drunk, I was deeply concerned. She continued to demonstrate behavior that was so unlike the person I had known for so long.

At that time in my career I don't think I had ever talked to a client from home and, if so, never on a weekend. The agency where I worked had 24-hour emergency coverage which allowed outpatient therapists to maintain strict limits in terms of client contact. I had never heard any of my colleagues say they had talked to a client from home. Work time was work time. After work, we let the emergency services department cover for us. These boundaries allowed for re-energizing between long, stressful days of seeing five or six therapy clients per day, and served as a way to help clients keep from becoming overly dependent on us. When Robin was clearly worried about getting through the weekend on that Friday in March 2003, it never crossed my mind to suggest we talk while I was at home...despite me saying earlier in the week that I would be much more available to her.

When I got the voice mail from Robin saying "I'm going to drink until I pass out," I immediately called her.

"I've already started drinking," she said. I asked her to stop. She refused.

"Robin, you are depressed and suicidal," I said firmly. "Drinking decreases your impulse control. I'm worried about what you'll do once you are drunk." She was alone in her apartment and everyone in her life, other than me, thought the crisis had passed and she was doing fine. Knowing she would not tell her people she needed support from them, I was very concerned.

"If I feel too suicidal I'll call the emergency services," Robin said, obviously humoring me. We both knew there was no chance she would do this. I confronted her.

"You're right," she said, already feeling the effects of the vodka she was drinking. "That's unlikely."

"Do you need to be back in the hospital?" I asked. It was actually the last thing I wanted to have happen, as I did not want to have to deal with the hospital staff again about Robin being difficult. But, I was genuinely worried for her safety...more than I had been since the day of her meltdown two months earlier. Robin was adamant that she did not want to go back to the hospital.

"I'm just going to drink and go to sleep," she said, trying to reassure me. "I'm sure I'll wake up tomorrow feeling better." Not likely, I thought. But, we hung up, as I knew we were at an impasse. I needed to think.

I was in a horrible position. I did not want to hospitalize Robin against her will. That would require having the police go to her apartment and forcibly bring her to the hospital. I did not think she actually met the criteria for being "detained" anyway, as she was denying any plans of hurting herself in the immediate future. Robin had signed Release of Information forms for me to talk to family and friends. I could have called one of them and asked them to go check on her, but I was concerned this would destroy the new level of trust we were developing. I knew I could not just leave things the way they were and go home for the weekend. I was too worried, knowing Robin was so

depressed, isolated, suicidal and drinking. Judgment calls about suicidal clients were a routine part of being a full-time therapist at a big
mental health agency. I knew I needed to do something, but I wasn't
sure what that was.

I was happy to discover my supervisor was still at work late on
that Friday afternoon. I needed to consult with someone I trusted.
We had worked together for a number of years, and Judith had been
a mentor to me. She had lots of experience and was highly regarded
by clinicians within the agency and throughout the community. She
knew about Robin's meltdown, as I had been consulting with her from
the beginning.

"Judith, I need your help," I said, and explained the situation. "I'm
really concerned about Robin's safety." Judith was one of the people
I had consulted about the issue of whether to extend the boundaries
with Robin. We had talked through my belief that she did not have borderline personality disorder despite the hospital staff's opinion. Like
my friend Giselle had earlier in the week, Judith helped me immensely
on that Friday afternoon by making a simple, obvious statement.

"Sharon," said Judith, "Why don't you just plan to check in with
Robin by phone over the weekend?"

Of course. What a wake-up call! It is unbelievable to me now that
I felt so unable to make this decision for myself. But, it was as if I
needed Judith's permission to violate what felt like an absolute rule
of therapy, at least at that agency at that time. My own obsessive-
compulsiveness kept me from being able to be more flexible. I had
told Robin earlier in the week I was going to be more available, and
then when she was vulnerably saying she was worried about getting
through the weekend I had stayed within my usual rigid boundaries.
I will forever be grateful to Judith for helping me look past my own
rigidity. I called Robin back.

"Robin, it's me. I didn't like the way we left things when we talked
earlier." She was still drinking and sounded slightly intoxicated, but
was still relatively coherent.

"I'm horrified by how fast I crashed," she said. "I know I'll have trouble facing you on Monday after behaving so badly."

Okay, there was a moment of clarity about the destructiveness of what she was doing. I tried again to get her to agree to stop drinking and pour out her alcohol. After some negotiation she did agree to stop drinking for the evening, and I promised to touch base with her by phone in the morning.

I was very glad I had consulted with Judith and realized I needed to be more flexible. Being able to talk to Robin on the phone after work hours was a significant shift for me that would become crucial to keeping her alive over the subsequent months. In the case of that particular weekend it was instrumental in helping me realize that Robin had been misdiagnosed...for the previous decade.

• • •

The next morning, I called Robin as planned. "I screwed up," she said sheepishly. "I'm completely hung over. I know drinking was a huge mistake."

"Do you need to be in the hospital, Robin?"

"I've been wondering that myself," she said. "I can't believe how I acted yesterday. I'm not stable. It scares me how fast I crashed and how stupid I was." She seemed genuinely frightened by her own behavior.

We talked about the pros and cons of having her go to the hospital and mutually decided the only benefit would be keeping her safe, which seemed like less of an issue than it had the previous day. "It would just cause more problems," Robin said. "I'd have to take more time off work, when I just went back." She was also worried about the financial obligation of returning to the hospital, since she did not know yet what she would owe from her previous three-week hospital stay.

We talked about her plans for the weekend. "I was throwing up all night after drinking so much," she said. "I don't think I could kill myself now even if I wanted to, because I'd just throw up whatever pills I take." We discussed this and made sure she had no other viable methods for killing herself available.

Robin then said yet another surprising thing. "I'm wondering if I subconsciously got drunk to make you mad enough to ditch me. It would be easier to kill myself if you would just ditch me."

Wow! There was the insightful Robin I knew. Not only were we having a rational discussion about whether she should be hospitalized, but she was thinking about and openly discussing her feelings about our relationship. I had gotten through to her! It was impacting her to know she would hurt me if she killed herself. Inside, part of me was cheering. The rest of me was still very worried about Robin's safety.

I was just beginning to grasp the degree to which Robin felt unable to control herself, and the fear this caused for her. She seemed to be trying to make sense of her own behavior. Robin felt bad enough about drinking the night before, and guilty enough about me calling her on the weekend, that she assured me she would be okay until our scheduled session on Monday. I believed her. She was sounding more rational than she had in a long time.

In our Monday session, Robin continued to talk openly. "I feel out of control," she said. "I'm worried about what'll happen if I get any more bad news. I'm not planning to kill myself at this point, but I still hate myself, hate my life, and wish I were dead."

Robin said her obsessive brain was continuing to focus on suicide. She was able to verbalize the internal battle being waged in her mind. She said she had gotten online over the weekend to research more specifics about ways to kill herself. At the same time, she said "It makes me uncomfortable to get more attached to you because it'll only make it harder to kill myself. But I keep coming to therapy and taking my meds. And I called you last Friday even though I usually would never do that. Part of me clearly wants help and wants to live."

What a relief it was to hear Robin say this. Thank God! It was her willingness to finally be completely open that allowed me to think about her situation and symptoms differently. Her very sudden mood shift, followed by impulsive self-destructive behavior and then genuine fear about feeling so completely unable to control herself, made me start thinking she might benefit from a mood stabilizing medication. Robin was scheduled to meet with Dr. Greene two days later, and I planned to talk to him about this option.

The next evening, I was at home thinking about Robin and what had happened. Mood stabilizing medications are usually used for people with bipolar disorder. I started thinking about bipolar disorder. All of a sudden my brain was reeling with a stunning realization! It felt like I couldn't keep up with my thoughts as I was instantly processing many things all at the same time.

Bipolar Disorder comes in several forms. Most people are familiar with the typical bipolar pattern of depression alternating with mania. During an episode of mania people feel very happy, energetic, don't need sleep and often do impulsive things they later regret. In its more severe form, bipolar mania often causes psychotic symptoms including hallucinations (hearing or seeing things that are not there) or delusions (believing things that are not real). A milder version, hypomania, causes all the typical symptoms of mania but not psychosis.

Robin had never shown signs of typical mania or even hypomania, and she never had periods of elevated mood. The idea of her having bipolar disorder had never before entered my mind. But, there is a less well known version of bipolar disorder called "mixed mania," or "a mixed episode" in which people experience symptoms of both depression and mania at the same time. All of a sudden, as I was thinking about telling Dr. Greene I thought Robin needed a mood stabilizer, I had an "epiphany." That word came to my mind, even before I remembered this was the name of Robin's cat. Maybe Robin was having a mixed bipolar episode!

I had been to the conference in Florida on psychopharmacology two months earlier. I learned more about mixed bipolar episodes than I had known before. The presenter was making a big deal about the importance of distinguishing between a mixed bipolar episode and an episode of severe depression accompanied by significant anxiety. I remembered him saying it was crucial to make this distinction because, "giving antidepressant medications to someone with bipolar disorder, without a mood stabilizer on board first, can make their symptoms worse."

While trying to wrap my brain around the epiphany I was having, I ran to get the materials from that conference. I remembered the presenter talking about how to identify a mixed bipolar episode, but I didn't remember what he had said.

After some digging through the piles on my desk, I found the handouts which included copies of the slides from the presentations. There was one slide that said it all. It was suddenly clear. The slide had the four distinguishing characteristics of "a mixed state": "Unrelenting Dysphoria, Marked Irritability, Severe Agitation/Anxiety, Intractable Insomnia."

Holy shit, I thought. I couldn't believe it! For the first time since Robin's meltdown, things suddenly all made sense. Dysphoria is depressed mood, which certainly fit. Bipolar disorder would explain why Robin had not responded to multiple antidepressant medications for the past year. It explained why her affect had been completely flat for so long and she was so depressed. This was why she was irritable, which was so unlike her. It was why she was being so impulsively self-destructive and feeling unable to control herself. It was why her leg bounced all the time, a hallmark sign of psychomotor agitation. She was experiencing a mixed bipolar episode!

As I thought about it, Robin's reaction to all the medication changes Dr. Greene and I had collaboratively made in the previous year fit more and more with this diagnosis. The presenter at the conference had talked about the recent revelation that the newer antipsychotics, including Geodon, had somewhat of a mood stabilizing effect. Robin was only able to sleep when she took Geodon. She got worse when she had gone off of it. But Geodon was not known primarily as a mood stabilizer. That was a whole different category of medications, and Robin appeared to need one of them.

Thankfully, Robin was scheduled to see Dr. Greene at noon the next day. I called him first thing in the morning. "Dr. Greene, I had an epiphany about Robin!" I said.

"Oh good, I love epiphanies," he replied. We had a good working relationship, and he was eager to hear what I had to say.

"Think about everything that has happened with Robin. Now, think about it in the context of mixed bipolar disorder," I said. I went on to explain all the things I had realized. I talked about another symptom of mixed mania, racing thoughts, which in hindsight Robin had seemed to be experiencing when she was in the hospital, before Dr. Greene prescribed the Geodon.

"I think you may be right," he said. "That would explain a lot of things." We talked about the fact that he was scheduled to see her that day. I told him I needed to be the one to tell Robin what we were thinking, and I would call her before she saw him. He agreed to prescribe a mood stabilizer and to educate Robin about it.

I hung up, feeling relieved that Dr. Greene and I were on the same page. I had not been happy about him thinking Robin had borderline personality traits. Before we talked, I was not sure he would agree with my opinion about bipolar disorder. I had about a minute to feel relieved after our conversation. I had to make a phone call quickly so I could have a serious conversation with Robin before she saw Dr. Greene. I had been so focused on talking to him about my epiphany, I had not even begun to process the ramifications of telling Robin. All of a sudden it sunk in. I had to call Robin and tell her I thought she had bipolar disorder. Yikes!

Robin was home for the morning, as she was still working half-days following her meltdown. I nervously made the phone call, not having any idea how she would react to the news.

"Robin, I have something big to tell you," I said. "I had an epiphany last night. I think the reason you're feeling so out of control may be because you're having a mixed bipolar episode." I went on to tell her about the symptoms and how this would explain why we had been having so much trouble finding the right medication. "Dr. Greene agrees this may be what's going on, and he'll be talking to you about taking a mood stabilizer. If you have bipolar disorder, this could make all the difference. It could be the answer in terms of you getting back to feeling okay again." I was trying to focus on the positives of the news I was giving her, knowing what a big deal it was for her to have to wrap her brain around it.

She seemed stunned, which was to be expected. "It would be a big adjustment for me to get used to this," she said. I knew she would need some time to process this news. We made plans to talk on the phone later that day after she got home from work.

"I'm having a lot of anxiety," Robin said when I called early that evening. "I'm afraid I'm not going to sleep tonight." She acknowledged that the anxiety was likely related to the idea of having bipolar disorder. "I'm concerned about the side effects of Depakote."

Depakote was the mood stabilizer Dr. Greene had chosen, as it was especially effective for mixed bipolar symptoms. We talked about her session with him, her concerns about being on Depakote, and her anxiety. She assured me she was not suicidal and said she needed time to process this new development.

I also needed to process this development, which had happened quickly following my sudden epiphany. How did both Dr. Greene and I go so long without either of us thinking about the possibility that Robin might have bipolar disorder? I felt bad that she had been depressed for over a year, trying medication after medication, and had only gotten worse. This made complete sense in the context of bipolar disorder, since taking antidepressants without a mood stabilizer can exacerbate bipolar symptoms. In fact, Dr. Greene and I had decided to increase her antidepressant dose a few weeks prior to her meltdown, trying to get more aggressive about treating her ongoing, significant depression. That medication increase, I assumed, had probably contributed to her meltdown.

I felt bad about that possibility, but I was not beating myself up too badly. I knew why we had never considered bipolar disorder. Robin had never had a typical manic or hypomanic episode, with elevated mood. She had never told me she felt unable to control her impulses, which was a hallmark symptom of mania. Both severe depression and mixed bipolar disorder could show a depressed mood combined with enormous anxiety, agitation and persistent insomnia. Robin had a trauma history, obsessive-compulsive disorder, obsessive-compulsive personality disorder and avoidant personality disorder, all of which caused anxiety. Insomnia was common for her and could be completely explained by the severe anxiety that was an ongoing part of her life.

Most importantly, prior to the year before her meltdown Robin's depression symptoms had always been easily alleviated with antidepressants alone. These medications had never previously made her worse. Given all the facts, there had been no way for us to know she was experiencing bipolar symptoms until she got worse enough and was comfortable enough to tell me how out of control she felt. Her new willingness to be open about her symptoms, in addition to her symptoms worsening to the point where they were more obvious, had finally helped me shift. I was just sorry, for Robin's sake, that it had taken so long for it to become clear. She had suffered so much!

• • •

"If I have bipolar disorder I'd have to accept a whole new identity," Robin said in our session the next day. "I'm okay with having depression and taking medication for it. Lots of people take antidepressant medication. But having bipolar disorder would mean I'm chronically mentally ill. I'd have to take mood stabilizers and maybe antipsychotic meds for the rest of my life." We talked about the ramifications of this identity shift. Having worked in the mental health field for so long, Robin was acutely aware of what it meant to have a severe and chronic mental illness. Her knowledge about the stigma associated with her potential new identity made it hard for her to imagine ever feeling okay about it.

Robin expressed fear about her tendency to feel, at times, compelled by her own brain to skip her medications and about how this would be a bigger problem if she had bipolar disorder. She openly revealed that since adolescence she had felt "crazy" when she was especially depressed and anxious. This was consistent with the racing thoughts I suspected, in hindsight, she had been having while she was in the hospital. The perception that one's thoughts are racing is another symptom of mania. Robin acknowledged that racing thoughts had been an issue, which she had never before felt able to verbalize. She said when she had racing thoughts, she felt "crazy."

Robin asked me what she would experience if the Depakote started to work. I told her she would feel less crazy, more stable and hopefully would feel less despair.

"That would be a relief," she said with no emotion.

As the weekend was approaching, I was met with the dilemma of whether to plan to talk to Robin on the phone, as we had done the previous weekend. I was torn. She was trying to integrate her new reality, in the context of thinking irrationally. It seemed to warrant an extra phone call. But at the same time, I didn't want to push her to have more contact with me than she was comfortable having. I knew her avoidant personality traits caused her to feel very anxious about being more open with me. I didn't want to make things any worse for her. I decided I needed to let Robin make the decision about whether to talk that weekend. Her response was not surprising.

"I feel like I'm getting too dependent," she said. "It makes me uncomfortable." She was not interested in scheduling a time to talk. She was getting increasingly anxious as she continued to process the bipolar issue and as she thought about returning to work full-time the following week. She said it would cause too much anxiety for her to plan to talk to me on the weekend. "I probably won't call. But if I feel too unstable I'll try to call you."

It was the best I could expect. Robin was making herself very vulnerable by being so open. She said she was not used to talking to people about her self-proclaimed "craziness." I was very concerned as I went home that weekend, knowing Robin would likely not call me or anyone else if she started feeling worse. I also knew that during a weekend with no plans and too much time to try to wrap her brain around her new reality, the likelihood of her getting worse was high.

These are the situations outpatient therapists dread. I could not hospitalize Robin against her will. She was not psychotic, and was insisting she was not planning to kill herself that weekend. Under the circumstances Dr. Greene would certainly have hospitalized her if she would have gone voluntarily, but she didn't want this.

I spent most of the weekend feeling anxious and worried, knowing Robin needed me to leave her alone in her anxiety and despair. Part of me was surprised, and part of me was not surprised when she called on Sunday afternoon.

"I drank a couple of wine coolers to get my nerve up to call you," Robin admitted. "I went to my parents' house to tan and talked to my brother. I tried calling Christi but she wasn't home. I've been reading on-line about bipolar disorder but I don't understand mixed episodes. I don't know whether I have it or not."

"Robin, we need to take one step at a time," I replied. "Let's see if the Depakote helps. We should know in the next few days and that will help us know if bipolar disorder is the issue."

Robin talked about her anxiety and fear about returning to work full-time the next day. It had only been a week and a half since she had returned part-time following her hospitalization and medical leave, and it had been stressful. She said she was thinking about calling off work, saying she was sick. I asked whether she felt safe, or whether she needed to be in the hospital.

"I don't want to go the hospital and I'm not planning to kill myself," she said. "But I'll probably keep drinking." We began to debate about drinking, as we had the previous weekend. I expressed my concern about how this could impact her already fragile impulse control. She seemed to be trying to get me off the phone. I didn't want to battle with her and make her more likely to destabilize. I knew how hard it was for her to call me, and I didn't want this call to end badly. "I'll read some magazines and go to bed early," Robin said.

We hung up. What a nightmare! I knew Robin was not okay, but I had no good options. I argued with myself for a while, trying to figure out whether I should do something and, if so, what. I was still hesitant to involve Robin's family, who had no idea she was struggling. Robin would feel hurt, angry and betrayed if I involved them without telling her. If I was sure it was a life threatening situation, I wouldn't have hesitated. But I wasn't. It didn't make sense to violate Robin's trust.

During the time I was an outpatient therapist, as an anxious person I would almost always worry when I was in a situation with a depressed client who I knew was having serious suicidal thoughts. But as long as I felt I had done what I could do and they were telling me they were not planning to kill themselves, it was not up to me to do anything more. Making contact with a client just to relieve my own anxiety would be completely inappropriate. It would send the message that the client was too fragile to make his or her own decisions, and it would just contribute to fostering an unhealthy dependency within the relationship. On that Sunday, part of me was telling myself the right thing to do was to manage my own anxiety and trust Robin to make it through the evening.

But then there was my gut, screaming at me. This was not a typical situation. Robin had just been told she may have bipolar disorder, was aware of and trying to process the ramifications of that, and was facing an enormous stressor of having to go to work full-time the next day. If I was right about the bipolar diagnosis, her impulse control and judgment were impaired anyway. She had already started drinking, which would make it worse. And most importantly, Robin had called me. She had almost never called me, in our decade long relationship. It was a big deal. She had to drink wine coolers to "work up the nerve." There was something she wanted me to know.

An hour or two had passed after our phone conversation when my gut finally won the battle I was having with myself about what to do. I called her back.

"Robin, I'm so sorry if it makes you anxious to talk to me again, but something told me to call and find out if you're okay."

"I'm in my car driving around," Robin said. We talked for a while and she sounded even more depressed and hopeless than when we had talked earlier. But the insightful Robin was also still there. "I know I'm making bad decisions. I'm mad at myself. I'm out of control," she said.

"Robin, I think you need to be in the hospital," I immediately told her. And, just like the day of her meltdown, she did not argue. She agreed to go home, pack her things and meet me there. I called ahead, talked to the emergency services staff and told them we were coming. I was relieved, knowing Robin would be safe.

We met at the hospital where I again sat with her by the big fish tank in the lobby while the admissions staff worked to get approval from her insurance company. It was two months after the day she was first hospitalized. Robin looked both exhausted and anxious. Her leg was bouncing more vigorously than usual. Her affect, as it had been for the previous two months, was flat.

"I drank more than I told you," she confessed. It continued to be one of her obsessive-compulsive rules to tell me whenever she engaged in self-destructive behavior.

"How much?" I asked, horrified that she had driven home and back to the hospital. She had not sounded drunk on the phone when we had talked. She was not looking or acting intoxicated.

"I don't know," she replied. "But I'm pretty drunk."

Wow! Robin revealed she had been drinking vodka while she was driving around. She could have killed someone else in addition to herself! Thank God my gut had told me to call her back! I let the admissions counselor at the hospital know Robin had much more to drink than she had previously said. I wanted the staff on the unit to be aware she was intoxicated. I told Robin I would be in touch the next day.

Robin's second hospitalization, in March 2003, lasted three days. She was more open with the staff than she had been in her first hospitalization but did not attend the groups. Dr. Greene increased her dose of Depakote. Within two days, Robin said she wanted to go home.

"I screwed up by drinking," she said. "I need to work harder to avoid alcohol." Robin and I set up a safety plan which included getting rid of all the alcohol in her apartment, and making social plans to fill the next weekend so she would not be so isolated.

Robin was discharged from the hospital with the plan of returning to her job half-time the rest of that week and full-time the next week. Her affect actually appeared brighter than it had in a long time, and she said her suicidal thoughts were minimal. She was sleeping well. Her thoughts were no longer racing and her knee was no longer bouncing. I was sure the Depakote was starting to take effect.

For the first time in over a year, I felt hopeful that we were on the right track in terms of Robin's treatment. It was such a relief! I believed the mixed bipolar disorder diagnosis was the answer, and that as the Depakote continued to take effect Robin would soon be feeling and functioning much better than she had in a long time. I had no idea how wrong I would turn out to be.

Robin's Thoughts About the Diagnosis

When Sharon told me she and Dr. Greene had determined that I fit the criteria for bipolar disorder I was shocked, but a small part of me was relieved. I was relieved because it meant that somebody had finally figured out what was going on and had a plan to treat it. I didn't know much about mixed episodes at the time, despite my background in mental health. I did my own research online to get information aside from what Sharon and Dr. Greene had told me. It made perfect sense as a diagnosis, as I exhibited all the symptoms of a mixed bipolar episode. It also helped explain my "crazy" behavior of the past better than simple depression did.

However, the relieved part of me was small. The bigger part of me was overwhelmed initially, feeling too many emotions at once to identify them. I remember feeling a physical jolt in my body, like an electrical charge, when Sharon told me. I was still reeling from the fact that I had been in a psychiatric hospital for three weeks. I don't think I was remotely ready to integrate a chronic mental illness diagnosis too.

I had accepted my past diagnoses of depression and OCD without any issues. After all, I obviously met the criteria for each of these diagnoses and thought that they explained the neurotic behavior I'd exhibited since my teens. I was okay with it, and with being in therapy and on antidepressant medication. There was a stigma, sure, but it was small and I didn't mind those close to me knowing my mental health situation. My identity, as I saw it, was a depressed person who worked in the mental health field, and that was fine with me. In fact, this was common. It worked for me.

But being diagnosed with a chronic mental illness and having to take a mood stabilizer was a different scenario. I wasn't prepared for all that meant. I worried what people would think when they found out, and whether my job status would be impacted. Suddenly, I had a new reality as a truly mentally ill person. It's like I crossed a line between acceptable mental illness and truly being "crazy" (in the minds of society, not mine). I needed to change my identity, and change wasn't something I was good at.

I've suffered from depressive symptoms on and off since childhood. When I now look back, I believe there were signs of bipolar disorder from early on, that I could never have recognized and never talked about. The first time I can remember feeling depression was in fourth grade. We moved to a different school system half way through the year, and it was terrible for me. I had to face a new home with new neighborhood kids, as well as a new school, new teachers and new surroundings. My mom has said she thought I hated her at this time. I spent a lot of time alone in my room, crying and hating life. My twin brother, Bob, adjusted well, making new friends easily. I remember looking out my bedroom window at him playing with the neighborhood kids, and feeling depressed. It took the rest of the school year for me to adjust to this change.

I started self-mutilating when I was in junior high school. I think the first few times I cut on myself, it was attention seeking behavior. I made very superficial cuts on my arms. My family noticed but accepted my lame explanations about accidental scratches without further intervention. Eventually, I used the cutting to satisfy my need to punish myself (a frequent feeling for people who experience childhood molestation). It was satisfying to watch the blood stream from my arm. It didn't take very long for the cutting to become my response to any negative emotion. I also cut when I felt numb from dissociating. As I grew older the cutting became less superficial and caused scarring. Everyone continued to accept my explanations for the wounds, and it obviously made them uncomfortable to discuss it.

I took a psychology class in high school, which gave me a better understanding of depression. I felt validated after this class, as it reinforced that there were others like me. Also, I read *The Bell Jar* by Sylvia Plath in high school and was further reassured that the way I sometimes felt was not uncommon. I have reread this novel countless times, as Sylvia Plath does an excellent job of describing how depression feels.

I probably surprised some people by choosing to attend the University of Arizona, given that I was shy, lacked confidence, and had never been away from home for any length of time. My freshman year at U of A was very significant for me. I not only survived being over a thousand miles away from home, I made many friends there and became more confident.

Unfortunately, it was during my first year of college when I discovered alcohol. I began to drink, heavily and frequently, which did not help my emotional stability and increased my impulsive, self-destructive behavior. One of the most dangerous things I would do was drinking and driving. I would get drunk, become bored or depressed, and go for drives around Tucson listening to depressing music. Often, I would drink while I was driving around.

On one occasion, I chose not to go out with my friends but instead stayed at the dorm and drank until I became very depressed. I went for a drive, listening to depressing music and drinking. I was drinking cheap, grape wine which tasted vile. At one point, I poured the wine out my car window, streaking it down the side of the car door. I was so drunk, I stopped the car at the side of the road and urinated in the street.

At about this time I must have been driving erratically, because I was pulled over by a policeman. I know he must have noticed the grape wine on the car door. However, he was very nice to me. For some reason, he didn't arrest me. He simply told me to go to a nearby convenience store and have some coffee to sober up. I was too drunk to even be scared. I did what he said, and he left. Somehow, after sitting briefly at the store, I managed to find a familiar street and found my way back to the dorm. It was horribly negligent of this officer to not arrest me, as I could have gone on to kill myself or someone else. This was 1985, and attitudes toward drunk driving were just beginning to change. I don't believe this would ever happen today. I wish I could say this experience taught me a lesson and I never did it again, but that's not the case. I continued to drink and drive while listening to depressing music for years after this. It wasn't until the 1990's, when I was pulled over and had to do a Breathalyzer, that I stopped this dangerous behavior.

A significant result of my time at U of A was an increase in my tanning obsession. I was able to lay out longer in the fall, and sooner in the spring due to the warmer climate. Unfortunately, I had a class at 2 p.m., three days a week. The class was Introduction to Meteorology, and was very boring. I often skipped this class to lay out with my friends. I missed an exam, and ended up failing the class (for the first time in my life).

I didn't realize at the time that I would lose my federal loan because of this, which meant that I would be unable to return to Arizona for my sophomore year. I received the notification letter over the summer, while I was working in a bakery (which I called the Bakery from Hell, because it was so hot). There was no way I could afford out of state tuition and room and board at Arizona without the loan, and I freaked out. One day at work at the bakery, I got agitated thinking about the situation and started sobbing. I ran out of work, went home and packed a bag, and drove to Omaha, Nebraska to see my best friend from U of A.

My parents had gone on a camping trip and returned to find me gone, which I think freaked them out. I came home soon after, and my parents and I discussed my options. The smart choices would have been to go to Indiana University, or the local IU campus. However, I was obsessed with returning to Arizona. We decided I would return to U of A as a part-time student and get a job to save money toward going full-time again.

I returned to Arizona for my sophomore year in 1986, but things weren't the same as when I lived in the freshman dorm. All of my friends from the dorm were scattered around campus. My best friend was living off-campus with someone else, and I was living in a smaller dorm that had been converted from a hotel. It even had a swimming pool. I should've been happy to be back, but instead I was miserable. My roommate was weird (she vacuumed in the nude). I was only taking two classes and was afraid that the university would find out and kick me out. I was also not having any luck in finding a job.

I was depressed and drinking quite a bit, and had no money for food. I started having anxiety attacks and cried a lot. I felt very stressed as I started to come to the realization that I was not going to be able to stay. I finally called my parents and asked if I could come home. At first they wanted me to try to make it work, but I think they could tell I was losing it and eventually agreed that I should come home. It was about half way through the semester when I withdrew from my classes. I packed my car, sobbing, and drove the first five hours to New Mexico. I was despondent at having to leave and just wanted to die. I left early the next morning and drove straight through the rest of the way home.

I got a job at a factory in order to save money once I got home. About a month later, my friend from high school invited me to Indiana University to visit for Halloween. While I was there she invited me to move down there and get an apartment with her. So, by November I was leaving home again to move to Bloomington, Indiana. I didn't take any classes initially. I worked in a grocery store deli in order to save money.

I ended up staying at IU for two and a half years, mostly going to school part-time and working. My binge drinking continued at IU, especially after I turned 21 in 1988. The depressive episodes and self-destructive behavior also continued.

About half way through my time in Bloomington I had another mini-meltdown. I was working full-time and taking a couple classes at the time. I worked in a restaurant, doing salad bar preparation and set-up. I became very depressed, started drinking and cutting more and I spent more time in my room, listening to depressing music. One day I was supposed to work in the afternoon, but just couldn't make myself go. I didn't bother to call in, and ignored the phone when they tried calling me. I didn't go to work the next day or the day after that. They eventually called and talked to one of my roommates. Obviously, I should have been fired. However, I eventually called and arranged a meeting with the manager. I was honest with him about my emotional state and even showed him the cuts on my arm. He was very compassionate, and didn't fire me because I was a good worker. I was very lucky not to have lost this job.

My roommates graduated in the spring of 1989, so I returned home to work and attend Indiana University, South Bend (IUSB). Initially, I attended school full-time and worked in a daycare, which I really enjoyed. This lasted until July 1990, when I got hired in my first "real" job, as a live-in house parent in a group home for emotionally and behaviorally disturbed adolescent girls. This was a challenging job, but I learned quite a bit about working with mentally ill teens, and I was good at it. I became a more mature, responsible person because of this job. I didn't drink very often because of my work schedule. I stopped self-mutilating, because it would have been too difficult to hide or explain away. Some of the girls I worked with were self-mutilators, and they would have seen through any lame excuse I could have given.

After about thirteen months as a house parent I was promoted to a supervisor position, supervising the house parents of two group homes. This was an afternoon shift position, so I was able to return to classes in the mornings. I did well in this position (I was chosen as Employee of the Quarter twice, once as a houseparent, and once as a supervisor). I had minor depression and anxiety during this period, but overall I functioned pretty well.

However, in 1993 things started going downhill. I started to get depressed and have anxiety attacks, and was barely sleeping at night. I had nightmares and began dissociating. I was stressed out at work, only going through the motions. I started drinking heavily again and had obsessive suicidal thoughts. I was anxious about my impending graduation from college and about being an aunt for the first time. I was also getting ready to move from an apartment to a house with a roommate.

The inevitable mini-meltdown happened in April 1993. My roommate found me hiding in my closet, covered with a blanket. I was dissociating so I'm not sure how I ended up in the closet. I remember that I started drinking in the morning, and cutting on my arms. My roommate was understandably freaked out and wanted to call the police. I managed to talk her into calling my brother instead. He came right over, and I started sobbing when I saw him. I was extremely anxious and agitated. We talked for a while and I calmed down. My roommate wanted me to go to the hospital, I think, but my brother convinced her it wasn't necessary.

I didn't call my boss to say I wouldn't be at work. In retrospect, he would have been very understanding, but at the time I was panicked at the idea of talking to anyone at work. My roommate (also a supervisor at the same facility) called her supervisor and informed her about what had happened. My boss tried to call me for several days after this but I couldn't talk to him. Eventually, I resigned from this job because I couldn't face going back.

After failing to get my brother to take me to the hospital, my roommate made me agree to let her call the local community mental health center and make an appointment. She said she couldn't continue to live with me unless I was evaluated. So my first official contact with psychiatric services took place the following day.

I had an intake assessment completed by a very nice lady named Pam. I was able to convince her that I was not an imminent danger to myself or others, and didn't need to be hospitalized. My first appointment with Sharon was scheduled for May 10, 1993, and our long journey began.

Looking back, it's obvious I needed help long before 1993. There were significant red flags that I didn't acknowledge. For instance, the self-mutilating behavior which started in my early teens and intensified during college is obviously not "normal" behavior. It was a sign that something was wrong. My family and friends accepted my excuses for the self-harm, partly because of a lack of knowledge about this behavior, but also I don't think it was conceivable to my parents that I would intentionally harm myself, and they wanted to believe my excuses. They didn't know about my abuse experience so they had no context in which to put self-mutilation. Sexual abuse was not known about in the early '80's like it is now. I remember the TV movie *Something About Amelia* starring Ted Danson and Glenn Close was very controversial when it came out in 1984. The climate was very different then than it is now.

The heavy drinking was another red flag that was ignored. I was away at school in Arizona and at IU except for the summers during college, so my parents only knew what I told them about my drinking. I was living the college experience at party schools, and didn't realize that my drinking was so out of control. Looking back, it's obvious that binge drinking was another sign that I was in trouble. Everybody drank a lot though, so it didn't seem so out of place. The fact that I was driving around listening to depressing music made the situation much more troublesome, though. I could've killed someone very easily while driving drunk, which horrifies me now. Again, the climate in the late '80's and early '90's was more lenient about drinking and driving than it is now, which is the only rationale I can come up with for the police officer not arresting me when he pulled me over in Arizona.

There were a couple of occasions when people tried to get me to seek help prior to 1993. The first happened in Arizona after a night of very heavy drinking and self-harm. I had punched a wall so hard that my right hand swelled up. You couldn't even tell I had knuckles because they were so swollen the next day. My Resident Assistant in the dorm pulled me aside the following day and tried to talk to me. She suggested that I go to the student mental health center. I was extremely embarrassed and ashamed, and minimized the situation as I had always done with others. There's no way I was going to the mental health center. The stigma was even greater then than it is now, and I didn't want to be labeled "crazy" by my peers.

The other occasion in which someone tried to get me to go for help occurred while I was at IU. It was a difficult time for me, mainly because I didn't have as many friends as I had in Arizona. I didn't live in a dorm at IU which is the best chance to make friends in a college town. The only people I knew were my two roommates, and they had their own things going on. I'm not an outgoing person so it's hard for me to make friends on my own. I met people through my part time jobs and that was the extent of my social life. So I was very isolated, and I continued to drink heavily and drive around listening to depressing music. I had multiple depressive episodes while I was there. During one of these episodes, I was lying in bed in the dark listening to my depressing mix tape when one of my roommates came in. She lay on the bed next to me and tried to talk to me. She suggested that I go to the student mental health center, just as my Resident Assistant in Arizona had done. My response was the same as previously. I minimized the situation and didn't go for help.

Looking back on both of these situations I wish I had accepted the advice and gone for treatment. I could've gotten treatment sooner, rather than waiting until the mini-meltdown in 1993 which cost me my job. In spite of my education in psychology and my work in the mental health field for three years (at the time), I still didn't acknowledge I needed help until it got ugly. Even then it took an ultimatum from my roommate to finally get me to go to therapy.

Now, in hindsight, I see signs that I may have been experiencing bipolar symptoms as early as childhood. Unfortunately, because I never experienced mania without accompanying depression (I had mixed states) I never recognized the symptoms as bipolar and neither did anyone else. Because I've always had severe anxiety, I thought that explained my frequent insomnia. Because dissociating and self-mutilating often result from childhood trauma, which I experienced, and because alcohol got added to the mix which significantly affected my impulse control, there were many explanations for all of my symptoms other than bipolar disorder. And, I never told Sharon or anyone else how crazy I actually felt.

5
A New Approach in Therapy

WHEN ROBIN WAS discharged following her second hospitalization in March 2003, I was very relieved that she seemed to be doing better. I assumed the mood stabilizer, Depakote, was starting to take effect. "I feel more stable," she said during our first session after returning home. "I feel like I can control myself better, and like I'm less crazy. But I'm having a bad day because I found out it's going to cost about $500 more than I thought to get Chuck fixed and I don't have the money. I'm starting to getting really freaked out about my finances."

Robin had never talked much about her financial situation. She had made reference to having debt, mostly connected to periods of time between jobs. But she had never talked about being particularly stressed about money. "I don't really feel like I'm up to going back to work full-time," Robin went on to explain. "But, I have to. I can't afford to go any longer without my full income."

"Robin, how are you feeling about being more open and vulnerable with me?" I asked before we ended our session. I wanted to know how much contact she needed, so we could plan whether to schedule a phone call before our next session. "I feel like I'm getting too dependent," came Robin's standard answer to this question. "It makes me anxious." She was still unable to verbalize what being too dependent meant, but it didn't matter. Since she was more stable, I needed to back off and let her get some distance.

I felt like I needed distance too. I had been expending significant emotional energy for an extended time. Worrying about Robin's safety non-stop for over two months had taken a toll on me, and I needed to get back to my normal routine. She was finally doing better. I believed we had gotten her diagnosis right and things would continue to improve. I was just as ready as Robin was to tone down our contact, as long as she was safe.

Robin and I made a plan to return to once a week sessions. We had been meeting twice a week since her meltdown. She still had tremendous anxiety about calling me so we planned to talk briefly on the phone on Mondays and Fridays to stay connected, and have our therapy sessions on Wednesdays.

Robin called the next Monday after she finished her first full day at work. "I'm feeling worse," she said. "I felt like I was zoning out all day (dissociating). It was really hard to do what I needed to do. All I want to do is sleep."

This was terrible! If she couldn't work I knew she would start feeling more stressed about her finances. I knew she could not tolerate asking her family, who had already helped pay for the repairs to her Jeep, for any more money. I knew being unable to work would only compound her anxiety and depression and make it much harder for Dr. Greene and I to get and keep her stabilized. The brief relief and hopefulness I had felt the previous week disappeared instantly.

"Are you having suicidal thoughts?" I asked for what seemed like the millionth time. I felt like I knew the answer, but I needed to find out how severe her thoughts were and determine her level of immediate risk.

"Yes." Robin replied. "I'm not going to kill myself, but I don't think I can keep doing this much longer." I could hear the hopelessness in her voice. I understood it. She had been feeling so bad for such a long time. The reprieve we had both felt the previous week seemed very far away. I could feel her disappointment and overwhelming despair. I felt the disappointment too.

"Robin, I'll talk to Dr. Greene about how bad you're feeling. I don't know whether it's Depakote side effects or whether he needs to tweak your meds. But we'll do something and get you feeling better." I tried desperately to help her feel more hopeful, but I needed Dr. Greene's help. The Depakote seemed to be helping Robin feel more in control. She was more rational, was sleeping better, and was not being impulsive or self-destructive in any way. But she was exhausted and seemed to be stabilized at such a depressed level.

Before her second hospitalization Robin had been taking two different antidepressant medications, Paxil and Wellbutrin, in addition to the antipsychotic Geodon and an antianxiety medication, Ativan, which helped her sleep. When Dr. Greene agreed she was likely experiencing a bipolar mixed episode he added Depakote and stopped the Wellbutrin, which he feared was exacerbating her mixed mania.

"Tell Robin to decrease the Depakote from three times a day to two. And tell her to re-start Wellbutrin," Dr. Greene said when I called him. We agreed that while taking both Depakote and Geodon, it was more likely Wellbutrin would help Robin's depression without causing mania. And she was probably more depressed because Wellbutrin had been leaving her system. Things were starting to make sense.

I called Robin to let her know Dr. Greene's instructions. She agreed to follow them and said she was planning to talk to Jennifer, her supervisor, at work that day. "I'll have her call you if she wants to. You can tell her anything," Robin said. "I need her to understand what's going on, and I don't think I can explain it very well. I'll be too nervous about talking to her."

I received a call from Jennifer later that day. "Robin's psychiatrist and I both believe we are finally on the right track in terms of getting her stabilized," I said to her. "We believe she has bipolar disorder, and now that we are treating it I think she will finally get better." As I said it, I was desperately hoping I was right. "Robin is really worried about losing her job. Does she need to worry about that?"

"Robin and I talked today about ways to decrease her caseload so her days aren't so long," Jennifer replied. "We don't want to lose her. She's a great case manager." We went on to discuss Jennifer's opinion that Robin always seemed to have good judgment about what she should and should not do with her clients, despite her symptoms.

"I trust Robin to let me know if she's feeling unable to manage the responsibilities of her job," Jennifer said. I was relieved to hear this. I had always found Robin to be very insightful, and her ability to fake it even in the midst of a mixed bipolar episode was astonishing to me. But it was good to have confirmation that Robin was a valued employee, that her judgment was trusted, and that she didn't have to worry about losing her job. I looked forward to telling Robin this, as she needed some good news.

I felt fairly confident that Dr. Greene's decision to re-start Wellbutrin would help Robin's depression and that the combination of Depakote and Geodon would keep the mania under control. I tried to reassure Robin that this was likely. I decided to talk about the big picture of our treatment to help her feel more hopeful that her life, overall, could improve.

"Robin, I still think a big part of your depression is that you've been completely isolated," I said. "Now that you've been more open with me, and we are on the right track with the medications, I think you'll start to feel better. I know it makes you anxious to be so vulnerable with me, but I do think it will get easier."

"I want to be closer to people," Robin bravely admitted. "But it's really hard for me to trust. And it just makes me uncomfortable. I feel too dependent because I know it isn't realistic to continue to be close to you. I'm just another one of your crazy patients."

Good for her for saying this! I was shocked she was willing to be so vulnerable and so direct. This was great progress. "Robin, therapy is a process. Right now it's okay for you to be dependent on me as you get used to feeling close to someone. But you also have to work on being more open with other people in your life. I can't be the only one, because then it does become unhealthy. At some point, when you're more comfortable being close to other people, it will feel okay to distance yourself from me." I suggested a session with her parents to help her begin to stop faking it with the important people in her life. I was surprised and pleased when she agreed. She said she would talk to them about scheduling something.

Before Robin left our session that day, she anxiously pulled something from the large tote-bag purse she always carried with her. I had no idea what was coming. "I made a CD of songs I listen to when I'm really depressed," Robin said. "I have a hard time explaining how I feel then. If you want to listen, these songs reflect it."

I was honored. Robin continued to make herself more vulnerable even though it made her very anxious. I told her I would be glad to listen to the CD over the weekend, and we would talk about it in our session the following week.

I was unfamiliar with the majority of the songs Robin had chosen. Although I was an avid listener of music and had my own share of melancholy songs in my library, I was not drawn to the kind of music Robin shared with me and I did not expect my reaction when listening to the CD.

It was the beginning of April 2003. I had devoted much emotional energy to riding the rollercoaster of Robin's intense despair, self-destructiveness, hopelessness and complete isolation for over two months. My gut told me I had been doing the right thing by serving as a life-line for Robin. I knew intellectually I was the only person in her life who could have tolerated hearing the details of her obsessive self-destructive thinking. But while listening to Robin's CD I suddenly, for the first time, began to fully grasp her reality on an emotional level. I realized she was only just beginning to be able to share her real experience. Feeling it was overwhelming to me.

The CD was titled *Sorrow*. The songs reflected enormous amounts of pain, loneliness, hopelessness and despair. The first two songs, *Torn* by Toad the Wet Sprocket and *Institutionalized* by Suicidal Tendencies, were representative of the whole CD. Most of the music was unfamiliar to me. Robin and I had very different music tastes, reflecting our different realities and world views.

As I sat alone in my house, listening to the CD and grasping on a whole new emotional level the degree of pain she had felt for so long, I believed we were finally on the right track in terms of her treatment. But, I also knew that even after her brain chemistry was stabilized it would be a long process, and not an easy one, to help Robin become more open with and feel close to other people. I didn't know if she was going to be able to hang on long enough or tolerate the anxiety it would cause for her to get there. As I sat in my living room, feeling deeply moved by the pain reflected in Robin's CD, I honestly didn't know if she was going to survive.

• • •

The agency where I worked was the community mental health center (CMHC) for the small Midwestern city in which we lived. Being a CMHC meant the agency had the mission of treating anyone from the county who needed mental health treatment, regardless of their ability to pay for those services. Insurance was accepted, a sliding fee based on income was in place, and some state funds defrayed the costs of providing a variety of care ranging from outpatient treatment to inpatient or residential care for all ages. It was a large, rapidly growing agency which, at its height, served 18,000 clients per year.

Working at this agency meant I saw a large variety of adult outpatient clients. In order to make the budget work, the administrators of the agency expected full-time clinicians to see a certain number of clients per week. This expectation helped ensure enough billing was done to help keep the agency financially stable.

My obsessive-compulsive personality traits mean I have always been a responsible, reliable, detail-oriented person and employee. I always made sure I met the expectations placed on me by the agency, including seeing the appropriate number of clients and completing my paperwork in a timely fashion. To not meet those expectations created anxiety for me, as I always worried about job security and about the approval of those for whom I worked.

The administrators of the agency kept trying to promote me to a management position, because I was meeting my job expectations and they wanted me to help make sure others did as well. Like Robin, though, my obsessive-compulsive personality traits meant I was easily stressed by change. I liked being a therapist and was reluctant to do anything else. I didn't want to take on the stress of being responsible for other people. The agency was financially stable, and I knew as long as I met my expectations I didn't have to worry about job security. I felt comfortable with the predictable routine of seeing my clients and doing my paperwork.

It was rewarding for me to be a therapist, and I was receiving good feedback from clients, colleagues and referral sources about my work. But, I was struggling with spending every day, day after day and year after year, immersed in the depths of other people's pain.

After growing up in a relatively religious family, I stopped attending church regularly as an adult. But, I became very motivated to read spiritual books. In hindsight, I think I needed to find a way to make sense of the excruciating pain I witnessed during my work as a therapist. It was not completely conscious, but I needed to believe people endured unfathomable suffering for some ultimately good reason. This allowed me to maintain appropriate distance, gave me more energy for my work, and helped me keep from becoming cynical and disillusioned with life. As I kept immersing myself in spiritual material, it began to increasingly inform my work.

By the time Robin had her meltdown in 2003, I was firmly entrenched in a spiritual framework that came from years of reading various books and listening to the CDs of many spiritual teachers. I believe we are all evolving as souls with the purpose of learning to love ourselves and others and to connect with other souls (we are all one). I believe we are here to set a good example for others in terms of being kind, compassionate and loving. The more we are able to do this consciously and purposefully, the more of a positive impact we can have. Because we are all connected, each person who sets this example has an impact, energetically, on the global consciousness.

In my spiritual framework, all the negative, painful things that happen both globally and within our individual lives are serving the ultimate purpose of helping us to experience ourselves as souls. In the absence of pain, we cannot fully appreciate joy and love. Life is a process of change, offering many opportunities for us to grow and learn and evolve. I believe the key to being happy and at peace, is to welcome change and 'go with the flow.' I strongly believe we are constantly being spiritually guided through our emotions or our 'gut' feelings. Part of the key to going with the flow is to trust this guidance and follow it.

Although years of spiritual studying led me to intellectually believe all of the above, it remained a struggle for me to actually live these beliefs. As an anxious person by nature, maintaining this perspective was a constant challenge. I had to frequently re-read the books that were most helpful and consciously remind myself of my spiritual beliefs.

I mostly did not talk about any of this with my professional colleagues or my clients. I did not want to risk being too vulnerable with my colleagues, not knowing how I would be judged as a proclaimed "spiritual person." And, It was generally not appropriate to share my spiritual beliefs with clients. I would frequently tell clients to "trust their gut," without saying I believed this was a way to tune into their spiritual guidance. At times my gut told me to talk to various clients about spirituality, and I did so carefully and selectively. Mostly though, I kept my spiritual beliefs to myself and shared them only with a few trusted, like minded friends.

Living through the first few months following Robin's meltdown in 2003 caused me to feel overwhelmed on many levels. My spiritual beliefs were being seriously challenged. Any sense of balance I had found in terms of managing my therapy sessions and paperwork was completely gone. I was spending a lot of time and energy thinking about Robin, talking to her, and documenting our conversations in detail, while at the same time seeing all of my other clients.

My anxiety issues had always caused me to worry whenever I had a client who was seriously suicidal. Robin was seriously suicidal for many months and I found myself constantly worrying about her safety. I knew, spiritually, that I needed to stay in close contact with her and extend the boundaries to help her connect with someone. But I was exhausted and stressed and scared about Robin's survival. I was worried about how her family and I would be impacted if she actually killed herself.

On the Monday after I listened to Robin's CD entitled *Sorrow*, we had our scheduled phone call. We were still meeting in therapy once a week on Wednesdays and talking on the phone on Mondays and Fridays. I asked her how her weekend had gone.

"I almost killed myself," Robin said matter of factly. "I got really depressed on Saturday. I had the Tylenol all lined up and drank three wine coolers to prepare myself."

What? What the hell? I certainly did not expect this. For God's sake, why was she not getting better? Robin just continued to shock and scare me. I knew she had been feeling more depressed and was stressed about her job. But in our phone conversation the previous Friday she had assured me if she felt worse over the weekend she would call. Obviously that didn't happen. Inside, I was frightened by how close she had come to attempting suicide and worried that she had not honored our agreement. Outwardly, I remained calm as usual. "What stopped you from going through with it?" I asked, completely afraid of what I would hear.

"I was worried about Epiphany," said Robin. "I actually started thinking seriously about taking her to the Humane Society so I wouldn't have to worry about her anymore. But then I couldn't do that either."

Okay, now I was starting to freak out. Robin had talked several times about her cat being the barrier keeping her from killing herself. But she had never talked about removing that barrier by taking Epiphany to the Humane Society. Her obsessive suicidal thoughts appeared to be getting more severe. "So Robin, on a 1-10 scale where are your suicidal thoughts today?" I asked, worried that we were going to have to battle about her going back to the hospital.

"I'd say they're at an eight today, compared to Saturday when they were at a ten. I feel a little better," she said. "Obviously there must be part of me that doesn't want to kill myself since something keeps stopping me. But I'm not consciously aware of it."

Robin went on to tell me she drank three wine coolers again on Sunday. She said she was just tired of feeling depressed and hopeless. I was somewhat confrontational with her about sabotaging her treatment by drinking, but did not want to be too confrontational and push her away. She was insightful and able to admit she was fighting an internal battle between wanting to live, allowing herself to get closer to me and other people, and fearing being vulnerable. Mostly, she said, she still just wanted to die.

I was relieved to hear that Robin's internal battle was partly about wanting to live and experience feeling connected to people. This helped confirm that my strategy about extending the boundaries in our relationship was on target. Her willingness to admit that part of her wanted to connect with people was a relief to hear. But, mostly it was eclipsed by my fear for her safety.

In our next therapy session Robin and I talked more about her struggle with constant suicidal thoughts. As we talked, she acknowledged that the changes Dr. Greene made to her medications were helping many of her symptoms. She said she was sleeping well, functioning adequately at work, feeling more able to think rationally, and was experiencing less anxiety and more energy. She was feeling more able to control her impulses. This was all good news. But she remained severely depressed, felt completely hopeless about her life getting any better, and could not stop her obsessive brain from focusing on suicide. She continued to display completely flat affect.

Unlike when she was in the midst of a mixed bipolar episode and had impaired impulse control, Robin now seemed to be choosing to sabotage her treatment by drinking. This was typical of her past self-destructive behavior while severely depressed. She stopped caring about getting better overall, and just wanted to numb herself to feel better in the moment. I knew she could not continue this pattern, especially when her suicidal thoughts were so constant and so intense. She could easily end up killing herself impulsively if she drank too much.

As a therapist, I constantly needed to make decisions during sessions about what to do. Therapists develop the skill of listening to the client talking in front of them, while simultaneously processing what to say next. It is one of those automatic skills that must be learned for someone to be a good therapist. We certainly can't say, "Okay, what you just said is completely freaking me out. Give me a minute to think about what to do about it." If the situation was not urgent I would wait and consult with my supervisor or colleagues after the session. But Robin was in danger at that time. With her increasing alcohol use it would not take long for her to destabilize her bipolar symptoms and become an even bigger suicide risk. What a nightmare! She was communicating that she needed me to do something. I trusted my gut.

"Robin, I want to talk about your CD." I had promised we would discuss it in our session that day. "I want you to know it touched me, very much. It helped me understand more fully how much pain you're experiencing."

When I had been listening to Robin's CD that previous weekend, I had thought about making her a CD in return to give her something positive to listen to when we were not in communication. But this is not something I would ever have done for a client before. I was unsure about it, since I didn't want to foster too much dependence or make Robin too anxious by increasing the emotional intimacy between us. I had been planning to consult with my colleagues about it.

At that time, though, when I needed to make a quick decision about how to help Robin stop sabotaging treatment, I decided I couldn't wait to get reassurance or opinions from other people. I knew what I was thinking about doing would be a risk. It could have gone either way in terms of causing her to work harder in treatment, or causing her to get too anxious, to distance from me, and to be more at risk of acting on her obsessive suicidal thoughts.

In making my decision, it didn't matter that I was anxious and stressed about continuing to be there for Robin, or whether I had no idea when my life would ever feel balanced again. My feelings and needs felt irrelevant to me. My spiritual guidance felt clear. I was completely driven to do what Robin needed in order to stay alive. In that moment, I knew I needed to take the risk of trusting my gut and extend the therapeutic boundaries yet again.

"Robin," I said. "I'm working on a CD for you."

"What?" She seemed very surprised. "I didn't know you made CDs."

"I love listening to music too, and do it as a way of connecting to my own emotions just like you," I said. "I want to give you a CD, but I have a problem. I can't reinforce self-destructive behavior, and I can't do anything that is unhealthy. You are drinking and sabotaging treatment. I can't give you a CD when you're doing this or I'll feel like I'm reinforcing self-destructiveness."

"I'll make a deal with you," I went on. "First, if you are willing, I want you to write a short note about each of the songs on your CD explaining what about the song affected you. I'll do the same about the songs I give you. Second, I want to get that session with your parents scheduled. And, I need you to get rid of your alcohol, stop drinking, and work harder to stay busy and distracted when you aren't at work. If you do all of that, I will give you a CD."

I told Robin I knew I was asking her to change life-long patterns, and that this caused significant anxiety. I told her I knew she needed my support in order to make these changes, and that I was prepared to offer that support as long as she kept doing her part and stopped sabotaging herself. Robin, desperate to feel better, and probably partly relieved that I was getting more directive, agreed to the deal. I went home to start working on my CD.

• • •

I gave Robin uplifting and comforting music to distract her from her suicidal thoughts. I also figured listening to a CD from me would help her feel connected when we were not in contact, which would hopefully help her feel less compelled to kill herself. I wanted her to remember that someone would be affected by her death, specifically, me.

There was another reason, however, to make Robin a CD. While I had developed a spiritual belief system that provided perspective and guidance for me, Robin had a horrible world view. We had talked around the issue for years prior to her meltdown. She had described reading existential literature in high school and defined herself as agnostic. She had acknowledged for years that her pessimistic view of the world likely contributed to her depression. I had repeatedly encouraged her to read about spirituality, hoping it would help shift her thinking in this area. But I purposely hadn't recommended specific books, because I didn't want to impose my beliefs on her. Despite my consistent suggestion that she do so, Robin had never started to read about spirituality on her own.

Cognitive techniques, a usually helpful therapeutic strategy, had never worked well for Robin's very rigid brain. My CD was a new way to try shifting her thinking by accessing her feelings. Robin had tremendous difficulty identifying and talking about her emotions. I asked her to make notes about what affected her about each song on her CD because I wanted to know more about what was going on in her head. Then I could begin to try helping her reconsider her negative world view.

Desperate times called for desperate measures. With Robin's life on the line, I suddenly didn't worry as much about suggesting a specific new way for her to view the world and the purpose of life, or about imposing my own beliefs onto her. I had many songs with subtle spiritual messages (if they were too blatant I knew Robin would not relate to them). I chose some of them for my CD and I wrote my thoughts about the messages within the lyrics. It was a new and different way to attempt to shift her thinking.

At the time of the CD exchange Robin had just confessed that she would have attempted suicide if it were not for her worries about her cat, Epiphany. She continued to be very isolated. She was still not letting her family or friends know how depressed she was, which is why I asked her to bring her parents into a session. They needed to know she was not okay. Although she was still somehow managing to do her job during the week, she was spending way too much time alone on the weekends obsessing about suicide.

On weekends at that time, I was spending several hours on either Saturday or Sunday in my office working on paperwork. I couldn't do therapy notes from home due to confidentiality issues, and I usually could not complete them all during the week. I actually enjoyed the quiet time in my office, and I liked being able to work on my paperwork without time pressure. Not feeling the pressure to get it all done during the week helped me to retain the balance I needed by working shorter days and not being too exhausted in the evenings.

Because Robin agreed to work harder to avoid being self-destructive as part of our CD exchange, I decided to reinforce these efforts by planning to briefly talk on the phone sometime during the weekend, which was her most dangerous time. Robin was adamant that she would not be comfortable talking to me from my home. This was one of her obsessive-compulsive rules. Somehow it was just more acceptable for her to have a phone conversation on the weekend if it came from my office. I was going to be there anyway, so we made plans for me to call during that time.

Robin took our agreement very seriously. She worked harder at staying busy and to stop drinking. She reported a corresponding decrease in the intensity of her suicidal thoughts, from an eight or ten on the 1-10 scale down to a five. However, the improvement was short-lived. It was not long before I learned that Robin working really hard and me making her a CD were not enough to overcome the severe depression and obsessive suicidal thinking that were consistently torturing her.

"I feel like I'm having a mini-meltdown," Robin said. She continued to show completely flat affect and her leg was back to bouncing up and down. "I feel very sad, and I don't feel like I'm in control of myself as much. I'm not planning to kill myself and I don't think I need to go to the hospital, but I don't feel like I can go to work and not act crazy." She said she planned to call off sick from work the next day. I was instantly concerned that my extending the therapeutic boundaries further had made her too anxious and was contributing to her feeling worse. I asked her about it.

"Actually, I feel more comfortable about opening up to you," she said. "It's helping, and I'm starting to get more used to it. The fact that you'd make me a CD helps me trust it. I've been thinking about the fact that you are my Virgil." I instantly understood her reference to Dante's *Inferno*. She was referring to me being her guide through hell. I hoped that meant she felt like we would eventually get out of hell, as Dante and Virgil did, but I didn't want to focus on it. I let her know I understood the reference, and was honored to be her "Virgil."

Robin Discusses Her World View

Prior to and during my Meltdown year, if I had been asked directly about my religious beliefs I would have identified myself as agnostic. My dad attended the Methodist Church while he was a child, and I was baptized in that church as an infant. My maternal grandfather was a pastor in the Missionary Church, so my mom attended church three times a week while growing up. In spite of my parents being raised with regular church attendance, we didn't go to church regularly when I was a child. I'm not sure exactly why this was the case, but I think this lack of religious education left a place for me to develop beliefs based on my own experience of the world rather than any particular religious doctrine. Unfortunately, my experience of the world as a child involved personal trauma and the death of my brother, Eddie. Both of these life impacting events led to my belief that the world is a harsh place and to me questioning the existence of God in light of such terrible events.

I don't wish to offend anyone of any religious faith. Religion works for many people all over the world. But everyone has their own beliefs and I personally do not support organized religion. Too much hypocrisy, hate, killing and war has been done in the name of, and with the support of various religions over the course of history. I believe a person can be spiritual without going to church.

However, even though I would have said I was agnostic before 2003 I suppose I could have been called a Cafeteria Christian, as I believed in a few concepts consistent with Christianity. For instance, I believed in heaven and angels. I think I incorporated these into my belief system as a child in response to Eddie's death from cancer at the age of four and a half. I was told then by my parents and all of my extended family members that Eddie had gone to heaven and had become an angel. This was a comforting thought to me as a child, and remains comforting to me as an adult as I've lost other loved ones.

When I was a senior in high school, I was introduced to Existential philosophy in an Advanced Placement English class. Existentialism isn't an inherently negative philosophy, but the concepts that attracted me reinforced my negative belief system. The phrase used to describe Existentialism is "existence precedes essence." In other words, we are not born with meaning or purpose to our lives, so we must create it ourselves. Adolescence was a particularly vulnerable time for me, in hindsight, as I was dealing with the impact of sexual abuse and probably the beginning of bipolar symptoms. It's not surprising that I became particularly interested in Existential philosophy, as it felt consistent with my depression and many of my life experiences. In creating a purpose for myself and meaning in my life, I focused on helping abused and neglected children. I did this through my career in mental health. This purpose, which had become my identity, was threatened by my Meltdown which contributed to my despair. Also, when I was younger I assumed that I would create meaning in my life by getting married, maybe having children, and owning a home. The fact that I had none of these things also added more and more to my sense of despair as I got older. I compared myself to peers who did have these things, and it depressed me.

Absurdity, another existential concept that caught my attention, refers to the fact that the world is a harsh and indifferent place, uncaring whether someone deserves to have something bad happen to them. What happens just happens. Things like child abuse, genocide, and the death of innocent children all exist because of the absurdity of life, according to existential philosophy. In my experience, Eddie was just a child so he obviously did nothing to deserve to suffer with cancer and die. My parents were a young, hardworking couple when Eddie got sick. They did nothing to deserve the pain of watching their innocent child die. Growing up with the legacy of Eddie's death as well as my personal experience with trauma contributed to my negative view of the world as an absurd place, as did my work with abused and neglected children.

In existentialism, human beings have free will which causes anxiety, or angst. An example of existential angst that my high school teacher described is a situation in which you are standing on a cliff. You are not only afraid you will fall, you are also afraid you might jump. I have often experienced this when I'm depressed while driving my car. During the summers while I was in college I worked at the "The Bakery from Hell." The twenty-minute drive to work took me along a curvy stretch of road along the river that was lined with trees. As I drove to work I sometimes pictured myself driving into one of the trees along the route. This example of angst, along with many others, continued to happen whenever I was depressed. I have experienced a lot of angst during my lifetime. So, in 2003, my world view was pretty ugly. My beliefs could be summed up by the phrase "life sucks and then you die." I questioned the existence of God in such a hostile world in which horrible things happened to innocent people. Working with abused children and their families reinforced this issue. I was pessimistic in general, and expected the worst of life.

This is the world view Sharon tried to address by making me CDs in response to the CDs I made for her. Accessing and expressing my emotions was not something I did well. I related to my emotions through music, and making CDs for Sharon allowed me to express to her how I felt. My songs were filled with negativity and pain and reflected my dark world view. Sharon countered my negativity with positive songs and notes, full of hope and life. A couple of her songs that were particularly helpful were *Never Give Up* by Yolanda Adams, and *Calling All Angels* by Train. Rather than listening to my depressing CDs when I was feeling suicidal, I could listen to one of the CDs she made.

Examples of notes to Sharon from my CDs:

Leave Me Alone (New Order) – *"Early 80's song, expresses in sound and lyrics the feelings of isolation and loneliness that accompany my depressed moods. Also emotes hopelessness and a sense that nobody understands, so why bother."*

Torn (Toad the Wet Sprocket) – *"This song re-creates the essence of* The Bell Jar, *both in sound and lyric. I connected emotionally with this song, in fact the whole CD, the first time I heard it.*

Somebody (Depeche Mode) – *"This may be the anguished anthem of thirty-something single females everywhere, and is almost too angst filled to be taken seriously. But it still affects me emotionally every time I hear it. Love the heartbeat sounds in the background."*

Unwell (Matchbox Twenty) – *"I listen to this song repeatedly, trying to internalize the message that I'm not crazy, and that I can go back to the way I used to be. I'm still not there yet. I still haven't assimilated the bipolar piece, for one thing. I know you don't think I should desire to go back to the way things were before, but it was better than it is now, and I'm not hopeful enough at this point to see my life getting better than before. I don't want to be one of my former clients...on a gaggle of meds, on disability and going to partial hospital just to fill the time. I have to think that I still have something to contribute, or I don't want to live."*

Heaven Knows I'm Miserable Now (The Smiths) – *"This song is almost a caricature of misery, it overdoes it so badly with the whining. No further comments required, I hope."*

Free to Decide (Cranberries) – *"This song outright talks about being suicidal and being free to decide about it. It perfectly illustrates my ambivalence."*

Examples of notes from Sharon's CDs to me:

Truth of the Heart (Melissa Etheridge) – *"I have always liked this song and I believe its messages. One of the main keys to healing is to open ourselves up to the truth of our emotions. As this song highlights, we all struggle but people are good, people can change, and deep down we are all the same."*

Hands (Jewel) – *"This is a song about how every person can change the world in a positive way. I think we are all here partly to do what we can to help other people and set a good example. We are all connected. Every small act of kindness affects the global consciousness positively. We are God's hands."*

All That We Let In (Indigo Girls) – *"I love this song and its message. We are better off when we let people in. You have made and are making huge progress in this regard. I feel honored and grateful that you have let me in."*

Utopia (Alanis Morissette) – *"Leave it to Alanis to write the perfect song to outline what I think we should all be working toward. I agree with her about the things that will lead us to Utopia. It is important to remember this when you are comparing yourself to other people in terms of their jobs, material possessions, etc. What leads to true happiness has nothing to do with those things. It has to do with all the things Alanis sings about in this song."*

Be Somebody (Paula Cole Band) – *"This song acknowledges that life involves a lot of madness and pain, but that making a positive difference for others is an important response to the negativity in the world. The most important message, I think, is to work on getting to a point where the negative events in the world do not kill the joy inside us. Obviously*

*we first need to help you find the joy, Robin, but we will get
there."*
<u>When You Believe (Whitney Houston and Mariah Carey)</u> –
*"This song may be a bit much for you right now, but I do think
we can get to a point where you are happy, which would feel
like a miracle to you, I assume. If you can't believe in a higher
power right now, work on believing in yourself, your strength
and the power of the process."*

Sharon and I ended up exchanging many different CDs and notes
about them during 2003 and the following couple of years. It didn't
have an immediate impact on my world view, but it at least wasn't
reinforcing my dark thoughts like listening to hopeless music did. As
I kept listening, with Sharon's perspective about each song in mind,
my negative world view began to slowly tilt toward a more positive
outlook on life.

The CDs and the notes that accompanied them became an inte-
gral part of my treatment. Changing my negative world view, which
was accomplished through the use of music and also reading spiritual
books, became an intervention that helped me, over time, become
less prone to depression and more able to bounce back from it when
it happened.

6
The Treatment of Last Resort

IN APRIL 2003 Robin had been hospitalized twice. It had become apparent that she had been misdiagnosed, and Dr. Greene had changed her medication to treat her symptoms. But I was baffled about why Robin was still so severely depressed and getting worse. I was grasping.

"Are you feeling stressed about the session with your parents next week?" I asked, trying to figure out what was causing her to feel worse. "Because if you're not feeling up to it we can always reschedule or put it off until you feel better."

"I haven't even thought that far ahead," said Robin. "I'm just trying to stop thinking about killing myself." She was more able to acknowledge the part of her that "doesn't want to do it," but she could not stop herself from obsessing about it. Her severe OCD was completely taking over her thoughts.

Robin had seen Dr. Greene earlier that day, and he had raised her dose of the antidepressant medication Wellbutrin. She was happy about this and was hoping it would help. I hoped so too, although I knew it would take several weeks. It didn't seem like Robin could wait that long to feel better.

The next day I received a voice mail from her. She had called on a day when we had not planned to talk, which was highly unusual. Her voice mail was very disturbing.

> *"Hi Sharon, it's just me, Robin. I think one of the reasons I'm more depressed is because when I saw Dr. Greene yesterday he told me he's assuming I'm bipolar. I'm having trouble with the idea of being chronically mentally ill. I don't think I'm hallucinating, I think I'm just talking to myself in my head and I'm just thinking about suicide too much. You don't need to call me back. I'll just plan to talk to you tomorrow like we planned."*

There was not a chance I was going to wait until the next day to talk to her! Robin never left voice mails. She hated making phone calls. And she had absolutely never talked about having hallucinations, ever. I was very concerned and immediately called her back. It was early evening and she sounded very drowsy.

"Robin, I got your message. What's going on? Are you okay?" I asked. "Why do you sound so tired?"

"I already took my night meds," Robin said. "I just want to go to bed."

"Why were you talking about hallucinating?" I asked nervously.

"I don't think I'm hallucinating," she replied. "I just can't get the suicidal thoughts out of my head. I've decided to change my method of suicide to drowning. Something I was reading about it made me decide it wouldn't be too bad."

Good God! She thought drowning herself would not be bad? I couldn't believe what I was hearing! Then, she kept talking and it kept getting worse. "I've been thinking about going through my stuff and getting rid of some things," she said. "I don't want my family to have to deal with as much stuff if something happens to me."

Okay, now she had a new plan and was thinking about getting rid of things, a clear sign of preparing for suicide. But, why on earth was she telling me this? Robin was smart enough to know she couldn't say these things to me without alarming me. She was still not remotely herself. The relentless depression just continued. I felt completely helpless in terms of trying to impact it.

We talked about Dr. Greene's comment about bipolar disorder. I realized we hadn't talked enough about this. When we initially brought it up the previous month, Dr. Greene and I both told Robin we weren't completely sure about the bipolar diagnosis. But, her positive response to Depakote in terms of stabilizing her manic symptoms had pretty much confirmed we were right. I guess I'd been assuming Robin knew this, but in hindsight I'm not sure how I thought she would have come to this conclusion. I had been too busy focusing on her being disconnected from people, her return to work and her suicidal thoughts. I hadn't been processing her feelings about her diagnosis. Apparently she was hanging on to the hope that we were wrong, and Dr. Greene's comment had dashed her hopes. It made sense why this was causing her to feel worse.

As we talked on the phone that evening, Robin started sounding a bit more rational. We talked, again, about whether she needed to be in the hospital. She assured me she wasn't going to kill herself that night and said she was going to try to go to work the next morning.

"I went to work today," Robin said when we talked the next afternoon. "I stayed only long enough to count the day, and then I left and went home. I spent some time this afternoon at work cleaning out my desk. I have too much stuff."

"What? Robin, you are focusing on getting rid of things? Last night you said you were thinking about getting rid of things in your apartment. Now at work? It sounds to me like you are planning to kill yourself. Do you have a date picked?"

"What do you mean our conversation last night?" Robin asked, sounding surprised. She had no memory of our long phone call. I told her about the voice mail message she left and our talk afterward.

"Oh my God! I can't believe I called you and said that stuff," Robin said. "I'm mortified!" She insisted she had not been drinking when we talked, and we discussed that she was likely dissociating.

I asked the question that was becoming a routine part of every conversation. "Do you think you need to be in the hospital?"

"No, I'll be okay. I have lots of plans this weekend. My niece has a soccer game tomorrow, and then we have Easter dinner at Bob's house on Sunday."

Robin assured me she had no alcohol in her apartment and would not drink. We made plans to talk over the weekend. It no longer mattered whether I was at home or at my office when we talked on the phone. And I was not okay waiting until the following Monday to have contact. Not a chance.

I was increasingly worried about Robin's safety and would have felt less anxious if she had agreed to go to the hospital. But, I also knew the hospital wouldn't solve anything in the long run. Dr. Greene had increased the Wellbutrin, and we were waiting for it to take effect. Robin was not being self-destructive and was sleeping, so she did not appear to be manic. If she could stay safe at home and continue to work until the Wellbutrin took effect, it would be better than her missing work and having to deal with the ramifications of that. But her depression was just so severe! She could not stop thinking about suicide. Her brain was torturing her. I knew I needed to stay in close contact, and if she got any worse I would be pushing harder for hospitalization.

It didn't take long for things to get worse. On Easter Sunday Robin and I talked on the phone after her family gathering. "I'm having a harder time fighting my suicidal thoughts," she said. "I found out a guy who lives in my apartment complex killed himself by drowning. It just confirmed my plan will work. I can't stop thinking about it."

Robin went on to tell me the new, extremely specific, detailed and lethal suicide plan she was obsessing about. It was well thought out and would definitely have been successful if she chose to act on it.

"I didn't want to write a suicide note before, but now I've decided I should," she said. "I want people to understand why I'm doing it in case they're angry or have questions. I don't want to do it until after my birthday because I don't want to ruin my niece's birthday or Mother's Day or Bob's birthday. I really want to hang on until after that, but I don't know if I can. I can't think about anything else."

I was starting to believe Robin did not really want to kill herself. If she did, she would never have told me her specific, lethal plan. She would have just done it. Her reason for delaying it was to minimize the pain for her family, again not realizing they would be devastated if she killed herself no matter when it happened. But, whether she wanted to wait for irrational reasons or not, Robin was telling me she couldn't hang on any longer.

It was time, yet again, for me to do something. I dreaded even bringing it up, but I believed I knew what needed to happen. I'd been thinking about it for the previous couple of weeks when Robin was getting worse.

"Robin, I think it's time to consider ECTs," I said. "I think you need to be in the hospital, and I'll talk to Dr. Greene about getting your insurance to cover ECTs since it appears the medication is not working."

As with her previous two hospitalizations, Robin did not argue with me. I was surprised. "Nothing else is working," she said. "I can't keep going on like this."

Robin and I talked about whether she needed to be in the hospital that evening. She wanted to wait, and said she would go in the morning. I did not insist she go to the hospital, trusting my gut she would be okay. Robin continued to be open with me rather than act on her obsessive suicidal thoughts. She did not want to hurt her family members. She was working very hard not to be self-destructive. She was ready to try anything, including ECTs, to feel better. She assured me she was going to take her meds, leave a voice mail for her supervisor that she would not be going to work the next day, and go to bed. I told her I'd call her in the morning after I talked to Dr. Greene.

• • •

In 1985, after graduating from college, I took a job as a Mental Health Technician (MHT) at a psychiatric hospital in my home town. I wanted experience to help decide whether I should pursue a Ph.D. in psychology. This job was a good choice, as I was exposed to many realities I never could have experienced in other settings.

As an MHT at that hospital, one of my assigned tasks was to assist with electroconvulsive therapy (ECT) treatments. There were three of us involved with these procedures, and we rotated our roles including preparation (getting patients to the procedure room and taking their vital signs), helping with the procedure (holding the electrodes on the patient's forehead while the doctor activated the machine to produce a seizure), and recovery (monitoring vital signs while the patient came out of anesthesia). Every Monday, Wednesday and Friday morning there were between three and ten patients, some of whom were staying at the hospital and some who came in as outpatients, receiving these treatments.

I was young, completely inexperienced and had no substantial knowledge about ECT. Of course, I was aware there was a stigma associated with it and had seen the antiquated portrayal of the treatment in the movie *One Flew Over the Cuckoo's Nest*. But I performed the responsibilities of my job as I was instructed to do, with no strong opinion about whether it was a good idea for people have these treatments. All I knew was that the procedure was quick and seemed painless.

I witnessed many of these procedures over the course of a year in this job. I never heard after the treatments were completed whether patients experienced lasting side effects. What I did know was that ECT worked. I'd see people come for treatments three days a week for two or three weeks, and during the course of that short time frame I would see person after person get better...dramatically better. People would often start their procedures with completely flat affect, unable to function. Within two weeks I would see them start smiling, laughing and telling me they felt much better. Whether the improvement lasted, or whether they later regretted having ECT due to any memory loss that accompanied it, I'll never know.

In 2003, the agency where I worked had just recently added ECT to its treatment options. Many of my colleagues expressed negative feelings about this, as they were either aware of the controversy surrounding memory loss (there was debate in the field about whether ECT caused permanent or temporary memory issues) or they were caught up in the stigma associated with this treatment. I simply told people my opinion; that it was a treatment of last resort, to be used sparingly and only after other treatment options had been exhausted. I told them about my prior experience with ECT and that it seemed to significantly help people.

Robin was the only client during my long career as an outpatient therapist for whom I recommended ECT. In April 2003, we were out of options. She was already on five medications and her severe depression had been unrelenting for over a year. We were at the point where the treatment of last resort needed to happen. Her life was at stake. On the morning after our phone conversation on Easter, I went to work and immediately paged Dr. Greene.

"It's Sharon. Robin is worse. She's still obsessing about suicide, and she is now stuck on a very specific, lethal plan." I told Dr. Greene the details of the well thought out suicide plan that Robin could not get out of her head. "She is desperate to feel better and is ready to try ECTs, if we can get her insurance company to approve them."

"Is she willing to go into the hospital?" asked Dr. Greene. "I'd feel most comfortable starting them as an inpatient." I assured him Robin would voluntarily admit herself to the hospital. Dr. Greene agreed that ECT was the best option given how many medications he had tried and how depressed Robin continued to be. He agreed to talk to her insurance company, if necessary, to gain approval.

Unfortunately, overnight Robin had changed her mind. "I don't want to go to the hospital," she said when I called to tell her about my conversation with Dr. Greene.

"Robin, we talked about this. I'm very concerned about how stuck your brain is and about your suicide plan. You told me last night you didn't think you could wait any longer." I pleaded with her not to make it difficult for us to help her.

"I agree I need to try ECTs," she said, sounding exhausted. "But I'm afraid if I'm in the hospital I'll just get worse. I hate being there, and I'm afraid I'll lose my job. Will you detain me if I don't agree to come in?" She knew very well how the system worked.

What? No, Robin, don't make me answer this question, I thought to myself. I was astonished that we were having this conversation. She had told me she would come to the hospital! The last thing I wanted to do was have her brought in against her will. What a nightmare! Based on everything she had said to me, I assumed Dr. Greene would agree Robin needed to be detained if she wouldn't come in voluntarily.

I had to make another quick judgment call. To tell Robin I would detain her was a huge risk. Under these circumstances, some depressed and suicidal people would have gone and hidden somewhere to avoid having the police find them. My options were to tell Robin the truth and risk this happening, or lie to her and risk damaging the new level of trust we had only recently established. It was a difficult judgment to make. As usual, I trusted my gut. I trusted what I had begun to understand the previous evening. Robin really did not want to die.

"Yes, Robin," I reluctantly said. "I'd have to talk to Dr. Greene, but we'd probably detain you."

"All right," she said, clearly angry. "I'll be there. Can you call Jennifer, though, and explain things? I'm really afraid I'm going to lose my job for having to take more time off work." She wasn't thinking well enough to process that she wasn't going to be able to work if she had ECTs, whether she was in the hospital or not.

I agreed to call Robin's supervisor after she got settled into the hospital and then I waited, very anxiously. I mostly trusted Robin to honor her word and come to the hospital as she promised. But, I also knew she was scared and not thinking rationally.

I watched from the lobby of the hospital, where I had a view of the main entrance to the agency's campus. I walked around, in and out of the lobby, so it wasn't too obvious to anyone that I was hovering. I desperately waited to see Robin's Jeep turn the corner and drive into the parking lot. It suddenly sank in...all the anxiety, energy and angst I had put into being there for Robin during the previous three months. I was nervous, wondering if I had made a huge mistake by not talking her into being hospitalized the previous evening. I started imagining the possibility of Robin not coming and having to make a terrible phone call to her parents. Finally, she arrived, and I breathed a huge sigh of relief.

I watched Robin pull into the parking lot and take her bag of belongings from her Jeep. She walked slowly, with her head down, into the building. I met her in the lobby where we sat next to the big fish tank, as usual. Robin appeared very angry. Her affect remained flat, her leg was bouncing, and she looked exhausted.

"I'm not mad at you," Robin said. "I'm mad at the situation."

"Robin, I'm so sorry you're going through this," I replied, feeling completely helpless. "I promise I'll call Jennifer this afternoon and talk about your job. Dr. Greene is working on getting approval for ECTs from your insurance company." Robin, clearly angry, did not want to talk. I was just relieved she was safe. We sat silently until the staff came to take her up to the unit.

Once her insurance company approved the treatments, Robin appeared to be less angry and to feel more optimistic. She started campaigning to be discharged from the hospital before she even had her first ECT.

"I don't want to be here anymore," she said. "It's unnecessary." Unfortunately, her brain was still obsessing and she was still rigidly stuck in her thoughts. The thoughts had simply shifted to getting out of the hospital before the weekend rather than killing herself. But, discharging her seemed like a horrible idea.

"I'll arrange to stay with my parents or have my mom stay with me at my apartment. I'll make sure I'm not alone," she pleaded.

Although I was quite reluctant to support Robin's request to be discharged, my gut continued to tell me she did not want to kill herself. I had to make another judgment call, this time about whether I felt safe about letting her leave the hospital. I knew if I didn't support her idea, Dr. Greene wouldn't either. I decided to stall. "If you work on putting a safety plan in place, and your first ECT goes okay tomorrow, I'll talk to Dr. Greene about it."

The next afternoon, I went to see Robin. She sat on her bed in the hospital room while I stood. Her affect, as it had been for months, was completely flat. She had received her first treatment of ECT early that morning and she said she was feeling a bit disoriented. She was having some difficulty remembering the events of the previous day. Otherwise, she was still singularly focused on being discharged from the hospital as soon as possible. She started crying as she talked about her most recent conversation with Dr. Greene, who told her she needed to stay in the hospital for the next three ECTs the following week.

"Why is it so important for you to be discharged?" I asked. "It would be easier and safer for you to stay while you get ECTs. Your insurance has approved it all. Help me understand."

"I hate being locked up and not being able to distract myself," she explained. "When I'm at home I can get out of my apartment and go somewhere...even driving around helps. I can't even listen to music here. Sharon, I promise I'm not going to kill myself while I'm having ECTs. I really want to give them a chance to work."

I believed her, and I suddenly understood. I'd always known Robin hated being in the hospital because it forced her out of her familiar routine, causing more anxiety. But I suddenly realized it also took away her most effective ways to manage her anxiety. Robin was attending no groups, as usual, and was staying in her room where she felt safe. But, staying in her room for hours on end kept her trapped and unable to do what she normally did to distract herself from her brain's torture. Her anxiety was magnified, and her effective coping skills taken away. I suddenly had a new awareness of Robin's obsessive-compulsive reality and why she was so desperate to go home.

I would have preferred Robin stay in the hospital. I was stressed and exhausted from the intensity of her most recent suicidal crisis. Knowing she was safe worked much better for me. But once she talked openly about why she so desperately wanted to be discharged, I wanted to help her. I trusted her promise not to kill herself while she was getting ECTs.

I paged Dr. Greene and was able to convince him it would be therapeutic for Robin to allow her family and friends to support her through the ECT process on an outpatient basis. I told him she wanted to give the ECTs a chance to work. Dr. Greene reluctantly agreed to take the risk, as long as I communicated clearly with Robin's mother about the possibility of confusion and memory loss surrounding the ECT procedures and the importance of monitoring Robin's safety.

• • •

Robin was discharged the following morning to the care of her parents, with whom she agreed to stay. Her father agreed to transport her to and from the hospital to receive ECTs on an outpatient basis. Her mother reassured me they would make sure she took her medications as prescribed. Robin and I did not have contact over the weekend. She had her second treatment of ECT early on Monday morning and called that afternoon.

"I don't feel any better yet," Robin said.

"You haven't even recovered from your second treatment," I replied. "It usually takes a few treatments before people start to notice a difference."

"I got a call from Jennifer today. I only have three more days left of medical leave after this week," she said without emotion. Robin explained that she had almost exhausted her time guaranteed by the Family Medical Leave Act, a federal law which forced employers to hold someone's job for up to twelve weeks per year if they had a medical problem or needed to care for a family member. "I have to meet with Jennifer tomorrow to talk about my job."

Robin was very upset about the prospect of losing her job. "I can't go back to living with my parents," she said. "I'd have to get rid of Epiphany." Her parents had a dog who would not easily adjust to having a cat in the house. "And I have too much debt. I can't go without income."

"Robin, let's just take one step at a time," I said, trying to reassure her despite my own worry about what her supervisor would say. "Just see what Jennifer has to say tomorrow. Try not to make any assumptions." It was the worst possible timing for Robin to have a job crisis. She had just started receiving ECTs. Having to worry about her job and financial situation was the last thing she needed.

"So, who makes the decision about how many ECTs I need? And when will that decision be made?" Robin seemed to be thinking more clearly after having had her second ECT procedure earlier that day. It was a good question. I told her I assumed the decision would be made by Dr. Sanchez, the psychiatrist who was administering the ECTs. Since I also wondered what he was thinking, I told Robin I would talk to Dr. Sanchez the following day.

"Usually by the second or third treatment I can tell whether the ECTs are helping," Dr. Sanchez said when we talked. "By the end of the week I'll decide whether we should schedule more treatments for next week." This was helpful information, but I was concerned he would be making a decision so quickly. Robin was so depressed, and we were out of other options. I did not want him to decide prematurely that ECTs were not helping. We didn't have a backup plan.

The next day, Robin called after meeting with her supervisor, obviously upset. "I'm blowing it," she said. "Jennifer said they're reassigning all my cases. If I don't go back to work by the end of next week, they can't guarantee my job. And if I go back and can't do my job, I'll lose it. I have to let them know by early next week what I'm doing. I don't think the ECTs are working. This just feels like another sign that I'm supposed to kill myself."

I couldn't blame Jennifer who was, I was sure, speaking for the administrators of the agency where Robin worked. I didn't blame them either. They had all been very supportive and flexible about Robin's need for time off. I understood why, as her protected medical leave was expiring, they felt they needed to push the issue. But this ultimatum could not have been more poorly timed for Robin, or for me in my efforts to help her get stabilized.

Despite the job crisis, Robin was showing subtle signs of improvement. Psychomotor agitation and retardation are both signs of significant depression. Robin had demonstrated agitation when she was experiencing her mixed bipolar symptoms. Once the Depakote stabilized her mania, she had begun to show significant psychomotor retardation. When people experience this they are noticeably slowed down. They respond to questions more slowly and they move more slowly. Robin was not only significantly slowed down, but there was also her completely flat affect which had been present for months. I noticed a difference in Robin in terms of these issues, even on the phone, after her second ECT. She was responding to questions more quickly, indicating that her brain was processing things more easily. Her voice sounded more animated. She wasn't as "flat" as she had been for so long. I had spoken to her mother on the phone earlier that day, who also said she felt Robin seemed less depressed during the previous few days.

"Robin, other people often see signs of improvement before the depressed person feels better," I said. "I think you're showing these signs." We talked about what I had noticed, and what her mother had said. I acknowledged that the bad job news had not helped her mood, but reassured her that I still thought the ECTs were starting to decrease her depression.

"I'm planning to have the next one on Friday," Robin said. "I'll see what Dr. Sanchez recommends. I don't have much choice. Just so you know, I told my parents I'll let them know if I feel like I need to go to the hospital." Wow. This was huge. The fact that Robin had this conversation with her parents was an indication of improvement on many levels. She was being open and letting them help her. She recognized she may need to go back to the hospital, and was willing to do so if necessary. She was saying, again, that she wanted to stay alive. I was encouraged.

Robin and I met the following day, later in the day after her third ECT. She was tolerating the treatments well. They were being done early in the morning and she said she was a bit groggy for several hours afterward, but then felt okay. There had been no signs of significant memory loss or confusion. She seemed to be processing the ramifications of the discussion she and Jennifer had the previous day. I already planned to call Jennifer to ensure Robin was remembering and processing the conversation they had accurately.

"I feel like they're trying to push me out the door. It's making my depression worse, not better," Robin said. "I understand why they need to reassign my cases, but it upsets me. I don't know how I'm supposed to decide anything about my job by next week, when I may be continuing to have ECTs."

I reassured her I would call Jennifer to find out what the administrators at her place of employment were thinking. This seemed to calm her down for the moment. I decided to ask about the financial pressure Robin was feeling.

Robin and I had previously talked in general about her financial stress. On that day, when she was so worried about losing her job, we talked more specifically. She told me how much credit card debt she had and that she was only able to pay the minimum payments, even when she was making her full-time income.

"If I lose my job, I won't even be able to make the minimum payments," she said. "I have no savings. I'd have to move in with my parents and get rid of Epiphany!"

I needed to, somehow, combat the enormous pressure and hopelessness Robin was feeling about her job, her financial situation and her future. I needed her to be okay with the possibility of having to tell Jennifer she could not return to work the next week, since I knew she would not be ready by then. Robin desperately needed a way to relieve some pressure.

"Have you ever considered filing bankruptcy?" I asked tentatively, not knowing how she would react to the question.

"I actually have thought about it," Robin replied. "I've never seriously considered it, though. I'm afraid I'd feel too much like a failure."

"Think about it as a way to get a fresh start," I responded. "Your whole meltdown is creating a fresh start in many ways. Now that we know what we need to do in treatment, I still think you'll eventually end up feeling better than ever before. Since you are so seriously thinking about killing yourself anyway, why don't you at least consider bankruptcy as an option so you can see how much it helps to get out from under all the financial pressure. You really have nothing to lose." I would not usually be so casual in talking with a client about suicidal thoughts or so direct about recommending a step as drastic as bankruptcy. But I was desperate and I needed Robin to feel like she had options other than killing herself.

"Maybe I'll talk to Bob about it," she said. I was surprised she was even willing to consider it.

I called Robin's supervisor the next day. I needed to help Jennifer understand that Robin would not be ready to return to work the following week, and to see if there were any options that would allow her to keep her job. I left a voice mail for Jennifer, and received a call back from the Director of Human Resources at Robin's place of employment.

"We value Robin as an employee," she said. "But we can only guarantee someone's specific job position for twelve weeks. Robin's twelve weeks is done next Wednesday. If we make an exception for one person, we'd have to do the same for others." We clarified the bottom line. If Robin was unable to return to work the following Thursday, she would lose her job. The HR Director was kind to say they would gladly hire Robin for a different position in the future, if they had an opening and she was ready to perform the job. But this was little comfort.

"I have to say, this puts us in a very difficult position," I said, pleading with her. "Robin is definitely showing signs of improvement and we think ECT is what she needs to get stabilized. But she will not be ready to return to work next week. If she knows she's going to lose her job, I'm afraid it will make it impossible for her to recover." I didn't want to be too dramatic, or to make her feel guilty. But I had nothing to lose by spelling out the reality of Robin's situation. After some discussion, the HR Director seemed to understand the dilemma and said she would talk to Robin's supervisors.

My head was spinning. I couldn't believe this was happening! After months of Robin being severely depressed and suicidal, and then reluctantly agreeing to ECTs which were undoubtedly starting to help, she could lose her job before we even got a chance to stabilize her! This would mean she couldn't pay her bills, and she'd lose her apartment and have to move in with her parents or her brother. It would be difficult for Robin's rigid brain to integrate this even if she wasn't deeply depressed. In her current state, I could not imagine her surviving this reality. What a complete and total disaster! It felt like all the forces in the Universe were conspiring against both Robin and I, and I actually wondered if she was supposed to kill herself. I am an optimist by nature. But my optimism was waning in the face of Robin's reality.

I again felt like I had to do something, and went to see Dr. Sanchez. I wanted to know how many more treatments he was planning, and how long after her last ECT Robin would need to recover before she'd be okay to work. "A week should be enough," Dr. Sanchez said. "I want to do three more treatments."

Miraculously, the administrators at Robin's place of employment were willing to make an exception to their policy for her, to allow for three more ECTs and a week to recover. The agreement was that Robin would return to her job half-time for the four days following Memorial Day, and then full-time the following week. They wanted to make sure, though, she knew that if she was unable to do her job at that time, she would lose the position.

Robin was relieved to hear this news. After four ECTs she continued to show signs of decreased psychomotor retardation and brighter affect. She was processing more quickly and thinking more clearly. Unfortunately, she was also starting to show signs of memory loss. Because she was thinking more rationally, she was beginning to process and attempt to integrate the reality of everything she had experienced during the previous three months.

"I've been doing some research on ECTs," she said in one of our sessions. "I'm surprised I agreed to them without knowing more about them. I can't remember a lot of things about the last few months." She asked many factual questions about events and time frames, and I provided honest answers. She was relieved that as we talked, most of the time her memory came back.

"Robin, this is a perfect example of the progress you're making. Researching ECTs and asking questions means you're thinking more clearly. You're starting to process what you've been through, which is huge. I know you hate the memory loss, but the ECTs are helping," I said. "You have no idea how much better you are compared to where you were."

"I guess, but I'm still depressed," she said. "I still can't stop think-ing about suicide. I have too much time to think when I'm not work-ing." Robin was still experiencing another significant depression symptom, anhedonia, which is an inability to feel pleasure or to have interest in activities that are usually enjoyable. For over three months Robin had not watched television, read books or done any of the things she normally did to pass the time. With ECTs, as her brain was beginning to experience relief from such a profound state of despair, she was beginning to recognize more definitively that she was still not herself.

"I know I completely lost control," she said. "I don't feel like I have it back yet. I want to go back to work. I want to get my life back to normal." It concerned me that Robin's rigid brain saw getting back to work full-time as the only way for her to feel back in control. I under-stood, though, why she couldn't deal with the alternative of giving up her job, which would cause her to lose her independence.

With more ECTs, Robin's affect continued to brighten. She began to joke about things for the first time in months. And most impor-tantly, she finally began to acknowledge she was feeling better. "I'm actually looking forward to going back to work," she said. "But I'm worried about the stress. I'm not sure if I can handle it. I'm still tired and don't have much motivation to do anything." She verbalized the same concerns I was having. I tried to be reassuring about how much her depression symptoms had improved.

After seven ECT treatments, although she was dramatically bet-ter, Robin continued to report feeling depressed and having some sui-cidal thoughts. She continued to show signs of depression, although they were much less severe. Because of the ECTs, she couldn't remember how bad things had gotten just prior to her most recent hospitalization, which meant she couldn't fully understand the progress she had made.

Although I felt it would be better if she could have more ECTs before returning to work, we didn't have a choice. Robin needed to try going back to the job with which she was familiar, with the co-workers who knew and supported her. It wouldn't have worked well to give up her job and then have the pressure of knowing she'd have to start over. New jobs were always incredibly stressful for her, even when she wasn't depressed. Dr. Greene had made a recent adjustment to her antidepressant medication, which hadn't yet taken effect. I was hopeful this would alleviate her remaining depression symptoms over time.

I tried to be optimistic, and at the same time prepare myself for the possibility of having to keep being Robin's life-line if she lost her job. We were continuing to have frequent contact. It had been a very stressful and exhausting few months, but I remained sure I was doing what I needed to do. Robin was coming out of a severe depression, did not want to die, and was still not able to be open with her family or friends. I knew she'd need to stay connected to me until her symptoms, her job and her financial situation were stabilized. Once that happened, I trusted we would be able to return to a more typical degree of contact and work on her anxiety about being more open with others.

I had plans to leave town for the Memorial Day weekend to attend a friend's wedding. I looked forward to the much needed break. As I was preparing to leave, Robin and I discussed her anxiety about starting work the following Tuesday. I offered to talk over the phone during the weekend, and was relieved by her response.

"It's a holiday weekend for God's sake!" she said. "If I can't go three days without talking to you, we definitely have a problem." And then, she laughed. It was so good to hear her laugh. Robin was finally returning.

Robin Discusses ECT

Electroconvulsive Therapy (ECT) is a treatment method that comes with huge stigma, because of the way it was originally used and because of its dramatization in movies such as *One Flew Over the Cuckoo's Nest*. The prospect of having ECT was very scary for me, but nothing else was working to decrease my deep depression and control my obsessive suicidal thoughts. So I was ready to try just about anything.

My psychiatrist wanted to use ECT treatments as soon as he saw me during the Meltdown (my first hospital stay) because I was so deeply depressed. I was too out of it to really make a decision, but that became a moot point when my insurance refused to cover the treatments. It was determined that therapy and medications should be tried instead. I was frightened when ECTs were revisited as the best option for treating my intractable depression during my third hospital stay. I had researched it on the internet to get a more reliable impression than what I knew was misleading on TV and in movies. I trusted Sharon and Dr. Greene, so I agreed to do ECT in April 2003.

I don't remember every detail about having ECTs, partly because I was in such a crazy place emotionally and partly because the most common side effect is short-term memory loss. I remember enough to give the highlights though. I was still in the hospital for my first treatment. Early in the morning a man came to my room to escort me to the ECT suite on the third floor. I remember he was in charge of the ECT process and he always wore Hawaiian print shirts. In the ECT suite I put on a hospital gown and signed a form (probably a consent for treatment. I don't remember). While a nurse inserted an IV line into me another person asked me several questions. The only question I recall is whether or not I had any loose teeth, which seemed like a strange question (in hindsight it makes sense, since they were planning to induce a grand mal seizure).

Then, electrodes were put on my head. If you have unilateral ECT they are placed only on one side of your head; they are placed on both sides if you have bilateral ECT. I don't know whether I had unilateral or bilateral, I just remember the electrode was cold. I was also hooked up to monitoring devices, which monitored heart activity (EKG) and brain activity (EEG), and measured the electrical discharges of the muscles. I was given muscle relaxants through the IV, and I was given anesthesia which quickly made me unconscious. I didn't feel any of the seizure that was stimulated in my brain by the electrical current passing through it. Soon after the ECT was completed, I woke up in the recovery area and the nurse helped me change back into my clothes. I felt no pain, but I was a little fuzzy in the head and disoriented afterwards for a while. I was tired, whether from the ECT or the anesthesia I don't know.

After the first treatment, the rest of the ECTs I had on an outpatient basis, and my dad transported me to them. At that time I was still not being very open with my parents about what was going on. I don't think my dad knew what to say to me, and neither of my parents asked a lot of questions. I think taking me to my ECT appointments was my dad's way of being helpful. He took me faithfully despite having to be there really early in the morning, like at five or six a.m. He sat around in the waiting room for the duration of the ECT procedure, and took me home afterward. I was grateful that my dad did this for me, as I would've had to do the ECT on an inpatient basis otherwise. None of my other friends or family would've been able to take this much time off from work to be with me.

I was given a sheet of Discharge Instructions after each outpatient ECT procedure. It included things like "don't drive until cleared by your doctor, avoid extremes of activity, refrain from making important decisions, and avoid emotional subjects in conversations or on TV." My favorite instruction, though, was "avoid crowded public places, such as the grocery store or the mall. However, car rides with a family member, away from heavy traffic, are recommended as pleasurable relaxation." This struck me as funny. Seriously, who does that? Car rides with family as "pleasurable relaxation?" The only pleasurable car rides I took back then were the ones I took while I was drinking and listening to depressing music, which I'm pretty sure they'd discourage.

Before I returned to work, I had a total of seven ECTs. I went every Monday, Wednesday, and Friday for two weeks, and had one more the following Monday. I suffered no ill effects from having ECT. It didn't kill my brain cells, making me suddenly stupid. The only long term effects are the hazy memory I have of that time, which I might have experienced without ECT because it was such a freaked out time for me. It didn't cause brain damage, or ongoing seizures, or any of the other things people fear when they hear the word ECT. There was no pain involved, other than a slight headache after each treatment for a couple of hours. The best part about ECT is that it worked. Not imme-diately, obviously, but I have no doubt that it sped up my recovery.

The fact that I had ECT is probably what I would've kept secret in my story, if that were possible, because of the enormous stigma about it. The image of ECT in the movies and on TV is very negative and misleading. Let's face it, people believe something is SERIOUSLY wrong with you if you have to have ECTs, right? It is not used lightly. It's often the treatment used when nothing else works. I'm hoping that by revealing that I've had ECT, I can help to normalize it a little bit. I don't regret having this treatment. I believe that it played a large role in helping me get my life back. It's not used casually, or to control behavior as some might think. It's a safe, effective treatment modal-ity for medication resistant depression like I had. I was not instantly cured, because it doesn't work like that. But without ECTs I may not have survived.

7
Rock Bottom

ROBIN RETURNED TO her job half-time on the Tuesday after Memorial Day in 2003. After seven ECT treatments and a week to recover, she was less depressed than she had been in many months. She was, however, very apprehensive about her return to work. The stakes were high and she felt enormous pressure, knowing she would lose her job if she could not do it successfully.

I actually had no idea whether Robin was ready to do her job successfully. She had improved significantly with the ECTs. But she was still experiencing depression symptoms and intrusive suicidal thoughts. I was afraid she needed a few more ECTs in order to really alleviate her depression. Dr. Greene and I had released Robin to return to work partly because she would not have dealt well with losing her job. We needed to give her a chance to get her life back. I hoped getting back into her usual routine, surrounded by supportive colleagues and supervisors, would help Robin keep the momentum going in terms of the progress that had begun with the ECTs.

"I know I look like I'm doing better on the outside. Everyone keeps telling me how much better I am." She said in our session during her first week of work. Her family, friends and co-workers had been noticing and commenting on the improvement. Her affect was definitely brighter and the psychomotor retardation was gone. This was very noticeable to everyone, and her sarcastic sense of humor, which is typically a big part of who she is, had returned.

"I may be better, but I still feel the same on the inside," she explained, with her voice cracking slightly. "I hate myself and I hate my life." She looked like she was trying not to cry. I desperately wanted her to feel some hope, so she would feel motivated to keep from drinking.

"Robin, remember there's a difference between biological and psychological depression," I said. "Your biological depression is definitely better. The medication is managing the mania. The ECTs have helped the depression. You're joking around for the first time in months, and all the outward signs of depression have decreased. That's what everyone sees. But the psychological depression is related to all the stress and uncertainty about your job and your finances, and still being so isolated. I think you still feel depressed because of these issues. We'll keep working on all of this."

After finishing her first week at work, Robin and I talked on the phone.

"I have to tell you something," she confessed. She was still feeling compelled to tell me when she behaved self-destructively. "I drank a wine cooler last night to help me sleep." Robin talked about her concern about the upcoming weekend, and her fear about having no plans and "too much time to think."

Although I offered to plan a time to talk, she did not want to have contact with me over the weekend. Robin was trying to decrease our contact so she did not feel "too dependent" on our connection. I would have preferred waiting until she was settled into her job to decrease our contact, but I knew Robin needed to feel like her life was returning to normal. As she had gotten better, she felt more uncomfortable depending on me so much. I needed to honor her need to distance from me. We made plans to touch base by phone after her first full day of work the following Monday.

"I've been thinking about everything that's happened in the last six months," she said at that time. "I don't know if I'm going to be able to handle the stress of working full-time." Robin went on to say she had not slept much the night before and had "forgotten" to take her medications that morning. She admitted she had been thinking all day the previous day about overdosing on Depakote, but did not because of her cat, Epiphany. She said she was also worried she would be unsuccessful in her suicide attempt and make things worse.

I sighed to myself, as I dreaded her response to my next question. It was like I already knew the answer. "Did you take your meds last night?" I asked, suspecting this may have contributed to her lack of sleep and increasing instability.

There was a moment of silence. "No," Robin quietly confessed.

"Robin, you are sabotaging yourself. What's going on?" I was calm on the phone, but inside I was suddenly scared. I tried not to show it in my voice. I began to think Robin was not ready to work full-time. Just when I thought things were getting better. The ECTs had so clearly been helping!

"I don't know. Maybe I'm subconsciously trying to lose my job to give myself a reason to kill myself," she said. "I just don't want to be on all these meds. I know it doesn't make any sense. I just feel too much pressure."

In order to honor Robin's need to determine how much contact we maintained, I had decided to shift from automatically scheduling regular phone calls, to asking her to tell me when she wanted to talk next. This allowed her to have control and flexibility about the frequency of our conversations without having to be the one to initiate calling me after hours (which was still hard for her). She could stay connected or distance, depending on how she felt. As she was trying to transition back to her full-time job, I was relieved that she continued to want frequent contact. She was not clearly not doing well.

"I broke down and took Depakote last night, but I didn't take the rest of my meds." Robin said in one of our phone calls during her second week of work. "I didn't sleep at all." I suddenly felt my own anxiety in the pit of my stomach. I stood and began pacing around my office as we talked. I already sensed that Robin was not going to be able to manage the stress of her job. More importantly, though, I was very concerned about whether she would survive if she lost it.

"Robin, I'm really worried about you sabotaging yourself. You're setting yourself up to lose your job. Why do you think you're doing this?" I asked.

"I know it's not rational," she replied. "I'm just not ready to give in to having to take all those meds. I think the reality of everything I've been through in the last six months is really starting to sink in. I'm trying to assimilate it all."

"We have a lot to process about what's happened and I know this feels overwhelming. But if you don't take your medication tonight, and you continue to go without any sleep, you'll be seriously jeopardizing your chances to succeed at work." I was firm in the tone of my voice. I kept pacing. Thankfully, my office phone had a long phone cord.

I was concerned. After everything we had been through in the previous six months and after all the extra effort it had taken to arrange the opportunity to return to her job, I was very frustrated with her blatant self-destructive behavior. Part of me understood she was reacting to the enormous stress she felt, along with grief about having to accept her new diagnosis. But she was not giving herself a fair chance to get back to work successfully. It didn't make sense that she was setting herself up for disaster. I think she could sense the anger in my tone.

"I'll take my meds tonight," she said. "I don't want you to be mad at me."

Good, I thought. Thank God for that.

• • •

In our session that week Robin admitted she had again skipped all of her meds the previous night because she was drinking, and had then called in sick to work. She was not purposely sabotaging herself. The stress of trying to work full-time and process everything she had been through, as well as the financial pressure she was feeling as a result of not receiving her full pay for a number of months, was overwhelming and destabilizing her.

Despite the drinking, the stress, and the lack of sleep, Robin's affect continued to remain brighter than it was prior to the ECTs. She said she felt okay at work, even with little sleep. She was more focused on the future despite ongoing obsessive suicidal thoughts. She reassured me she was not planning to kill herself, and she began to take all of her medications again.

The improvement, though, was short lived. In our session during her third week of full-time work, Robin admitted that on the previous Friday night she took "much more" Ativan than she was supposed to. She did not know how many pills she had taken, but said she woke up "groggy and thick headed."

"Robin, on Friday you said you were going to take your meds as prescribed." I couldn't hide my surprise. She had overdosed? For God's sake, really? I thought. "What happened?" I asked. I rolled my office chair toward her, and leaned forward. I think she knew I was upset.

"I know it makes no sense," she said, her leg bouncing with anxiety. "It was impulsive. I just wanted to make sure I slept, and I wanted to see what would happen."

"You seem to be trying to create a crisis!" I confronted her, emphatically, with my stomach beginning to tighten. "You are pushing me to have to do something, and you are clearly jeopardizing your job. What's going on?"

"It's not conscious," Robin insisted, looking more and more uncomfortable as she could sense my alarm. "I don't know what's going on. I just can't stop obsessing about suicide. I guess I haven't decided about living or dying yet. Part of me wants to live and watch my nieces and nephew grow up, but I'm having a harder time controlling the other part."

Thank God she was talking to me about her ambivalence. I was grateful for that. But, it was hard for me not to get scared by the conversation. Robin was basically telling me she had impulsively overdosed. She could have easily misjudged the amount and killed herself by accident that night. We talked about the hospital, and she was adamant about not wanting to go. She insisted she was going to go to work the next day. She looked at me and said nothing, as if she was waiting to see what I was going to do.

We sat in silence for a minute, as I made a decision. I started wondering, again, whether I needed to have Robin detained. I didn't want to put her in the hospital, knowing it wouldn't solve anything. It would cause her to lose her job which would make everything worse. At that point, after we had been through this so many times before, I knew I needed to trust that if Robin truly wanted to kill herself, she would already be dead. My gut told me that to detain her would be a bad idea.

Overall I was feeling completely helpless, exhausted, and frustrated by Robin's ongoing self-destructive behavior. In my own mind I started questioning whether I was doing her any good. I think she could sense my frustration as I again talked about the dilemma her behavior caused for me.

"Robin, you're putting me in a bad position again. Now you're overdosing. What am I supposed to do about that?"

"I'm really sorry," she said, wringing her hands...a common habit when she was especially anxious. "I'm not trying to upset you. I can understand why you might be angry at me." Great, I thought. Robin is depressed and suicidal and now thinks I'm angry at her, which will just give her one more reason to kill herself. This was not going well.

"I'll try harder," Robin insisted. "I'll take my meds and I promise I won't drink tonight."

I decided I needed to trust her. But things were coming to a head. I had no idea what the outcome would be, but I was running out of optimism. Robin was clearly in control of her own destiny, and the probability of her keeping her job was looking bleak. I didn't think she'd kill herself that night, but I went to bed and contemplated the very real possibility that after all we had been through, Robin could still end up dead.

The next day, at around noon, she called me at a time when we had not planned to talk. I immediately knew something was wrong.

"I called in sick to work today," she said. "I feel like I'm losing control again." She confessed she drank vodka and skipped most of her medications the previous night, even after promising not to do this. "I wondered last night if I need to be in the hospital," said Robin. "This morning I went to the river and had the urge to jump in. I was able to stop myself, but I realize I'm overwhelmed and not in control."

My reaction to this news was a mixture of emotions. Obviously, I was very relieved she had not jumped in the river! I was thrilled she had called me instead, and was initiating the conversation about the hospital this time. But, I was also filled with dread as it was now a given that Robin would be losing her job. I took a deep breath, and said what I needed to say.

"Robin, I really think you need more ECTs," I said. "You didn't have enough of them before. I think it's time we really get your depression under control." I was indirectly telling her she needed to quit her job. I knew what a big deal this was. But, it was obvious she wasn't going to be able to keep it. As we talked, she realized it too. She knew she had no choice but to undergo more ECTs if she wanted to survive. I told her I would call her supervisor to find out what her options were in terms of her job and disability benefits, and that I would call Dr. Sanchez about scheduling more ECT treatments.

• • •

In June 2003, six months after her meltdown, Robin lost her beloved job with the team of co-workers and supervisors who were so supportive to her. Thankfully, her supervisor said they would "hire her back in a minute" if they had a position open and she was well enough to perform the job. The Human Resources manager at Robin's place of employment said she still had three months of short-term disability benefits left and she would retain her health insurance coverage during that time. She also had long-term disability benefits which she could apply for if needed.

"I guess it's better to take time off and get well rather than go to work, act crazy, and get fired," Robin said when she learned about how her benefits worked. This was another example of her thinking more clearly despite her self-destructiveness in the face of the work pressure. We had a rational discussion about whether she needed to be in the hospital.

"I want to avoid going there if I can," she said. "But I'll go if I need to." She admitted she was feeling more depressed about the reality of losing her job. She admitted her impulse control was weak, and she agreed to pour out all of her alcohol. And most importantly, Robin actually acknowledged she really did not want to kill herself.

Dr. Sanchez was able to get insurance approval for three more ECT treatments, which were scheduled to start on the Friday after she lost her job. She wanted to stay out of the hospital, and they were arranged on an outpatient basis. I was not able to get Robin to agree to stay with her parents or her brother. But, she did agree to allow me to talk to her mother and her brother about calling every evening to check in with her, which would provide accountability in terms of making sure she wasn't drinking.

I was especially concerned because I was again scheduled to leave for a vacation, this time to spend time with my family. Although I planned to check in with Robin periodically by phone, I would be many hours away and it would be difficult for me to help facilitate a hospitalization if she needed it. Robin's mother and brother were very willing to check in with her, and her father agreed to transport her to the early morning outpatient ECT treatments.

Robin was definitely better, but still very depressed. She admitted she didn't want to kill herself, but still could not stop obsessing about it. All I knew for sure at that time, was that I needed a break. I was exhausted...mentally, physically and emotionally. I knew I desperately needed some distance to get perspective about the life and death struggle I continued to witness.

I knew the vacation to visit my family in Northern Michigan would bring some much needed time away to get refreshed and regrouped.

When I left for vacation on the day Robin began her second round of ECTs in June 2003, I drove alone. My husband needed to work and planned to drive separately to my parents' house. Having five hours of alone time in the car was a much needed luxury for me. For the first time in months I had some extended time to myself with nothing to distract me.

The timing of the trip was ironic. Robin had just hit rock bottom. Although I knew that Robin, deep down, did not want to kill herself, I also knew she felt her life had completely fallen apart. I knew how bad she felt about the reality of needing to file for bankruptcy, and I knew she had no confidence that doing so would make things better. She was reeling from the sudden change in her diagnosis, the fact that she had been hospitalized three times, the loss of her job, and especially that she had undergone ECTs and was still having constant suicidal thoughts. I had done everything I could possibly do, for such a long time, and she was still at significant risk for suicide as Dr. Rios had said so many years before. There was no way for me to trust that more ECTs would get Robin feeling better enough to stop thinking about killing herself. There was certainly no way for her to trust this either. I felt completely powerless.

During that five hour drive it felt like the emotions I had been unable to process during the previous six months hit me all at once. I felt overwhelmed with sadness. There was the therapist part of me, who knew I had done everything I could do for Robin and that if she killed herself it was not my fault. But the rest of me just felt bad...mostly for Robin who was completely at the mercy of her rigid brain and the depression that had consumed her. I felt bad for her parents and her brother, who knew at some level that Robin was struggling but had no idea how dangerous her depression had become. I thought about how shocked and completely shattered they would be if she committed suicide. I thought about her nieces and nephews, who she saw frequently, who would be confused and traumatized if she suddenly died. And, I tried to imagine my own feelings if it came to that.

My overwhelming emotions that day in the car were about more than just Robin. Although I had been a psychotherapist for a decade and had treated many people with severe mental illness, rarely had I experienced so intimately the devastating effects mental illness can have on someone's life. Robin just wanted to be able to live her life, do her job, pay her bills and be okay. She was completely at the mercy of her own brain. No matter what I, Dr. Greene, or Dr. Sanchez did as her treatment providers, and no matter how hard she fought to get back to just living her life, her mental illness could still kill her. It was unfathomable. I thought with a new perspective about all the patients I had treated over the course of my career and the impact their illnesses had on their ability to function in various ways.

I thought about members of my own family, going back generations, who had struggled with significant anxiety and probably also depression, without treatment (including a great uncle who committed suicide). I thought about how different all of their lives could have been if effective treatments had been readily available and the stigma of mental illness had not kept them from realizing they had these symptoms. It made me very sad to think about all of it.

When I arrived at my parent's house, I was immediately surrounded by family. Parents, siblings, nieces and nephews filled the house with lots of activity. After such an emotional drive, it was very good to be distracted by all the children in my life who I love dearly. Over the subsequent week I was able to feel some distance from Robin, which was helpful. But, in the midst of the time with my family, per her request, I made time to talk to Robin on the phone every other day. I would go to the guest room of my parents' house where I was staying, for privacy. I stood and stared out the window into the thick woods behind their house, as I dialed Robin's phone number.

"My life is a financial, occupational, social and emotional fiasco," Robin said in one of our phone calls. She acknowledged she still felt depressed, and was still having some suicidal thoughts. "I'm stressed because I know I need to file bankruptcy."

"I think it's time to talk to an attorney," I told her. "I know the name of one who is really supportive and easy to talk to. I think getting more information about the whole process will help." Robin agreed, and I gave her the name. Two days later when we talked, she felt better.

"I talked to the attorney. I have an appointment scheduled to see her, which helps," Robin said, sounding relieved and more relaxed than I had heard in a while.

"I'm glad. How did the ECTs go?" Her insurance company had only approved three treatments, and she had the third one that morning.

"The procedures themselves were fine," Robin said. "But I'm concerned they don't seem to have helped enough."

"How bad are the suicidal thoughts?" I asked, assuming she was still having them.

"They're always there," she said. "But I know my parents and my brother would be devastated if I killed myself." I was surprised and thrilled to hear her say this. It was the first time her family members, not her cat, had been the biggest barrier for her in terms of suicide. It was the first time she was able to say they would be "devastated" and not just "upset." Thank God, she was finally thinking rationally enough to realize this. The Robin I had known for so long, who was very sensitive to other people's feelings, was finally coming back!

• • •

When we met following my vacation, we continued to process Robin's new reality. "How are you feeling about the bipolar diagnosis?" I asked, wanting to get a sense of where she was in terms of processing her new identity.

"I actually think I'd rather have people know I have bipolar disorder at this point," Robin said, surprisingly. "It would explain why I had such a hard time at work and had to quit." Wow! Even though she was still feeling depressed, Robin was thinking so much more rationally. She may not feel like herself, but she was starting to sound like herself. The additional ECTs seemed to have helped, thank God.

I was surprised further to hear Robin say she had investigated the amount of money she would receive in the form of Social Security Disability benefits if it came to this. She actually said she was beginning to accept that she would not likely be ready to return to her job as soon as she had hoped.

"I've been thinking about what I could do instead," she said. "Maybe I could help my brother and sister-in-law by watching my nephew a couple days a week. Or maybe I could volunteer as a court-appointed special advocate at some point to use my skills and stay in touch with people I know through work."

It was fantastic to hear Robin say these things. Although I knew she wasn't ready to volunteer anywhere due to the stress this would cause, the fact that she was thinking about this was miraculous. I couldn't believe she was actually allowing herself to consider ways in which being on disability could be okay. I took the opportunity to suggest what I knew needed to happen. I had previously been afraid to bring it up.

"Robin, I think it's time to find out more about your long-term disability benefits," I said, knowing she was going to exhaust short-term disability in a couple of months. She reluctantly agreed and said she would look into it.

A few days later, Robin called after talking to the Human Resources Director at her former place of employment. "I have to go back to work!" she said emphatically. She sounded very upset. "If I go on long-term disability I'd make only 60% of what I made before, but now my $400 health insurance premium would come out of it. I'd never be able to afford to stay in my apartment. And I can't afford my meds without health insurance. She's sending the paperwork in case I decide to apply, and she said it usually takes about a month to process it. But I can't do it. I have to go back to work!"

I was not prepared for this. Robin had just gotten to the point where she was able to consider being on long-term disability. As she explained what she had learned, I knew Robin was not remotely okay with the idea of losing her apartment and her financial independence.

It was the beginning of July 2003. Robin had been without a job, trying to wrap her brain around this reality, for several weeks. Over the next month she experienced ups and downs as she dealt with the enormous stress associated with being in complete limbo. The stakes were high. She was thinking more clearly and was therefore able to process things mostly realistically.

Understandably, Robin wanted to return to her pre-meltdown life where she was working full-time in a career she enjoyed and was able to support herself. She had embraced the concept of bankruptcy, which meant financial relief, and the idea of earning her previous full-time income without the pressure of paying off past debts contributed to her desire to return to work. Obviously this was her strong preference, as this would prevent her from having to accept any significant limitations imposed by her new identity as someone with a severe and chronic mental illness.

Robin's supervisor, Jennifer, was open to the idea of Robin returning to a position similar to the one she had lost. But, she sent Robin a letter outlining all the responsibilities of this position and said she would need a written statement from her treatment team (i.e., me or Dr. Greene) confirming she was ready to perform all of these responsibilities before she would be hired. It was not clear, though, whether there would actually be an opening before short-term disability ended. Robin had significant difficulty with all of the uncertainty. But, she tried to set this aside and work on her issues.

Robin and I had many conversations about her long-time patterns of social isolation and self-destructiveness, the big picture of her treatment (that she was improving in many ways despite all the ups and downs), and how to continue making progress. Because her bio-logical depression was better, she was able to read and watch television for the first time in many months, which served as distractions. I had her reading books on specific ways to overcome depression. She began to walk for exercise. We worked on cognitive and behavioral techniques, which had always been difficult for her, to help shift her ingrained patterns.

Robin had her last ECT procedure at the end of July 2003. Dr. Sanchez believed it would be helpful for her to have one treatment about a month after her previous series, in order to ensure that the biological changes in her brain continued. Because Robin was still struggling with ongoing, obsessive suicidal thoughts, Dr. Greene decided to increase one of her five medications, Celexa, to a higher dose. We were continuing to attack her significant depression from every possible angle.

Robin was trying to process the reality of her meltdown, her job loss, and the continuing uncertainty about whether she would be able to return to her previous career. I was disappointed to learn she was blaming herself for "not controlling her emotions enough" when she was first hospitalized in January 2003. She then insightfully said, however, "if I don't blame myself I have to acknowledge the degree to which I lost my defenses and went crazy." Robin was seemingly, painfully, beginning to come to terms with her illness.

I was relieved by Robin's progress. Very relieved. But I knew we were not out of the woods yet. I knew, deep down, that until Robin was settled...either back at work in the mental health field or on long-term disability in a situation that felt okay to her, things could still get dangerous again very quickly.

• • •

In August 2003, from Robin's perspective her life was ruined. In seven months she had gone from living in her own apartment and working full-time at a job she felt good about, with co-workers who liked and respected her, to facing the reality of being chronically mentally ill, bankrupt, and potentially unable to support herself in the near future. Along with her job she had lost both her income and her primary social support network, and her family members had no idea she might need their help. She had not shared with them the details of what would happen financially if she began to receive long-term disability benefits.

Robin was thinking rationally enough to understand she needed to apply for long-term disability benefits in order to keep this option open. But she remained focused on her desire to return to work with her previous employer by September 2003, when her short-term disability benefits would end. In her mind, this was the only option to live in a way that felt tolerable.

In mid-August she had lunch with some of her former co-workers in order to stay in touch with them as well as distract herself. She wanted to stay up-to-date about the potential for starting a new position in September. A few days later, we had a session.

"I've been feeling more depressed since we had lunch," she said. "Everyone was talking about how slow their caseloads have been. I know they won't need to fill any empty positions any time soon. And as much as I hate to admit it, I know I'm not ready to go back to work."

Robin started to cry. While other clients cried routinely in my office, Robin did not. It was highly unusual for her to allow herself to be this vulnerable outside of the hospital. I knew her tears were not a reflection of biological depression that required more medication or ECTs. Her tears were, plainly and simply, an expression of profound grief.

"My job was the only thing I had," Robin said with tears running down her cheeks. "I'm losing my independence, my friends, and my identity." She was right. I had nothing to say to make it any better. I let her cry. I offered Kleenex, which she accepted but didn't use. I empathized with her pain to the best of my ability. I could not imagine the fear she was feeling underneath the enormous sadness she was expressing.

This was a more vulnerable version of the Robin I had known for so many years...the Robin who was smart, insightful, and able to think very rationally. I had not seen the Robin I knew for eight long months, because she had been completely overwhelmed by her mental illness. The rational Robin I knew was back, but she had no good options for getting back to any semblance of the life she had previously known. I was actually feeling pretty discouraged myself. After we had worked so hard to finally get her brain functioning again, now Robin was facing the monumental task of building a new life for herself as a person with a severe, disabling (at least for the moment) mental illness. I did not have any easy answers in terms of how to do this.

As we continued to talk, Robin reluctantly admitted she was back to having more intense suicidal thoughts as she felt the hopelessness of her situation. "I'm tired of having to ask for help. I'm tired of fighting. It's too hard," she said quietly. She was staring at the floor. Her legs were back to bouncing, as they often did during times of increased anxiety. She was fidgeting with the Kleenex. And then, she asked a heartbreaking question. "Will you be mad at me if I end up back in the hospital?"

"Robin, of course I wouldn't be mad at you!" I said, insistently. "Do you think you need to be there?"

"I'm not going to do anything this week," she replied. "I have to get through the meeting with my lawyer about the bankruptcy."

Robin had always been reluctant to leave a financial mess for her family. She felt strongly that she needed to get the bankruptcy finalized in order to prevent this. Personally, I was happy for any barriers that existed in her mind to help keep her from suicide.

"I know I need to go on disability," she said. "I can accept that. But I don't want to ask either my brother or my parents if I can move in with them. And I don't see any way to make things work financially on my own. I don't know what to do!"

We were able to talk practically about whether Robin's brother Bob and his wife needed help with child care or other things that Robin could do for them in exchange for money. She said she would consider talking to him about this. Because Robin was obsessing about her situation and not sleeping well, I told her I would talk to Dr. Greene about a medication change to help with sleep. And I told her I would do some investigating about ways to cover her medical costs without her previous job's expensive insurance, which might make it possible for her to stay in her apartment. All of this problem solving helped her to feel a bit more hopeful, for the time being.

• • •

I can't emphasize enough how important it is for therapists, when they are in a situation with a client that is emotionally intense, confusing, or overwhelming in any way, to get outside of themselves. Feedback from trusted colleagues or supervisors is absolutely crucial in terms of maintaining perspective during the enormously difficult situations we therapists encounter with our clients. I will never be able to express to my former treatment team the gratitude I feel for their support and guidance during the long journey of stabilizing Robin's symptoms in 2003. During our weekly meetings I kept them updated on all of the developments, and they had ridden the roller-coaster of emotions along with me. It was in August, when Robin's life truly hit rock bottom, that I felt their support most sincerely.

Judith, my supervisor at the time, sat in on the team meetings. The rest of the team consisted of two women and two men, all psychologists and licensed social workers who had been therapists themselves for many years. We all liked each other and respected each other's opinions. Our meetings involved giving each other feedback and suggestions about how to handle particularly difficult client situations, commiserating about agency politics and mental health system difficulties, and providing support to each other about the realities of our professional and sometimes our personal lives. We met in one of the rooms in our department that was used for group therapy and other meetings. There were a number of chairs in this large room, and the six of us always arranged our chairs in the middle of the room in a circle...as if we were in our own little group therapy session. Sometimes it felt like that.

I was particularly anxious in August 2003 to problem solve Robin's dilemma with my treatment team members. I needed their help. I outlined the details of her financial reality following the loss of her job, and her willingness to say she did not feel ready to return to work.

"I know Robin isn't ready to deal with this reality," said Gwen, one of the most wise and most experienced team members. "But I had a client once who reminds me a lot of Robin. She was a physician. She functioned well for many years, and then had a complete breakdown. Her stress tolerance was never the same after that. It took her a while to get through the adjustment, of course, but last I knew she was on disability and working part-time in a grocery store. It wasn't ideal, but it worked for her."

Wow! Gwen was right. Robin was not ready to deal with this possible reality. And, although I didn't say it, neither was I. Robin had just gotten stabilized with the last round of ECTs the previous month! It felt premature to assume she would need to be on disability forever, never to return to her chosen career. After all, she had been able to do her job very competently right up to her meltdown and we now had much more accurate information about her correct diagnosis. It seemed that, with some time and continued work in treatment, maybe Robin could get back to working full-time. I certainly wasn't sure, but I knew she would need to try.

Maybe I was grasping and my ability to be objective was questionable, but debating Robin's long-term prognosis was not what I needed to focus on. I needed suggestions about how to get her through the immediate crisis.

"Even if long-term disability and part-time work is what Robin will need to do eventually, she is definitely not ready yet to accept this." I said. "She is going to apply for long-term disability, and knows she is not ready to work full-time. But she will likely need to attempt to return to her previous job at some point. She is pretty determined to get back to working in the mental health field. She feels like her job is her identity, and she's not ready to lose that. Right now, she just needs a way to stay in her apartment and maintain her independence."

Something suddenly shifted in the room. It was as if everyone, including me, understood Robin's pain on a new level. For eight months, what she had experienced was so extreme, we could not really begin to relate to it. But, suddenly we were more generally talking about the reality that mental illness can shatter the lives of professional people, to the point where they can no longer do the jobs that define who they are. No one in the room admitted they were thinking about how awful it would be to have that happen for themselves. But, from the tone of the conversation and the sudden energy everyone felt about helping Robin, I suspect we were all feeling that vulnerability on some level. We all acknowledged what we often witnessed in our work…that mental illness can be devastating.

All of a sudden, the suggestions came from all directions. Discussion of applying for Medicaid, or pharmacy discount plans, or possible ways to get the administrators from the agency to reduce Robin's fees, etc. came forward. Practical suggestions I had not considered, which could potentially allow Robin to get her medical costs covered without insurance (allowing her the possibility of staying in her apartment, maybe with a little help from her family until she could get a part-time job). Now, I felt more hopeful. I wasn't ready to talk to Robin about any of these options, but I now had some possible solutions I could explore.

After doing some investigating, Robin and I had a difficult session in which we talked about options for continuing to cover the costs of her mental health treatment without insurance.

"Robin, I've learned you would probably be eligible for Medicaid if you aren't working and you would qualify for a state funded program which enables you to have a 95% discount for all the services provided here (at the agency). Without income, you'd also probably be able to get your medications free through the drug companies that manufacture them. They have what are called patient assistance programs," I explained some of the details of these options, which could theoretically allow her to give up the expensive insurance through her former employer and still be able to live in her apartment. Thank God she was physically healthy and had no health costs other than mental health treatment.

Robin was silent for a few moments as she took in the information I was telling her. "It'll take me a while to accept being on the other side," she said. "I'm used to being the one helping people get government assistance, not the one receiving it."

She was silent for a while longer, staring at the floor. She was wringing her hands, anxiously. She seemed to be processing the reality she was facing. Then she said, "When do you think I'll be ready to go back to work again? Do you think it'll be six weeks? Or do you think it'll be more like six months or even longer?"

I knew I had to be honest with her. I was afraid of upsetting her, but I knew she needed to hear the truth. I shifted in my seat. "I don't think it will be six weeks," I said tentatively.

"I agree," said Robin, still staring at the floor.

We both acknowledged her sadness about this, and how hard it was for her to admit the degree to which her stress tolerance had been affected by the previous eight months. I wanted her to feel some hope, however, as she tried to accept that she would be unlikely to return to her previous job in the near future.

"I think you'll get approved for long-term disability, Robin. And, you should probably apply for Social Security disability at some point too. If you got approved for that, I think you could work part-time in addition. This might be a good option for a while so we can focus more in therapy on helping you really heal. Not just heal enough to get back to a full-time job, but really heal. So you are happier with yourself and your life."

"That seems impossible," she said. She was sitting in the same crappy green chair in my office where she always sat during our sessions. She stared at the floor, bouncing her leg, and fighting back tears.

I assured Robin we would talk much more about all of the situational and psychological issues that contributed to her ongoing depression. I wanted her to have a sense that life on disability benefits could actually be an improvement over her life prior to her meltdown. I knew she couldn't possibly imagine it at that time. But I hoped she would stick around to let us work on helping her get there.

It was August 2003. Robin still had a few more weeks of short-term disability income she could count on, and was waiting to hear about whether she was approved for long-term disability benefits through her former employer. She met with her attorney and learned it would likely be the end of September before the hearing would be scheduled to finalize the bankruptcy process.

Robin continued to report ongoing, daily suicidal thoughts. She managed to avoid alcohol, and spent lots of time with her family and friends to distract herself. But, as the days went on and Robin continued to experience the ambiguity associated with not knowing whether long-term disability would be approved in time for her to avoid a gap in her income, she began to become more anxious and depressed. Her suicidal thoughts intensified. When we talked about them, Robin made it clear she had no intention of killing herself before the bankruptcy was finalized. Despite the increase in suicidal thinking, she was still sleeping okay and drinking only an occasional social drink.

Things changed, however, dramatically and quickly. We talked in a planned phone call on a Monday in late August.

"I'm more depressed," Robin said. "I drank three beers on Saturday night and then I couldn't sleep all night. I was thinking about what I'd write in a suicide note." I got a sinking feeling in the pit of my stomach that we were going down a familiar and dangerous road.

"How much sleep did you get last night?" I asked.

"Very little," Robin said. "I didn't take Trazodone because I don't want to be on any more medication. I know I'm not thinking very clearly."

All of a sudden I had a horrifying thought. I wasn't sure at all, because her situation could easily be causing her to have increased depression. But, I remembered that Dr. Greene had increased Robin's Celexa dose in mid-July, and added Trazodone for sleep in mid-August. Both of these were anti-depressant medications, and in the absence of enough mood stabilizing medication, could cause someone who has bipolar disorder to experience symptoms of mania. Dr. Greene and I had discussed this possibility, but he believed the Depakote and Geodon she was taking would prevent this from happening. I didn't want to alarm Robin, partly because I was not at all sure that mania was part of the issue. But, it came to my mind.

The next morning, my suspicion was confirmed. Robin was obviously experiencing a mixed bipolar episode.

"I slept better with the Trazodone," she said in a phone call. "But I'm still having trouble thinking clearly. I feel crazy and out of control." Thank God, Robin and I had gotten to a point where she felt comfortable telling me this was how she was feeling.

"Robin, I'm concerned that the Celexa increase a few weeks ago, coupled with the Trazodone, is destabilizing you," I said. She acknowledged she was experiencing all the symptoms of mixed mania including irritability, increased anxiety, racing thoughts, and difficulty controlling her impulses.

"All I want to do is go buy some vodka and get drunk," she said.

After some discussion about options for keeping her safe while we stabilized her symptoms, and Robin refusing to consider staying with a family member, she agreed to re-enter the hospital. It was her fourth hospitalization in eight months.

Robin's Thoughts About Rock Bottom

It was a horrible six months for me at the start of 2003. I had a major Meltdown, was hospitalized in a psychiatric hospital for the first time, went on short-term disability, was diagnosed with a severe and chronic mental illness, was prescribed anti-psychotic and mood stabilizing medications, and had ECTs. All of these events were completely contrary to my previous identity as a person who had depression magnified by childhood trauma, who just needed to take antidepressant medication (like, it seemed, most people I know). I was reeling from all of these developments, while at the same time I remained deeply depressed. It was unimaginable that things could get much worse for me, but it wasn't over yet.

Going back to work was a consistent goal for me throughout 2003. I've never done well with life changes, even minor ones. I certainly wasn't ready for all the changes that happened to me that year.

I wanted my old life back, and latched onto my career as the only way I could achieve this. However, the timing of my return to work six months after the Meltdown was terrible. I had only finished my first few ECT treatments when I was informed that I needed to return to my job or lose my position. My employer had been very accommodating to that point, holding my position past the length of my FMLA (Family Medical Leave Act) time period. So I couldn't complain much when I was told my time was up. I was grateful to Dr. Sanchez for understanding my need to stop the ECTs soon enough for me to return to work, and to Sharon for arranging it all with my supervisor. I did feel better after the seven ECT treatments I received, and was hoping it was enough for me to get back to work successfully.

Unfortunately, I didn't return to the best situation. The day I returned to work, my supervisor told me I'd need to address my team of coworkers. Apparently I'd made comments during my leave from work which made some of them uncomfortable. I had fairly regular contact with my team while I was off of work, usually meeting some of them for lunch on Fridays. I have a sarcastic, self-deprecating sense of humor, and I think I was trying to break the tension with my co-workers by joking about what I was going through. I have no memory of anything I said, but I guess some of them did not find my attempts to make light of my situation funny. I was never told exactly what I said which made them uncomfortable. Not even knowing what I was apologizing for agitated my anxiety even more.

Talk about a nightmare during my first week back! I was already anxious enough about returning to work. Being open with people under the best of circumstances made me very nervous and uncomfortable. It was okay to make jokes about myself in small groups of people, but to be forced to discuss my very painful issues seriously in front of the whole team of about fifteen people at once was terrifying for me. It magnified my already overwhelming anxiety. Somehow I was able to do it, and to say what I needed to say. I survived it, and was relieved.

Another factor which made returning to work at this time difficult was that I had to start over with a totally new case load. I had been gone so long, my clients had to be transferred to other case managers so they could get the help they needed. While I understood and expected this, it was hard for me to begin working with all new families. My social anxiety issues made working with new clients hard even when I wasn't depressed. Taking on new clients in the emotional state I was in at that time was extremely stressful.

To make matters worse, one of the new families was very resistant to working with my program. It was a case that had been referred by the probation department, so they were court-ordered to comply. Court-ordered clients were frequently resistant, but these people were very angry about it and very vocal about their anger. I don't do confrontation well. I'd been really stressed by resistant clients prior to my Meltdown, and being depressed and anxious one week after finishing a course of ECT certainly didn't put me in the best possible place to deal with them.

I lasted about a month before the stress became too much and I had to give up my job. Sharon wrote about all the ways I was being self-destructive during that time, seemingly sabotaging myself in my efforts to get my life back to normal and succeed at work. I really don't remember all of that. The ECTs I had before and after that time make all of it a blur. But it doesn't surprise me when I read Sharon's recounting of my out of control behavior of drinking and skipping medications during the time I was working. This is what I did back then when I was depressed, or too anxious, or in hindsight, experiencing mixed mania. I suspect it was probably clear to me, deep down, shortly after I started back at my job that I wasn't going to be able to manage it. I couldn't face that reality, and escaped by drinking. I wasn't thinking clearly, obviously, when I made the decision to skip my meds. I probably skipped them because I knew that mixing medication with alcohol meant bad side effects. The bottom line is that I was overwhelmed, still depressed, unable to process the reality of what was happening to my life, and just trying to go to work every day and survive. It finally caught up. I'm surprised I was able to avoid going to the hospital when I lost my job, since it felt like the end of the world to me. But, Sharon quickly convinced me to resume the ECTs, and my brain refocused my anxiety on that.

Losing my job was obviously very difficult. I remember cleaning out my desk and carrying my belongings out to Chuck on my last day. I was crying quietly, and couldn't look at my coworkers as I packed. I was close to my team, and was devastated to leave them. My supervisor, Jennifer, said she'd hire me back if I got to a place where I could return, but I think deep down I knew I wasn't going back.

• • •

Around this time, Sharon and I had been discussing the possibility of filing for bankruptcy to alleviate some of my financial pressure. I was lucky I had short-term disability benefits through my employer, so I still had some income while I was off of work. However, I only received a percentage of my regular income, which was causing me greater financial stress. Aside from my usual debt, I now had medical bills for my time in the psychiatric hospital, ECTs, and increases in medication and therapy.

I made decent money as a case manager (I was at the highest salary for the position at my place of employment) and I didn't have children, so I should've been in a tolerable financial position at the time of my Meltdown. Unfortunately, though, I had quite a bit of credit card debt and I didn't have any savings or extra money to pay for these additional expenses. I had accumulated a large amount of debt partly due to impulsive spending habits on my part, and partly due to the fact that I had to live on my credit cards for periods of unemployment because of mini-meltdowns. I'm not making excuses. I never should've had as many credit cards as I had. I had a VISA, MasterCard, Discover, and several department store credit cards. I made payments on time, but usually only made the minimum payments.

I was able to get by when I was earning my whole salary, but once I went on short-term disability and started to receive my bills for treatment from the Meltdown, it became really tight. I already owed my brother a ton of money for the repair bill for Chuck earlier in the year, so I wasn't about to ask to borrow any money from family. As I was beginning to be more open with Sharon, I started talking to her about how stressed I was about money. This had never been a topic we had talked about before. Filing for bankruptcy was not an option I had ever considered.

When Sharon suggested it as a way to alleviate some of my stress, I resisted the idea of filing for bankruptcy for quite a while. I think this is because of my family values and the attitude toward finances I learned from my parents. I come from a working class family, in which there was never a ton of extra money. We weren't poor, and I always had what I needed, but it wasn't always the expensive name brands like other kids had.

My parents married young. My dad worked in a factory and was taking night college classes, while my mom stayed home with us three kids. My brother, Eddie, was diagnosed with cancer when I was a toddler, which put a huge financial burden on my parents. My dad had to quit college (only 17 credit hours short of finishing), which then limited his occupational options from then on. My parents had many medical bills for Eddie, some of which were paid for by insurance, but not all. They also had to make a couple of trips to New York to see a specialist for the type of cancer Eddie had which was not cheap.

In spite of this financial crisis, my parents managed to pay their bills on time. My mom had to go to work after Eddie died, to help financially. As I was growing up, there were periods in which my dad was laid off from work, and money became very tight. However, my parents always managed to pay the bills without assistance from others. They never considered bankruptcy as an option.

This is the environment in which I grew up, so the thought of filing for bankruptcy was against everything I had been taught. I felt embarrassment and shame at the thought of it. But, I was reaching the level of financial crisis, and after Sharon and I talked about it, bankruptcy was the only option I could see to repair my financial situation. I hated to do it, but I couldn't see any other way out. I finally agreed to talk to an attorney, and borrowed the money from my brother to file for bankruptcy.

At that time, filing for bankruptcy meant easily being totally relieved of all debt, unlike today when the rules are stricter. So I was basically given a blank slate financially. My bankruptcy decision absolved me of all of my medical bills related to the Meltdown, as well as my credit card debt (except for one Visa card, which my dad had co-signed on. I didn't want to affect his credit by including it). I should've felt enormously relieved by this sudden financial freedom, but I didn't. I felt even more like a failure.

So in August 2003 as I entered the hospital for the fourth time, I could not imagine a way in which my life could ever be okay again. I felt like I had lost my career, my identity, my income, my friends, and any sense of stability I had begun to regain as my severe depression began to lift. I was trying to wrap my brain around the reality of having a severe and chronic mental illness. Of having ECTS. Of filing bankruptcy. Of applying for disability. I had no idea how I would pay my bills going forward. It makes sense to me, in hindsight, that I was so suicidal. As a person who had always been very stressed by uncertainty, I don't know how I was even functioning. In the context of Dante's Inferno and his nine circles of hell, the lowest circle is cold and isolating as it is the furthest away from God. At that time, it felt like I had reached the bottom of hell.

8
Stability Achieved

IT WAS THE end of August 2003, and Robin was in the hospital. Unfortunately, between the time we had the conversation about covering the costs of her medical care and the time she was hospitalized, I had learned some bad news. Really bad news. I decided to tell her while she was in the hospital and safe, so she could have time to integrate the new information and make some decisions.

The inpatient unit had an installment of phones on the wall in the hallway. From my office in the outpatient building I could call the nursing station in the adjoining hospital building, and the staff would find Robin and connect my call to one of the hallway phones. I hated to have this conversation on the phone where she had no privacy, but my schedule was packed that day and I couldn't get over to the hospital. More importantly, I needed her to know what I had learned as soon as possible, so she could rally support from her family.

"Robin, it's me," I said when I heard her answer the phone. It was the day after she had entered the hospital. Her voice sounded flat and sad. "How are you doing?"

"I just talked to my brother," she said. "He was trying to be supportive. He thinks working in mental health is too stressful. He agrees I should go on disability long-term and do something part-time that doesn't involve suffering." I cheered for Bob in my head. I agreed with him. But I couldn't be the one to tell Robin I thought she should stop working in mental health. She saw it as her identity and as her only real area of interest. I was happy to hear Bob was supportive of Robin collecting disability benefits. His support was crucial to the bad news I was about to share.

"Robin, I'm glad Bob is being supportive and you are being open with him. There's something I've learned that I need to tell you." I went on to share with Robin that if she chose to apply for Medicaid benefits, her income from long-term disability would result in a "spend down," the equivalent of a monthly deductible, of around $500 per month.

"You'd have to cover $500 of the costs every month, and then have Medicaid cover the rest. You'd still get the 95% discount for your services here at the agency, and I'm sure Dr. Greene would provide some samples. But that won't work as a long term solution. Robin, the bottom line is I'm not sure you can keep your apartment." I hated to have to say this to her. Robin said nothing, trying to process the news. "Your medications would cost over $500 per month. Being on Medicaid would disqualify you from getting the meds from the drug companies for free," I explained.

When Dr. Greene admitted Robin to the hospital he immediately lowered her Celexa dose, agreeing with my assumption that increasing it and adding Trazodone for sleep had triggered a mixed bipolar episode. He replaced Trazodone with Ambien, which was specifically a sleeping medication, not an antidepressant like Trazodone, and therefore unlikely to exacerbate her mania. He also stopped Geodon, the antipsychotic Robin had been taking since her first hospitalization in January, and replaced it with Abilify.

I had learned about Abilify, a new antipsychotic medication in 2003, at the psychopharmacology conference I attended in January immediately after Robin's first hospitalization. I didn't know specifically why Dr. Greene chose to make this change, but I remembered the presenter at the conference saying it was a brand new type of antipsychotic medication and was chemically unlike anything else that had ever been on the market.

The problem was Abilify and the other medications Robin was taking regularly (Celexa, Wellbutrin, and Depakote) were very expensive. Without insurance they would cost hundreds and hundreds of dollars per month. There was no way Robin would be able to afford to pay for them without insurance.

During our phone conversation I threw out the only other option I could think of, which could potentially allow her to continue to live in her apartment. "I don't think it's a good idea but the other option is to go without insurance. You'd qualify for free medications from the drug companies and for the 95% discount from the agency. Obviously there would still be some medical costs, but they'd be minimal as long as you only need treatment for mental health issues. If you had a car accident, or an injury or physical illness, you'd be uncovered. I'm concerned living on the edge to this extent would be really stressful."

Robin was silent on the other end of the phone. This was a lot of information to take in. She said she would have to talk to her family members about what she should do. I knew it was time for me to step out of the driver's seat somewhat. Robin, overall, was much better. Her mixed episode, which happened for very explainable reasons, was being treated and she was already improving after being in the hospital one night. I assumed this was because her family members were now aware of her financial dilemma, had rallied and were being supportive. Robin was still anxious and not sleeping well, but she said her mood was a bit better and her suicidal thoughts had dramatically decreased. It was time for both me and Robin to let her family help.

The next day, I was shocked by the changes. "I saw Dr. Greene this morning," she said. "He's discharging me today."

What? I had not expected this. I had no idea whether she was stable enough to leave the hospital. If Dr. Greene had told her he would send her home, without calling me first as he usually did, Robin must have been very convincing!

"I feel more stable and ready to go home," she said. "My parents and Bob and I all talked about what to do. They want to help me keep my insurance, and my apartment. Bob is going to pay me to help with the kids and do other stuff around their house. If it doesn't work out, we talked about me moving in with him if I need to."

Really? Wow. I couldn't have been more relieved to hear the news, but we were approaching the Labor Day holiday weekend, which made me nervous. Robin and I had decreased the frequency of our contact, partly because she was doing better overall and partly because she didn't want to become too dependent on me. I knew she wouldn't want to talk during the three-day weekend. I wanted to make sure she was actually safe to go home, and not just minimizing her symptoms with Dr. Greene because she wanted to get out of the hospital.

"Are you concerned that getting out of the hospital will cause your brain to shift back to thinking about suicide?" She had been experiencing a mixed bipolar episode, and she'd only been in the hospital two days!

"I'm feeling better," she said, "I'm hoping this was a wakeup call for me." She said she was still having significant trouble sleeping, typical for her during a mixed episode, but she assumed being at home would help. She always had trouble sleeping when she was not in her own apartment and bed. We had one night for her to test her theory before the holiday weekend. Robin was discharged from the hospital that day.

Shortly after her discharge, I received a call from her mom. "I'm just calling to see how Robin is really doing," she said. "I was surprised that she needed to go to the hospital and then got discharged so quickly."

No kidding...me too. Robin had given me permission to talk to her family members about anything other than her suicidal thoughts. I explained to her mom that she had been experiencing a mixed episode, and we were now completely certain that bipolar disorder was Robin's main issue. We talked about how stressed Robin had been about the financial ramifications of losing her job and applying for disability.

"Dr. Greene made medication changes that will help. But I also really think it helped that Robin feels supported by you and her dad and Bob," I said. "You have no idea how glad I am that she's allowing you to know what's going on. That is all huge progress."

"But is she okay to be out of the hospital?" she asked, sounding fearful. Robin's mom was apparently starting to understand the potential dangerousness of the situation. Thank God. It was such a relief to me. Robin was finally letting her family in!

"I think she's definitely better," I said, trying to reassure Robin's worried mom without painting an unrealistically rosy picture. "But I honestly don't know how much of the sudden change was real and how much was Robin faking it well enough to get out of the hospital. I promise I'll be talking to her tomorrow before the holiday weekend to make sure she is sleeping. If not, I can talk to Dr. Greene about options."

The next day, Robin and I talked by phone. "I'm feeling more stable. I'm less depressed than when I went to the hospital, but I'm still really anxious and tired. I slept last night but I kept waking up," she said. As we talked, I learned she had not taken the Ambien Dr. Greene prescribed for sleep.

I was instantly irritated. Part of the point of us talking that day was to see if the Ambien did what she needed it to do, so I could consult with Dr. Greene about a change before the weekend if necessary. Robin did not seem to understand we were trying to stabilize her brain chemistry, and not taking her medication as prescribed could jeopardize that. I was already frustrated that she had, without talking to me, gotten Dr. Greene to discharge her right before a holiday weekend.

Robin had, at some point after she started feeling better, rigidly decided talking on weekends was no longer necessary. This was fine, and preferable for me, except when I knew she not biologically stable.

Despite letting her family in, I knew she would never call them if she was feeling "crazy," suicidal, or having urges to be self-destructive. I knew she had little control over her rigid, unstable brain. But she was putting me in a difficult position, just as she had countless times the previous eight months. My patience was beginning to wear thin.

Trying my best to hide my irritation, I told Robin to take the Ambien. She agreed, and we talked about what she would do to stay busy over the weekend. She promised not to kill herself, or drink. This was hard for me to trust when I knew she was not yet stabilized.

As I drove home from my office that evening I reminded myself, for what felt like the billionth time, that I had done everything I could possibly do. Robin was making her own choices. I couldn't control everything.

• • •

After the Labor Day weekend, I drove my car into a parking space at work. Employees were required to leave the parking lot closest to the outpatient building free for clients and visitors, so it was a bit of a walk from the employee lot. On the beautiful agency campus, I walked along a tree lined drive, overlooking a large grassy area with a sculpture garden as I made my way. As I was walking, I found myself thinking about Robin and wondering how her weekend had gone. We planned to talk on the phone later that afternoon. I was trying to prepare myself to hear just about anything.

When we talked, Robin sounded exhausted and stressed. "I had a bad weekend," she said. "The weather was crappy and the plans I made fell through. I went out and bought some vodka yesterday and got drunk."

What the hell? I was instantly angry. It was the first time in my ten years as Robin's therapist that I was truly angry at her. Through all her times of self-destructive behavior during the previous eight months, I had been able to stay patient and focused on Robin's severe depression and difficulties with impulse control. I was able to empathize with how awful she must have felt, and could understand why she would want to numb herself with alcohol. At those times, I would calmly and firmly tell her I could not support or enable self-destructive behavior. I had always been able to stay professional and therapeutic. But on that day in September 2003, I reached my limit.

I had already been irritated the previous Friday after Robin campaigned with Dr. Greene to get out of the hospital without talking to me about it, and after she did not take the Ambien he prescribed for sleep. She had promised she would not drink. To hear that she not only drank, but purposely went and bought vodka with the plan of getting drunk, scared me. I knew things could get very ugly again, very quickly.

I was angry mostly because Robin made a choice to not call me, and to get drunk instead. After all the ways I had extended the boundaries to help overcome her severe anxiety about reaching out to people, I was hurt that she was still unwilling to call me to avoid being self-destructive. I would always tell my clients in therapy that underneath anger is usually hurt or fear. That day I was feeling a lot of both. But what I felt consciously, was just plain anger.

The rational part of me knew Robin wasn't thinking clearly, because she wasn't yet stabilized. The therapist part of me, had it been operating, would have been able to hide my anger from Robin on the phone. But I was a human being who had extended myself for her, in many ways, over a long period of time. I was getting tired. The therapist part of me wasn't able to override the hurt, scared, and angry human part.

"Are you ready to get back on track and stop being self-destructive?" I asked, with an angry tone in my voice.

"I'm not sure," Robin said sheepishly, her voice sounding flat. "I'm trying. I went to work today and packed up all my stuff from my desk. Then I went to lunch with my co-workers. I had to fight to keep from crying during lunch."

Of course. Robin was dealing with the enormous grief associated with losing her job. I wasn't surprised she had a hard time while packing her office and seeing her co-workers. But she did not have to do this today. From my angry perspective, I wondered whether she was choosing to immerse herself in the grief, almost as if she wanted an excuse to self-destruct. I knew I was taking it too personally that Robin drank. I had temporarily lost any ability to be therapeutic.

Our phone call was supposed to be a brief contact to discuss how things had gone over the weekend. We were scheduled to meet the next day. I knew I needed to get off the phone and get myself calmed down, so I could be therapeutic during our session.

"I need you to get rid of the rest of the vodka you bought," I said, emphatically.

"I'm not ready to do that," Robin said, just as firmly.

Wow, okay. This was not going to go well. I shifted enough to say, less angrily, that we would talk more about all of it when we met the next day. I asked Robin about her suicidal thoughts.

"They are low," she said. "I'm ruminating more about job stuff and what's happening financially." She assured me she would not kill herself before our appointment. I hung up, knowing I needed to get clear before our session the next day.

I needed to make a decision. I had made a very conscious judgment call shortly after Robin's meltdown to make part of the focus in therapy about our relationship. I realized the extent to which she had severe anxiety about being open with anyone. My decision to extend the boundaries within our relationship and talk about the fact that I cared about her, had gradually allowed her to feel more comfortable being open with me, and then more open with her family. I knew my gut had steered me in the right direction.

I needed to trust my gut again. Robin and I had developed a close enough connection that I hoped I could influence her positively by being honest about my anger. If I knew she was stable, it would have been an easy decision. I would have trusted the connection and used the situation as a "teaching moment" in the therapy process. But she wasn't stable. She was still not sleeping well, and her behavior over the weekend was evidence of impaired impulse control. There was a risk that if I expressed my anger and she was not able to process it rationally, she could use it as yet another reason to kill herself. I had used our close connection as a way to keep her alive until she stabilized and could let more of her own people in. If she felt like our connection was damaged in any way, I worried it could push her toward more self-destructiveness.

I didn't agonize very long about my decision. My gut felt clear. I trusted the connection. Robin had stayed alive through so much partly, I believed, because she felt good about being able to be completely open and feel accepted by me. I knew I needed to be honest and direct with her in our session. I felt it was worth the risk, since she was continuing to be self-destructive and I needed to do what I could to stop this. When she arrived, I was a bit nervous about saying what I needed to say.

"Robin, we've talked a lot about our relationship over the last eight months. I've been more open in order to help you feel comfortable in close relationships. Part of a healthy relationship is the ability to be direct about all feelings, both good and bad. I need you to know that yesterday, for the first time I was really angry at you," I said. I went on to explain why.

"I could tell you were angry," Robin replied. "I've already gotten rid of the vodka. I'm going to try to stop being self-destructive. I don't want you to be mad at me."

Praise God! All of a sudden I felt validated. After all my questioning earlier in the year about whether I was doing the right thing by opening up to Robin and extending the boundaries, I saw again that it had been the right decision. She cared enough about me and about not making me angry, that she was willing to work harder to stay alive. I was relieved. Very relieved.

We went on to have a long discussion about cleaning out her office, and losing her job. She cried as we talked. I was glad she was beginning to feel more comfortable showing her emotions in front of me. She was open about how hard it was for her to accept her inability to work.

"Robin, I think it's going to be important for you to have something productive to do. It doesn't work for you to have too much unstructured time and so little social contact. I know you are grieving many losses. But maybe volunteer work of some kind would be a good distraction. I think it will help if you can shift your focus to rebuilding your life, rather than on what you have lost."

"I agree," Robin said. "But first I need to get some things settled. I need to finalize the bankruptcy and know whether I'll be getting long-term disability. I've been thinking about it, and probably need to just go ahead and apply for Social Security Disability benefits too. There's no point in putting it off." She became tearful again, as she talked about how hard it was for her to admit that she needed to take this step.

I felt much better after this session. I was no longer angry. It helped that Robin was willing to consider volunteer work, and to apply for Social Security Disability benefits. This was all progress in terms of her accepting the reality of her situation, despite her enormous grief. The next day, I was even more encouraged by her progress.

Robin called, unexpectedly. I was shocked to hear why.

"I need to tell you about something you said in our session yesterday that hurt my feelings," Robin said, sounding nervous. Wow! This was amazing. For her to be this assertive and direct with me, was unheard of. It had never happened before. In the past, when I had encouraged her to be direct with people about her feelings she had always just said, "I don't do conflict."

"Please, tell me," I said.

Robin and I had been talking about how bad she felt over the weekend when she chose to go buy vodka and get drunk. At another time in the conversation she talked about making a CD of songs during the weekend.

"When I was telling you about my CD you asked if it was a drunk and depressing CD," she said. "I felt hurt because it took a lot for me to share my CDs with you. I felt like you were dismissing that."

Wow! What a monumental step for her! I was instantly sorry. She was completely right. I had obviously still been angry when we talked about her CD. I had crossed the line, was unprofessional, and said something hurtful. When therapy focuses on the relationship between client and therapist, the theory is that it provides a safe place for clients to practice these kinds of relationship skills. I was absolutely thrilled that Robin felt safe enough to say this to me. This was the person who, eight months earlier, had confessed in the middle of a severe mixed bipolar episode that she had kept many details of how she had felt from me for a decade. All the work we had done together during the previous eight months was paying off!

"Robin, I'm so sorry. You're right. That was very hurtful," I said apologetically. "I'm so happy you could tell me this, and that you called to say it rather than waiting. Good for you. Please, forgive me. If I'm ever angry at you in the future, I'll be more careful about what I say." I went on to explain that I had been very honored that she shared her very personal CDs with me, and did not mean to discount what a big step this was for her.

We were scheduled to meet the following week. Robin was sleeping better and appeared to be stabilizing following her hospitalization. We talked about her plans for the weekend, and she assured me she would not drink. She stated it very insistently, "I don't want to make you mad again."

It wasn't the best reason for her to avoid drinking. I would have preferred her to be internally motivated to stay stable and avoid relapse. But at that point, I wasn't going to argue. Progress was happening!

● ● ●

In mid-September 2003, approximately two weeks after her fourth hospitalization, Robin began to display noticeable signs of a further lessening of depression. Her affect was brighter. Her thinking continued to be more rational. She moved more quickly and responded to questions more easily and with more depth (less psychomotor retardation). She was beginning to look more and more like the Robin I had known before the year of depression that led up to her meltdown, rather than the depressed and slowed down version of Robin I had been seeing for many months. She had obviously been improving as a result of the ECTs, but this was a new level of "better." She even began to say she was feeling considerably less depressed.

"I really think the medication changes Dr. Greene made when you went into the hospital, lowering the Celexa and changing Geodon to Abilify, are helping," I said to her in a session one day.

"I actually don't feel out of control like I'd been feeling for so long," she said. "It's surprising."

"Robin, I hate to say it, but if there was any remaining doubt about whether you have bipolar disorder, this eliminates it." I said. "Otherwise you wouldn't be responding so well to these specific medication changes." We discussed that having bipolar disorder made it particularly important to eliminate self-destructive behavior, especially those things that sabotaged her brain's biological stability. We talked about the deep grief she continued to feel about losing her job, and the uncertainty her new diagnosis caused.

"I just don't know what I'm going to do with my life," Robin said. "And even though I'm less depressed, I'm still really anxious about whether I'll be approved for long-term disability. If I don't get approved, I have no idea what I'll do!"

Thankfully, the next day I received a phone call from a representative of the company that provided long-term disability insurance benefits for her former employer. He wanted me to fax copies of my therapy progress notes to them, as they were considering Robin's application. I was able to talk to him about her symptoms and meltdown. While I had him on the phone, I let him know how anxious she was to find out not only whether she'd be approved but also when she would receive her first check.

It did not take long for the reviewers at the insurance company to make the right decision. After reading the details of Robin's experiences, I think they realized that if anyone deserved long-term disability benefits, she did. It was the following day when I received a phone call from the same representative, telling me Robin had been approved and her first check would be mailed that day. I was very happy to call Robin to tell her the news.

"This is the first good thing that's happened in a long time," was Robin's reply. She was able to relax a bit, knowing she would continue to have income. Over the next few weeks, Robin began to try to integrate all that had happened to her during the previous eight months.

"I don't know why, but I'm having urges to stop taking all my medications in order to see what happens," she said one day. "I don't understand why I need to be on so many different ones." Robin did not remember much of what she had been through, partly due to the ECTs but also because she had been so deeply depressed. I explained the reasons each of the five medications she took had been added, and why each of them remained crucial to her ongoing stability. My hope was that reminding Robin how each medication had helped would motivate her to avoid sabotaging her brain chemistry.

"I hope it doesn't get really bad again," she said as she was beginning to understand the reality of how dangerous her illness had become. "I don't know how I would survive it."

Robin readily acknowledged that she was back to her previous pattern of minimizing her symptoms and issues with her friends and family, and presenting herself as doing better than she actually felt. Although her mood was definitely improved, she was sleeping better and her anxiety was decreased, the obsessive suicidal thoughts continued.

"I need to feel like things are getting back to normal," she said, justifying her pattern of minimizing her symptoms to others. "I want everybody to treat me like I'm okay, not like I'm crazy."

"That's fine, Robin, for now. As long as you aren't minimizing any-thing with me. I need you to keep working on getting more comfort-able being open with me, even though your defenses are returning and it would be easy for you to fall back to what seemed to work for so long. You have to be open with someone. Right now that's me. As you get more comfortable, we'll work on having you be more open with your friends and family."

Once Robin was able to stop worrying about getting approved for long-term disability, her anxiety was relieved but her mood became more depressed. As had been happening gradually over the previous few months since completing ECT treatments, she was recognizing more completely the implications of her illness. She was realizing on a new level the degree to which her life and her identity had been forever altered.

Part of the problem was that Robin lived alone and had nothing to do. She had too much time to think, and not enough contact with people. She continued to have suicidal thoughts on a regular basis, and her mood fluctuated depending on how much time she spent alone. Although I believed this depression was situational, it was worsening. Robin needed something positive in her life that served as a distraction, put her in contact with people and gave her a sense of purpose.

"I just wish things could go back to the way they were before," she said during a session in late September 2003.

"Robin, I hate to say it, but you really weren't happy with your life before the meltdown either," I said, trying to help her shift. "Your jobs in mental health have always been very stressful." I reminded her of some of the specific situations we had talked about through the years that caused her to feel stressed at work. "I'm not going to dismiss your enormous grief, and I want to help you work through that. But it may also help to look at being on disability as an opportunity to find a better balance in your life and not feel so stressed."

I frequently had clients accuse me of being too positive. I knew Robin probably wanted to throw something at me for suggesting that being on disability could actually be a good thing. But I believed what I was saying and I wanted to help her believe it too. It would become a frequent topic of conversation in the upcoming months and years. Robin's stress tolerance was not high. Working full-time in mental health had always caused anxiety for her. I believed if she could find the right part-time job or the right volunteer position or both, she would be much happier than if she went back to her previous full-time work in mental health.

"I know you can't imagine it right now," I said. "But if you had the right balance in your life, and could get to a place where neither your work nor your illness defines who you are, you could actually feel better than you probably ever have. And, you have many people who care about you. If you could feel more comfortable letting them in and feeling accepted by them for who you really are, this would make all the difference."

I was trying to paint a picture for Robin of a future that was very possible, and could allow her to be happier than she had ever been. But she couldn't imagine it.

"I don't think about the future," she said. "I never really have. I've always just assumed I'll end up killing myself. It seems unlikely that I'll ever get to a point where I'm actually happy."

In therapy I continued to try to help Robin shift her thinking. Her bankruptcy hearing, which finalized the process, took place in early October 2003. This further alleviated anxiety as she no longer needed to worry about the overwhelming debt from the past. It enabled her to stay in her apartment as long as we got the drug companies to provide her medications. But the bankruptcy contributed to Robin's feelings of failure, and highlighted all the negative life-changing experiences she had endured over a relatively short period of time. It caused her suicidal thoughts to increase.

"I'm tired of doing the suicidal battle in my head all the time," she said one day in a session.

"Robin, your depression is now much less biological and much more tied to situational events," I said. "I actually think suicidal thoughts have become your brain's way of experiencing strong negative emotions." We talked about the fact that in the past she had dissociated frequently and self-mutilated, in addition to using alcohol to numb herself when she was feeling particularly depressed. She was able to acknowledge that she had not self-mutilated at all during the past year and had dissociated relatively little, given what she was experiencing. She was able to give herself credit for these signs of healing. We talked about her efforts to continue to avoid numbing herself with alcohol. Mostly, we talked about the importance of finding the right balance in her life as a way to minimize her periods of depressed mood and the associated suicidal thoughts that always accompanied it.

● ● ●

In order to begin the process of rebuilding her life, Robin decided to start by finding a volunteer position that would work for her...in other words, that would not make her too anxious or stressed. It did not take long, with her credentials, to find a local agency that wanted her help. So, it was with enormous trepidation that Robin began a part-time volunteer position at an agency that helped people with AIDs in mid-October 2003.

"I'm going to start going there four hours every Monday and will be driving clients to appointments," she said. "I'm anxious about getting lost when I'm trying to find the offices, but as long as they don't pack too many appointments into one afternoon I'll be fine."

Robin said she felt positive after her first day and felt "briefly competent" afterward.

The next day, Robin called. "My brother got a questionnaire from Social Security. They're asking him a bunch of questions about me." I told her this was standard procedure when someone applied for Social Security Disability benefits, because they want objective information from someone who knows the applicant well.

"I didn't sleep at all last night," she said. "I was obsessing about a lot of different things, but mostly the Social Security paperwork made everything more real. I would prefer to be in 'la la land' where I believe I'll be going back to work whenever they have an opening. But I know this isn't true, which makes me depressed." Robin agreed to let me know if her sleep did not improve.

In our session the following week, Robin said she had gone to volunteer, but they had no clients who needed her to drive them anywhere. She said they had her do some filing, but she only stayed for a couple of hours.

Then, as we kept talking, Robin started saying things I was not expecting or prepared to hear. Although I shouldn't have been, I was probably more stunned than I had been during the previous eight months.

"I was feeling okay after volunteering, until I went to bed. "Then, I couldn't sleep. I began to obsess about suicide including what I'd write in a note, what songs I'd want to have played at my memorial service, and who'd need to be contacted after I am dead." She said it took her several hours to get to sleep.

"Robin, what happened? You've been feeling so much better overall! What caused your mood to shift so suddenly?"

"I was really anxious about going to volunteer on Monday. Then I felt let down when they didn't have much for me to do. I'm trying to accept that I won't be going back to my job. But I'm having trouble getting past this."

We talked again about the big picture of her life and her treatment, and about all the progress she had already made. We talked about all the progress she could continue to make in the future.

"It feels like it would be too hard to make the changes it would take to make things better enough," she said, sounding very hopeless.

Robin went on. As usual, thankfully, she felt compelled to confess self-destructiveness to me. "Yesterday I was seriously thinking about overdosing. I had everything ready. I even had the CD of songs made, the note written, and the list of people to contact."

What the hell? I couldn't believe it. I thought we were past this! Throughout the entire time since Robin's meltdown, she had never carried it this far. She had never written a note. She certainly had not made a CD of songs for her memorial service. It indicated that she had not only been obsessing, she had been meticulously planning to carry out an attempt! After hearing this, I was suddenly very anxious. But I relied on my ability, honed over many years of practice, to remain calm on the outside and ask the right questions.

"What stopped you?" I tentatively asked, not sure what I would hear.

"Well, Christi and I had plans to get together. After I decided to kill myself, I had to call her to cancel our plans so she wouldn't be worried about me. I expected to just leave a voice mail, but she picked up the phone. She was so disappointed about me canceling; I changed my mind and decided to go over there before I killed myself."

Thank God for Christi! Although I had never met Robin's friend, I had heard a lot about her and liked what I had heard. Inside, I was thinking I would give her a big hug if I could. She had no idea how helpful she was to Robin that night. I was trying to digest the reality that, again, Robin had planned a suicide attempt without me knowing it and could have easily, in an impulsive moment, carried it out. It was a painful reminder that no matter how hard I had worked to help her, and no matter how much progress she had made, Robin was still in danger.

"So, I'm assuming by the time you got home from Christi's place you had shifted enough to keep from carrying out your plan?" I asked.

"Yes. I guess part of me doesn't want to kill myself, because I don't want to hurt people. Besides, I think there is also part of me that is too chicken. I'm really afraid I'd just screw it up and make things worse."

In hindsight, I should not have been surprised by Robin's near suicide attempt. Not only are people often at high risk for suicide when they are coming out of a serious depression, but also I suddenly remembered that Robin had repeatedly talked about needing to finalize her bankruptcy as a barrier in terms of suicide so she did not leave a financial mess for her family. That barrier had recently been removed. Robin was feeling hopeless about being able to adjust to her new identity and losing her previous job. In hindsight, it made sense that she was having more suicidal thoughts.

I asked the question I had asked so many times before during that year. "Do you need to be in the hospital, Robin?"

"I really want to avoid that if I can," she said. We discussed the fact that she had not been drinking despite her increased depression, and was not showing significant signs of mixed mania. I told her I would talk to Dr. Greene the next day, and we would go from there.

"Dr. Greene, it's Sharon," I said after paging him the next morning. "Robin has been doing much better since her last hospitalization, but her sleep has started to get disrupted and she has been more depressed in the last week or so. She's back to ruminating about suicide."

After some discussion in which I told him about the events of the previous day, Dr. Greene made the decision to increase both Robin's Abilify and Depakote doses. Robin and I continued to talk through her grief issues as we waited to see what the medication changes would do. We continued to have some contact on the phone during the week, in addition to meeting in therapy once a week. She continued to refuse to talk on the weekends, as she did not want to feel "too dependent."

So, when she called me on a Sunday in late October 2003, I knew she must not be doing well. It remained highly unusual for her to contact me without a planned time to talk, especially on a weekend.

"I still can't stop thinking about suicide. I'm having a hard time and need to refocus away from those thoughts." Wow! This was a shift! Robin had overcome her anxiety about calling me in order to proactively try to avoid being self-destructive. I was surprised, and thrilled by the change despite my concern that she was not doing well. Robin described a clear pattern over the previous few days of doing okay during the day when she was busy and distracted, but getting more depressed toward evening and ruminating about suicide at night. Then, she said something truly remarkable.

"I don't want to kill myself," she said. Unambiguously and unqualified. For the first time since her meltdown she said it emphatically, and had called me because she felt so sure about it. Thank God. "I'm frustrated that my brain keeps going there," Robin explained. "I'm tired of trying to fill time to keep myself distracted. I just want to stop thinking about it."

I don't know what happened that caused Robin to suddenly be so sure she wanted to stay alive. I don't know whether her near miss the previous week had scared her, or whether she was beginning to benefit from the medication changes. But what a relief it was to hear those words. Robin finally knew, completely, that she did not want to die! And, she had called me to ask me to help her stay alive!

We talked about ways to help her brain shift. I suggested we think about ways to increase the barriers in terms of acting on her suicidal thoughts. "What do you think you could do that would make it harder for you to act on those thoughts in a weak moment?" I asked.

Robin revealed she had a stockpile of old medications she was no longer taking, which had been part of her plan for overdosing. She decided that night to get rid of all of the extra medications she had in her apartment. She reluctantly agreed to pour out all of her alcohol, even though she had not recently been drinking. And, after some discussion she agreed to delete her recently written suicide note, in which she gave final instructions, from her computer. Robin, thank God, was finally serious about staying alive!

• • •

One of the consistent themes of my many conversations with Robin throughout the course of her very painful year of despair was that her severe depression and obsessive suicidal thoughts had both biological and psychological components. The medication changes Dr. Greene made were an effort to continue to stabilize her brain's biology.

The biological factors contributing to her meltdown were her enormous obsessive-compulsive anxiety, and the unfortunate reality that we did not know she had bipolar disorder. When she became more depressed at the beginning of 2002, Dr. Greene and I collaboratively worked to try various combinations of antidepressant medications for a year with no real success. It never occurred to either of us that she might have bipolar disorder. We were actually making her mixed mania worse by adding more and more antidepressant medication without a mood stabilizer. The difficulty we had stabilizing the biology of her brain, I am convinced in hindsight, was partly due to her going so long without the proper treatment. I think it was also due to the prominent psychological factors that were contributing to her ongoing, significant depressed mood.

Robin's brain was stabilized biologically step by step over the course of 2003. Although Dr. Greene immediately wanted her to have ECTs, it was not an option. We were grasping when we talked about adding an antipsychotic medication and he started her on Geodon. We did not realize it would actually help because atypical antipsychotics are beneficial in stabilizing bipolar symptoms. When we finally figured out the bipolar diagnosis the addition of Depakote, a mood stabilizer, was extremely helpful in terms of improving Robin's sleep and decreasing her impulsivity. But, by this time her life was already falling apart and her mood, although stabilized, was stabilized at an extremely depressed level. She was on Paxil, which got changed to Celexa and increased to a high dose. She went on and off Wellbutrin, and did better with it than without it as long as she also had Depakote and Geodon. It was during her fourth hospitalization in August 2003 that Dr. Greene discontinued Geodon and started her on Abilify, a relatively new medication at that time.

I believe it was the ECTs that helped Robin turn the corner biologically. Without them I am not sure we would have been able stabilize her mood soon enough to keep her alive. The ECTs certainly did not solve everything. They did not change the fact that Robin now had to face her new reality as a severely mentally ill person. They did not address the enormous grief she felt about the loss of her job and her life as she knew it. But, the ECTs helped Robin get from a place of overwhelming biological depression (completely flat affect, psychomotor retardation, profound anhedonia, feelings of hopelessness and worthlessness, and unrelenting suicidal thoughts), to a place of being able to process reality more rationally. Her affect brightened, she began to enjoy activities again, and she began to think more clearly. The ECTs were an instrumental part of what finally allowed us to stabilize Robin's brain. But there was one more piece of the biological puzzle that needed to happen.

The medication adjustments made by Dr. Greene following her near suicide attempt in October 2003, were to increase her Depakote and Abilify doses. It quickly became apparent that the Depakote increase caused her to feel tired and lethargic, which had also happened the previous spring when she had been on that dose for a short period of time. At the same time, though, her mood was improving and her suicidal thoughts virtually disappeared for the first time in over a year. This happened within the timeframe that would be expected for Abilify to take effect. So, with a decrease in Depakote and the new, higher dose of Abilify, Robin finally, finally, finally came in to a session with me one day in late November 2003 and said, "I feel like myself again." There was no question...it was Abilify that was the final piece of the biological puzzle. The dosage increase got her to the place where she finally felt like herself. It caused her suicidal thoughts, which had been there mostly consistently for over a year, to stop. Completely. It felt too good to be true. Her suicidal thoughts simply stopped. Her brain was finally stabilized!

Robin felt like herself again! It seemed miraculous. It had been almost two years since she had felt that way. What an enormous relief for us both. Four hospitalizations, eleven ECT treatments, Celexa, Wellbutrin, Depakote and Abilify. And many, many months of despair and anguish. Robin finally felt like herself again.

Regarding the psychological factors contributing to Robin's depression symptoms, her anxiety about letting anyone know what she really experienced including me (avoidant personality disorder), was a huge issue. I knew she was more open with me than anyone else. Once I found out how much she had not been telling me I began to realize how alone she must have felt. I was sure this was a major contributing factor in terms of her severe depression.

Learning about her previous suicide attempt by carbon monoxide, and that it was her obsessive-compulsive need to be on time for work that saved her life, helped me to finally understand the extreme rigidity of Robin's brain. It helped me understand the extent to which she had no control over her own thoughts, and that when her brain locked onto suicide she had no ability to shift her thinking. Understanding this helped me know I needed to change my whole approach to her treatment.

Robin needed to connect with people, and at first it needed to be me. I knew she needed to talk to someone consistently about her persistent suicidal thoughts. Her family and friends would not have been able to handle this. I purposely and consciously extended the boundaries within our therapeutic relationship because I knew this was a crucial step for her going forward, and I knew she needed me to be her life line until we could get her stabilized. She needed to get past the painful anxiety it caused for her to be open with anyone about how she felt. I assumed once she was able to become comfortable being open and vulnerable with me, it would allow her to do the same with the other people in her life. Without this happening, I knew Robin would continue to feel alone and to be very prone to significant depression.

Robin and I, throughout the years of our work together, had occasionally talked about her very pessimistic world view...another psychological factor contributing to her tendency toward depression. She had never been proactive, though, about doing any reading that might challenge her basically agnostic, nihilistic and fatalistic perspective. While therapists generally refrain from imposing their beliefs onto their clients, Robin's meltdown encouraged me to be less rigid about this issue. I recommended some books and music with spiritual content.

When she was feeling like it was impossible to accept being on long-term disability, I focused on my belief that the biggest and most important purpose we all have in our lives is to love other people. I consistently reminded her that she still had this ability, no matter what her job or financial situation happened to be. In other words, her identity did not need to revolve around her career. She was a wonderful, caring, funny, smart person with much to offer the world, whether she was employed or not. Most importantly, I repeatedly gave her the message that having a severe mental illness did not keep her from fulfilling the purpose of loving others.

I wish I could say stabilizing the biology of Robin's brain, as evidenced by her statement "I feel like myself again," meant that all would be smooth going forward. But, it became apparent as her brain was stabilizing, that suicidal thoughts were an automatic response whenever she was feeling painful emotions. She had come so far from when we first met in 1993...she never cut herself and she rarely dissociated throughout all of 2003 despite the painful emotions she felt. But, we had more work to do in order to help her feel pain without her brain automatically locking onto suicidal thoughts and wanting to use alcohol to numb herself.

I also wish I could say that once Robin's brain was biologically stabilized she was able to agree that taking some time before attempting to return to work...to grieve, heal, and work on the psychological factors we identified, was the best next step. I tried desperately to convince her that being on disability was an opportunity to take some time and energy to work on the issues we needed to address in therapy. However, she remained singularly focused on returning to her previous position as a full-time case manager as soon as possible. She was not ready to grieve and move forward as a person disabled by chronic mental illness. Understandably, she wanted her old life back.

I knew Robin was going to have to make another attempt to return to her previous life, whether she was likely to succeed or not. I was very fearful that she was going to set herself up for another disappointment and potential meltdown. I was concerned for her, but also for me. I had extended myself for many months and was so relieved she was finally better. I wanted and needed a break from the intensity and the stress. But, Robin was stuck. I was not going to change her mind.

So, when Robin came to a session in December 2003 and told me there was an opening for a case manager at her previous place of employment, working in the same full-time capacity as before, my heart sunk. But I needed to support her in making her own decisions and living her own life. She wanted to apply for the job. Despite my gut feeling that it was not going to go well, I wrote a letter, co-signed by Dr. Greene, saying Robin was ready to return to full-time work. And then, I prepared myself for the next stage of our extraordinary journey.

Robin's Thoughts About 2003

Reflecting back on the Meltdown year is always difficult for me. Most of the time I don't let myself think about it. After all, it has been thirteen years. However, writing this book has forced me to transport myself back to that time. As a result, I've had to re-experience the grief I felt. Prior to working on this book, I had managed to tuck away my feelings about everything that happened that year, except for a small grieving period every year around the anniversary of the Meltdown. Aside from this, I haven't let myself dwell on that period of my life (or I would be in a perpetual state of depression). Since we began working on the book, though, I've had to consider the overwhelming losses I suffered in 2003 and the utter hopelessness I felt at that time. The crisis during that year led to emotional, occupational, financial, and social devastation for me. I was suddenly facing a new reality, one which I had never imagined myself living.

I had to attempt to integrate the fact that I had a serious and chronic mental illness, not simply the depression I had suffered at times. In my mind there was a huge difference between depression and chronic mental illness. Depression had become much more socially acceptable by 2003. I had several friends who had experienced depression and were taking antidepressants as a result. We could talk openly about seeing therapists, and even joked about it with each other. Being chronically mentally ill was a whole different story, though.

At that time my experience with people who had serious mental illnesses resulted mainly from my work as a group facilitator for adults at a community mental health center. The clients were predominantly diagnosed with schizophrenia and bipolar disorder. Most of them lived in group homes and did not have jobs, instead collecting Social Security Disability benefits due to an inability to sustain employment. I observed the attitude of people in the community toward these clients first hand, when the group met at the library. People stared and moved away from them, as many of the clients had poor hygiene or were overtly responding to auditory hallucinations. Although I was sympathetic to my clients and their experiences, I did not identify myself as one of them. Not in any way. They were the people that others either made fun of or felt sorry for. I was one of the people who helped them. In 2003 my vision of what it meant to be seriously mentally ill was forever changed, as I tried to grasp what it meant to be "one of them."

I also had to accept taking an antipsychotic medication for the first time. This was an issue because I didn't want any association with anything that had the word "psychotic" attached to it. In my experience with the clients in group therapy, those who had been prescribed antipsychotic medications for a long time sometimes had side effects such as tardive dyskinesia, which causes involuntary muscle movements. They often gained weight or had other side effects, and I was afraid I would experience these things too. But mostly, taking antipsychotic medication put me too close to that category where I didn't want to be. That category where people were laughed at or pitied, or both.

Being a patient in a psychiatric hospital, which I never considered as a possibility prior to my Meltdown, and having ECTs with the enormous stigma attached to them, were further blows to my identity as I had known it. It was very difficult to acknowledge these events as part of "me." I was familiar with being on the other side of the mental illness divide, as a helper and a professional. I wasn't even remotely ready to accept being on the side of the stigmatized patient. It terrified me.

I had to face the possibility that I might be unable to return to my job as a case manager at the facility where I had worked successfully for over four years. This completely impacted my social network, as much of my social life revolved around my job. There was uncertainty as to whether I could return to work as a case manager at any facility. Although I stayed focused on returning to my previous life, deep down I didn't know if I would ever again be able to work in mental health in any capacity. Losing my job and being uncertain about my ability to return to work in the mental health field crushed my identity...an identity which centered around my life as a respected mental health professional. My self-esteem and confidence were shot.

Filing for bankruptcy and applying for long-term disability were further blows to my self-image. More importantly, though, my independence was threatened. I had to face the possibility that I would no longer be able to afford to live on my own. I was in my mid-thirties and I certainly did not want to return to living with my parents. I had moved home ten years earlier after quitting a job (soon after the meltdown that led to my first appointment with Sharon). After that, I had lived with roommates or alone in my own apartment. It would have felt like an enormous step backward if I was forced to go back home to live, assuming my parents would have allowed me to move in. I also, obviously, had Epiphany to consider as my parents had a dog. I was still depressed, and having to try to grasp all of the ramifications of my newly diagnosed bipolar illness was completely overwhelming.

When I finally got stabilized and back to "feeling like myself" again, which meant my thoughts weren't going a million miles a minute, I wasn't obsessing about suicide, and my depression and anxiety symptoms felt manageable. I wasn't cured, but I finally felt like I was back to my baseline of stability. However, I was still completely uncertain about my future ability to work, to support myself, and to live independently. That year, 2003, ended with my reality being completely different compared to when it started. I was less depressed and felt more stable, but my life was in ruins.

Aside from grieving the losses that resulted from my Meltdown, as I reflect on that year I'm very surprised I did not actually kill myself. My surprise is due to the fact that I was so focused on suicide most of the time. I was completely obsessed with taking my life and spent hours on the internet, painstakingly researching methods that would allow me to do so successfully. Also, despite Sharon's efforts to get me to abstain, I drank alcohol frequently during that year. I drank in order to numb myself and get some form of relief from the painful depression I felt. But the combination of obsessive suicidal thoughts and drinking alcohol, when my impulse control was also being affected by my bipolar symptoms, was a potent recipe for disaster. I have no idea why I did not, in a weak moment, just do it. In my more coherent moments I knew I didn't want to hurt people or put Epiphany in a bad situation. But I had plenty of moments where I wasn't coherent and wanted very badly to be dead. I guess I was lucky, or something bigger than me was operating. I have no idea why I survived.

When I reflect back I feel enormous gratitude for my treatment team, especially Sharon. Her extraordinary efforts, going way above what is expected of a therapist, are a large part of the reason I am alive. I was very lucky to have treatment providers who worked well together to provide my care. Sharon and Dr. Greene were a cohesive team. If I went into the hospital, Sharon was able work with me and Dr. Greene remained my treating physician. There were no gaps in communication. This is not the case in many communities, especially not now after many changes have taken place in the funding of health care over the past decade.

If I had to be hospitalized today in my community, I would not have anything close to the level of continuity of care I had back in 2003. The large community mental health center where Sharon and Dr. Greene worked, ended up closing in 2011, largely due to financial issues. My current therapist and psychiatrist now work for a different agency than the new local psychiatric hospital. If I had to be hospitalized today, they would not be involved in my care in any way. I would be treated by a psychiatrist and therapist who don't know me, and who may or may not request information from my treating providers. This reality terrifies me, because there is no guarantee I'll never be hospitalized again. I'm still on most of the same medications that stabilized me in 2003, and have no idea what would happen if a doctor I don't know chose to change them. My fear about this possibility helps keep me motivated to do everything I can to keep my bipolar symptoms under control.

When reflecting on my Meltdown and the subsequent nightmare year I also have to consider the changes that happened in my close relationships, namely with my family and with Sharon. The change with my family was very slow and gradual, especially with my parents. I was slightly open with my brother, Bob, at the time of my Meltdown. I was able to tell him about my hospitalization after a few days. However, I was not open with my parents. They had no idea how emotionally unstable I was when I had the Meltdown, and I didn't inform them that I was in the hospital for quite a while. I was used to faking it with everyone so I wouldn't have to talk about how depressed or suicidal I was feeling. As the year progressed I was able to be more open with my family, although at the end of this year I still wasn't comfortable telling them when I was suicidal. I knew that the thought of me killing myself was hard for them to consider, and I didn't want to freak them out any more than I already had.

In terms of my relationship with Sharon, the change was more noticeable. I had been faking it with her to an extent for years in therapy. I let her know when I was depressed, but didn't reveal how suicidal or out of control I felt. It was important to me that she respect me, and I didn't want to be just another "crazy" client on her case load. I was very rigid in terms of boundaries, which I knew was important in therapy because of my own work in the mental health field. These issues all changed, however, when I had the Meltdown. Suddenly, my filter was gone and I said things I would never have previously said. I began to express my feelings more openly with her, like telling her when I was feeling like drinking or killing myself.

As Sharon stretched the boundaries of our relationship and encouraged me to continue to open up, I was initially very anxious because it was such a change from how I had always been in all of my relationships. I had never told anyone how I really felt. I actually didn't even know how to articulate it. Gradually, it got easier with Sharon's encouragement, although I worried about becoming too dependent on her because of the frequent contact. I knew it could not continue to be that way forever, and was afraid to be too open. I was afraid it would be too hard when things had to change back to a more normal pattern of contact. But, I think it was me knowing Sharon was willing to work so hard to help me that made me feel more able to be open with her. It made me anxious to talk about my feelings and thoughts, for many reasons, but Sharon motivated me to try harder and it eventually got easier. I truly feel like she was my "Virgil" and I was Dante, descending together to the bottom of hell and eventually back out again.

There are obvious lessons to be learned from my experiences during the Meltdown year. For instance, it is crucial to take medications as prescribed and not self-medicate with alcohol or non-prescribed drugs. Also, it is important to become as educated as possible about your mental illness. But, I think the most important take away from my experiences is the need to be open with treatment providers and develop a support system of family and/or friends. Had I been more open about my real issues with Sharon sooner, I could've been diagnosed correctly and received the proper treatment earlier in the process. I was lucky to have Sharon as a therapist for as long as I did, and that she put in the extraordinary time and effort to help and support me. However, this is not typical in therapy, and shouldn't be expected. It's crucial to have other sources of support. It took time, but I eventually became open with my family and some friends so that they could support me as Sharon gradually decreased her contact with me over the years.

If I had control over it, obviously I would never choose to have bipolar disorder, or obsessive-compulsive disorder, or any of the other symptoms I experience. However, I can now say that many good things came out of that nightmare year in 2003. Being correctly diagnosed and treated allowed me to begin the long process of healing and learning to accept my new reality. It was not an easy process rebuilding my life. It was painful, and involved many ups and downs. But, I can honestly say I am now happy to be alive. In 2003 I could not imagine feeling anything close to this.

Part Two:

Deliverance

9
Robin: Rebuilding My Life (2004-2007)

IN JANUARY 2004, after everything I had gone through in the previous year, I was determined to get my life back to some semblance of normal. The panacea, as I saw it, was returning to work as a case manager at my previous employer. This was my obsessive focus at that time. I was convinced I just needed to go back to work in case management and everything else would be resolved. Of course, it made no sense that I wanted to return to my prior life, as it really hadn't been working all that well for me. I don't deal well at all with change, though.

The thought of starting over at a new job caused me great anxiety, especially when I had no self-confidence and no way to trust my ability to manage stress. But at the same time, I did not want to continue to be on disability. I wanted to have a normal life again, with a full-time job and health insurance like all the other people I knew in my age group. The only feasible way to accomplish this, it seemed to me, was to go back to my previous job with my supportive co-workers as quickly as possible.

Unfortunately, there weren't any openings on my old case management team at that time, so I applied for the next best thing...a position on a different team with the same employer. Like my old job, this team also did home-based case management with children and adolescents. The difference was that the clients weren't referred by the welfare department's Office of Family and Children (OFC), so there wasn't a probation officer or caseworker from OFC involved in the cases. The clients were kids who had mental health issues and were seeing therapists and/or psychiatrists. The biggest difference for me was that I would have to start with all new co-workers. I wouldn't be able to go back to working with the people I knew, who were already very supportive to me.

Six weeks after submitting my application for a position on this team, a decision still had not been made about whether I, or anyone else, would be hired. There had been some delay in the funding of the position which dragged the whole process out. As time went on, I became more and more anxious. On the one hand I was afraid I wouldn't get the job. In my still depressed state I knew I would respond badly to the feelings of rejection I would experience if I didn't get the position. I also thought being turned down for this particular job would hurt my chances of getting another job at the agency if one came up (on my old team, for example).

Even scarier to me than the thought of not getting hired for this opening was the possibility of actually getting the job. This freaked me out, and should've been an indicator to me that I wasn't ready. I wasn't looking too deeply into my fear at that time, I just panicked at the idea that I would get a case management job on a new team. My fear revolved around being hired, then not being able to handle it. The possibility of failure loomed large in my mind. I knew it would be my last chance at this agency, as nobody else would hire me if I failed as a case manager again.

Finally, I couldn't take the uncertainty any longer, and left a voice-mail for the supervisor withdrawing myself from consideration for the position. I think I realized on some level that I could no longer be a full time mental health employee. I just was not ready to fully acknowledge it yet.

It was March 2004. I decided at that time, after plenty of feedback from Sharon, that it was a good idea to start out slowly rather than jump back into full time case management. With that as my new goal, I applied for a part time mental health tech (MHT) position at the child and adolescent inpatient hospital at the agency where I had previously worked. This was a very different role compared to my job in case management, but it was possible to vary the hours based on how I was doing. My past experience in a residential setting involved similar responsibilities, so the job felt doable. Also, a former coworker had been promoted to social worker on this unit, and even better, my former supervisor on the case management team had been promoted to manager of inpatient services at the agency. I had a positive relationship with him, and felt comfortable calling him about hiring me.

This person, knowing all I had been through in the previous year, was glad to give me a chance to be successful. I was quickly hired on a part time basis as an MHT. I worked eight hour shifts, shadowing the other MHTs on the inpatient unit to learn my role and responsibilities. As I expected, it really wasn't that different from my role in residential treatment in the past. It required supervision of the patients and de-escalating them when they acted out. The MHTs were also responsible for leading various therapeutic group activities with the patients. This position should've been easy for me compared to my previous job. Unfortunately, though, I only lasted a few days.

As one might expect, the patients acted out even more than the kids I worked with in residential treatment, and physical intervention was common as well as verbal de-escalation techniques. It was just too stressful for me. There was frequent verbal and physical acting out by the patients, often directed at the MHTs. The unit was often in chaos, and even when there wasn't any crisis playing out, I felt tense, waiting for it. I was simply unable to cope with the stress of the situation, so I resigned after several days. On some level I realized I had hurt my chances of going back as a case manager at this agency, but I didn't consciously acknowledge this. I was still not ready to face this reality.

Despite my failure at attempting a part time position as an MHT in the child and adolescent inpatient hospital, I remained focused on returning to the mental health field. I just wasn't ready to give it up. However, as it appeared I wasn't going to be able to do this immediately, Sharon convinced me to sign up for Vocational Rehabilitation (VR), in order to explore other opportunities. She initiated the referral for me, knowing that it would take a while for me to hear anything from them.

In the meantime, I obsessed about going back to work in my previous capacity, in spite of the continuing and increasing signs that this was a lousy idea. At that point I just couldn't shift away from this being the goal. I had no idea what else I would do. I couldn't see any future that did not include me being a case manager. I couldn't even fathom it.

My obsessing was rewarded when a friend and former case management peer informed me that there was an opening on my old team. This peer had been promoted to a team leader position and encouraged me to apply for the opening. She arranged a meeting with Jennifer, my former supervisor. I met with my friend and Jennifer in a small, windowless conference room at the agency. It quickly became clear that this was not going to result in a job offer. Jennifer was very clinical, not friendly like we knew each other already. It wasn't an interview so much as a chance for Jennifer to explain to me that she had no intention of hiring me for the position, because she doubted that I was ready to handle the responsibilities. She used my failure to cope with the stress of the child and adolescent MHT position as an example of my inability to perform the job.

I admit I was completely shocked by this meeting. I had been led to believe by my former coworker that I actually had a chance at getting hired in the position. I felt blindsided, and was hurt and very upset afterward. Never mind that Jennifer was actually right about her example of the MHT fiasco as a recent failure that likely meant I wasn't ready to return to mental health work. I felt like they had approached me and wanted me. I drove home crying and feeling set up. I'm sure my friend's efforts weren't malignant in intent; I think that she probably thought she was helping, and didn't consult with Jennifer before approaching me.

Regardless of her intent, the result was that I was still unemployed and my confidence had taken yet another hit. It would be a while before I could meet with the VR counselor to discuss my future, and I needed income as well as something to do to keep me occupied. Having too much unstructured time wasn't working well for me. My brain would shift to depressing themes and focus on all the losses I had experienced. Then, I would want to drink to numb myself. It was clear I needed to stay busy. I resorted to the easiest solution for finding employment...I spoke with my mom about getting back into "The Bakery from Hell," where I had worked many times before.

My mom and two aunts had worked at this wholesale bakery for decades, and it had been my summer job countless times in the past. I knew I only had to ask and I could have a job. In the past I had always worked in the bakery itself. This time, I was happy to get a position in the office, where one of my aunts worked. I could have worked in the office before, but the pay was less and the hours were part-time. At that time, though, this was exactly what I needed. It helped that the office was air conditioned, while the bakery was not. I did stuff like filing, mailing statements and completing credit memos for clients. I had to answer the phone (which I hated), but luckily they didn't get many phone calls in the afternoon. Answering the phone at jobs has always been an issue for me. I don't know who is calling or what they will ask. I am afraid I won't know the answer. The ambiguity of it is very anxiety provoking.

I did this job for about five months, until I started working with Vocational Rehabilitation. I could've continued working while meeting with VR, but they didn't really need me at the bakery and I didn't really like the tedium of the job. Also, it was summer, and I have to confess I wanted more time to lay in the sun.

• • •

Once Vocational Rehabilitation finally came through, they referred me to a program that provided employment seeking assistance. This program happened to be run by the agency where Sharon worked, and where I received treatment. They actually made it a point to try to help people find jobs at the agency if they were interested in working there, as their employees were more likely than others to be understanding about the struggles of people with chronic mental illnesses. The agency had many different programs in their many different buildings. As long as I didn't work in the departments where Sharon and Dr. Greene were working, it was okay for me to interview for jobs there. Because it was so large, and had so many different programs, there were actually quite a few options for me at that time.

I first applied for a job providing case management services to chronically mentally ill adults, a population that I worked with previously as a group facilitator. I did poorly in this interview, and was not hired. I was way too nervous. The VR counselor gave me feedback in order to help me present better. According to the person who interviewed me, I had flat affect and was fidgeting with my skirt. Apparently my low self-confidence was visible. This was not easy to hear, and caused me to feel more discouraged about the prospect of working in the mental health field. And, it made subsequent interviews even more anxiety provoking because I had to think consciously about not fidgeting. It was terrible!

I then applied for a position as a staff member at a day treatment program (a "Clubhouse") for chronically mentally ill adults. I did better in this interview. I worked harder at being engaging and personable, and to not move my hands so I would not be accused of fidgeting too much. The feedback from this interviewer to the VR counselor was better, but the supervisor was taking time to interview other prospects.

I also interviewed for a job as a staff member at an Alzheimer's assisted living program. The job would have involved the day to day care of patients with dementia including helping them with tasks of daily living like bathing, dressing and eating. I was offered and could've accepted this position, but it would only be temporary since the licensing expectations would change in a few months, requiring CNA certification which I lacked. I also had no experience working with the elderly population, which made this job seem much less comfortable for me.

In the meantime, I also interviewed for a child and adolescent case management position that came up. This had always remained my ultimate goal, and I must have done well in the interview, because I got the job.

It was January 2005, two years after my Meltdown. I was very excited to have finally achieved my long held goal of returning to a job in case management within the mental health field. At the same time, I was very anxious about whether I would be able to manage the stress involved in starting a whole new position in a new agency with a different system from what I had been used to. I was so anxious I was not sleeping well in the time leading up to my first day, and I got very little sleep the night before.

My new co-workers seemed like good people, but I was trying so hard to come across as a "normal" person, that it was stressful just to interact with them. I was terrified about not being able to handle the stress. I spent a couple weeks in training, shadowing other case managers and learning the paperwork. This was a helpful experience, but I felt like I was in the way. We would be going to clients' homes, where the case manager and client knew each other, and it felt awkward for me to be there. But this was a necessary part of learning the ropes of the job.

I was assigned my own clients gradually once training was over, and I was finally a case manager again. Unfortunately, though, I wasn't up to the task. The main difference between this job and what I had done previously was that this program required the case manager to lead meetings with members of the community and family supports. This was stressful for me, as I have social anxiety to begin with and my confidence was low from my experiences of the past few years. There was also a ton of paperwork with this position, more even than at my previous employer. Finally, the expectation in terms of the number of clients I would see was higher.

I always feel stressed at new jobs (who doesn't?), but I was overwhelmed quickly in my new position. My sleep was affected, which just made the overwhelming stress worse. I was extremely anxious and feeling depressed, and it didn't take long for the suicidal thoughts to kick in as I realized I couldn't do it anymore. I had to accept that I wasn't capable of doing case management any longer, which meant really having to give up my identity and start all over with a new life. I had struggled for two years, attempting and failing at interviewing and working, to get back to my old life in order to not have to accept the reality that it wasn't possible. To lose this hard earned job opportunity was devastating to me. The obsessive suicidal thoughts took over again, and I ended up in the hospital. I quit the job while I was hospitalized, knowing that I wouldn't be returning.

This was my first hospitalization since the Meltdown year. Needless to say I was not happy about being back there. But, I was not happy with anything at the time. I had failed at my ultimate goal. I had no idea what I would do next. I was in the hospital for six days, during which I refused to go to groups, as usual. The last thing I wanted to do was talk about losing what I perceived as my last chance to be "normal." Sharon and Dr. Greene met with me in the hospital and eventually my thoughts shifted away from suicide. I was deemed ready to go back home, where I had to figure out how to go on with my life.

• • •

It was March 2005 and I finally had come to the end of what I had considered my "old" life. I had to come up with a new goal, and a new idea of what normalcy meant for me. I was unemployed again, with no clue what direction to go in regards to seeking employment. I applied for a few part-time jobs, at the library and for an after school child care program, but remained unemployed. I really had no idea what type of job I was interested in since mental health work was all I had ever wanted to do.

Because I needed a positive focus, Sharon thought that summer would be a good time to try to work on my obsessive tanning issue, and I agreed. With no idea what direction to turn, I did not feel ready to begin a whole new job search. And, due to my ongoing OCD issues with tanning, with no job, this is what I would be focused on anyway.

We tried a few different interventions, including decreasing the time I laid in the sun, applying sunscreen after different amounts of time, and filling out a form Sharon created that tracked my thoughts and feelings about the various interventions as I did them. I was only moderately successful at the goal of decreasing my tanning time that summer, as my obsessive urges to lay in the sun were very overpowering. Unlike many OCD symptoms where people do not want to keep doing the compulsive behavior, I wanted to lie in the sun and enjoyed it as long as I wasn't too hot. My ambivalence made it more difficult, but that summer I managed to decrease tanning from five hours to no more than four hours a day.

Another stressor at that time was that my father had a recurrence of cancer in his neck. He'd had surgery on his mouth and throat quite a few years earlier for oral cancer, and it came back that summer. This was very stressful for me and my whole family. He had a series of chemotherapy and radiation treatments. As he grew weaker with the treatments, I would drive him to his appointments. I was glad to be able to do something to help, especially due to the fact that he had taken me to ECTs when I needed transportation. It felt like I was able to pay him back for the help he gave me when I needed it.

My mood vacillated between anxious and slightly depressed much of the time, but I overall maintained stability. However, as the end of the year approached I became increasingly depressed. Between my father's illness, the fact that I had no real plan for my life, no daily structure (tanning season was over), and minimal social contact, I began to have the familiar signs of depression.

Another stressor at that time was that Medicare Part D, the medication component to Medicare, was initiated. This made me ineligible for the Patient Assistance Plan help I had been receiving for my prescriptions, and meant I had to pay copays and a deductible. It also meant that after receiving a specified amount of financial help for my meds during a calendar year, there would be the so-called "donut hole" or "coverage gap," which was part of the whole Medicare Part D reality. This meant I would have to spend over $3,000 of my own money every year before receiving further assistance with payment of my meds for the rest of that year. I was getting generics for all of my meds except Abilify, which wasn't available as a generic, and was very expensive. All of a sudden, the safety net of services that allowed me to afford to maintain my independence was threatened. If I had to pay for Abilify, even for part of the year, I would not be able to afford my apartment without a job. It all completely overwhelmed me.

It was December 2005, and the negative thoughts and anxiety became a vicious circle. I was dwelling on the fact that the third anniversary of my Meltdown was approaching in January and I still had no life. I started to feel out of control and overwhelmed, and the obsessive suicidal thoughts returned. By early January 2006 it got bad enough that Sharon and I agreed the hospital was a necessary step to stabilize me once again.

This time, I was there for four days. I remember that as soon as I got there I regretted going. I hated being in the hospital with the pressure to go to groups, the loss of control over my daily activities, and having to talk to people I didn't know. It had been a long time since I'd been there, but it didn't take long for me to be reminded about why I hated it. However, being there did allow my brain to shift away from thinking about suicide.

For a while before this, Sharon had been talking to me about a therapy group she was planning, which would revolve around depression and anxiety. She said she had three other women who would benefit from such a group, and thought I was a good candidate for this as well. I was non-committal initially (like my refusal to attend groups in the hospital). Sharon had repeatedly suggested I attend groups through the years, and I had always completely resisted the idea. She saw therapy groups as a way for me to be more open, but I wanted no part of it. This was the avoidant part of my personality. Being open caused enormous anxiety and I didn't want to feel that. I was so isolated in my own world. I didn't let people know how I felt. It made me anxious to even imagine talking to people about what I really experienced. I didn't know what to say to people I didn't know, and I knew the expectation would be for me to be honest.

But, I was getting desperate to feel better, and the work Sharon and I had done since my Meltdown had helped to decrease the anxiety slightly. It helped that this group was to be small, women only, and specifically for clients with depression/anxiety who were disabled by their mental health issues. The first group session was held about a week after I was released from the hospital in January 2006.

With huge trepidation I managed to make it to the first session. The other group members were all very likeable, as Sharon had promised. This group turned out to be very beneficial to me, in many ways.

It gave me something to do every week, and something to look for-ward to. I had way too much free time without structure and although this was just an hour and a half, it was something. I met three funny, intelligent women who experienced symptoms of depression and anxiety similar to mine, and were on disability. While they all had dif-ferent contributing issues, they knew what it felt like to be anxious or depressed and unable to control one's own brain, and were able to empathize with me. It was a safe place to talk about mental health issues without being judged, and they were incredibly supportive. Most importantly, I liked them.

I was very anxious at first, not talking much and sitting there bouncing my leg. As time passed, I was more comfortable and was able to initiate conversation. The group was the first place where I actually talked openly about my symptoms, ECTs (one of the other members had experienced them), the stigma, being on disability, etc. The act of saying what I felt to people eventually got easier and allowed me to begin to be more open with other people in my life. It was an enormous turning point for me in terms of feeling less alone and less isolated. At one point, one of the group members referred to us as the Book Club, a name which stuck. To this day, some of the Book Club members get together on occasion for dinner and to catch up.

• • •

One of the life issues that Sharon determined was contributing to my ongoing depression was my negative world view. My view that "life sucks and then you die" was not helping me in the big picture of my treatment, so during this time of unemployment we decided to tackle this subject by having me read books on spiritual topics. Sharon sug-gested books, without regard to any particular religion. She did not push anything on me, just recommended titles she thought might give me material to think about as I clarified what I did and did not believe. This was not an intervention that worked overnight, as I still sometimes struggle with my spiritual outlook, but it did guide me in a more positive direction in my beliefs. It helped me see the bigger picture and stay in the present, rather than focusing on the past.

It is hard to fully articulate my new spiritual beliefs, but I definitely believe there is a higher power, or God. I usually believe things happen for a reason, although I can't say I have any answers about why I have a severe mental illness or had to go through the Meltdown. Before, I always questioned whether God existed, and didn't usually believe it. Whenever anything bad happened to me, I felt like and believed on some level that I was being punished. This was consistent with my belief that the world was a harsh place, and death just meant life was over. Though it was inconsistent with all of my other beliefs, I always believed in heaven and that my brother had gone there when he passed away. It made no sense. Now, I believe in life after death, and that we are living the lives we are supposed to be living. We are all on our own path.

My improved spiritual framework was tested in January of 2007, when my dad succumbed to the cancer that had been making his life hell for years. It obviously wasn't a surprise, but it was traumatic nevertheless. He collapsed at home prior to a doctor's appointment. My mom came home to take him to the appointment and found him in the bathroom. She called 911, then called me. It was early in the morning, and I've always hated early morning phone calls. They are almost never a good thing. I raced over to my parents' home, where the EMTs were providing CPR to my dad in the living room. It was a chaotic scene, with my parents' dog shut in a room, barking nonstop, not helping the situation. I followed the ambulance to the hospital. My brother and sister in law soon arrived, and we all sat in a private waiting room at the ER.

It wasn't very long before a hospital staffer came in and asked us if we had a priest or minister we wanted to contact. That's when it became real. It hit me that this was probably the end for my dad.

They intubated him and he was placed in the ICU. Phone calls were made to extended family members, who gathered in the waiting area outside his room. We took turns visiting him throughout the day, and my mom spent the night in the waiting room.

The next day, my dad's condition worsened. The doctor told us that he no longer had reflexes, and was not likely to wake up. My mom gathered with my brother and me, and said my dad wouldn't want to live this way. We agreed, and the decision was made to unhook the breathing tube. Prior to doing this, the extended family members were allowed in a couple at a time to say goodbye. Then they all left, and my immediate family was in the room when they unhooked the tube and my dad soon died. The whole experience was very surreal for me. The emotions were very intense, and at times I dissociated.

Prior to my Meltdown and the work Sharon and I did in terms of shifting my spiritual beliefs, my dad dying would have reinforced my "life sucks and then you die" philosophy. I would have seen it as yet another way in which I was being punished. But instead, when he died I was able to look at it from a bigger picture perspective. I believed that his death was about him, not me. It was his time, for whatever reason. It was part of his plan. This did not minimize my sadness over the loss of him. But I was sad…not suicidal, which showed me how far I had come since my Meltdown.

My dad died at the age of 60, coincidentally on my maternal aunt's birthday. This same aunt was ill at the time of his funeral, but everyone thought it was bronchitis. She was hospitalized a couple of days after my dad's funeral, and we were shocked to learn that she had to have immediate surgery due to stage 4 colon cancer. The cancer had traveled to her lungs, which caused the bronchitis-like symptoms. My family was devastated, but she started chemotherapy and we were ready to fight the fight with her. Her breathing worsened though, and she remained in the hospital where her health continued to deteriorate.

We decided as a family that someone should be with her overnight, and I insisted on doing it. Everyone else, besides my grandma, had to work, and I didn't want her to have to do it. I wasn't working, so it made the most sense for me to stay overnight with my aunt. I slept in a reclining chair with a blanket, brought into the room by the nurse. I had insomnia anyway, so I wasn't worried about disturbing my sleep.

One night, my aunt woke up in the middle of the night, struggling to breath and in obvious distress, so I alerted the nurse. The on-call doctor, who was a jerk, came in and said her breathing had deteriorated to the point where she needed to make the decision whether to go on a breathing tube, or just "be made comfortable." My aunt looked at me desperately, unsure what she should do, at which point the doctor snapped at her "Don't look at her, you need to decide." As I said, he was a jerk.

The doctor was basically telling her she had to decide between giving up or continuing to fight with no promise that it would do any good. She chose to be intubated, and was taken to the ICU. It was about 4:00 a.m. by this point, and I immediately called my mom, who then called the rest of the family who all came to the hospital. The nurse allowed us to go into the ICU room in bunches, even though policy allowed only two at a time. My aunt's condition worsened due to complications with her meds, and her blood sugar dropped considerably. She was miserable, and quite obviously dying.

Later that day my aunt finally made the decision to have the medications that were controlling her symptoms stopped, which made the jerk doctor angry, but he complied. We all crowded into the room to say our goodbyes to my aunt, and she died a little later, coincidentally on my other aunt's birthday. The whole situation was very agonizing, and brought up feelings about my dad's death three weeks earlier. I lost two very close family members within a month, in very traumatic situations.

The fact that I was the one from my family to stay with my aunt overnight, only three weeks after my dad's death, was a sign of how much progress I had made in treatment. I think I was still in shock about my dad, but I felt clear I needed to be the one to be there for my aunt. I just kept thinking about my belief that she would be going to heaven. The fact that I was able to do what I did during that time, without becoming overwhelmed, depressed or suicidal, helped me to gain some confidence. It made me feel better in a way, because I was able to be helpful and I suddenly felt like I had a purpose for the first time in a long time.

Before my Meltdown this whole traumatic time would have been completely overwhelming to me, and I would not have wanted to be any part of it. I hated hospitals and I would likely have had difficulty even going to visit my dad or my aunt. It would have just reinforced my whole negative belief system. It was a clear sign of progress that I was able to hold up through the crises.

Unfortunately, after the shock wore off and the reality of losing my dad and my aunt sunk in, the familiar depression returned. It took about six weeks before my grief turned to suicidal depression (not surprisingly), at which point I was hospitalized again. This time, Dr. Greene actually agreed to have me hospitalized on the Geriatric Unit. This was where I spent the first night in the hospital at the time of my Meltdown over four years earlier. Then, I remember feeling so terrified, but now this unit was my preference. On the Geriatric Unit I was not pressured to go to groups, since most of the elderly people were not able to participate in much programming. I was able to just stay in my room, safe from myself and unable to obtain alcohol. This time it took six days for my brain to get shifted, and I was ready to go back and face the world again. I remained sad about the deaths of the people I loved, but being in the hospital had helped me shift away from thinking about suicide.

● ● ●

Another issue that tested my spirituality was my initial skin cancer diagnosis in June 2007. I went to my family doctor because I had a small sore next to my nose, where my glasses sat, which wouldn't heal. My doctor referred me to a dermatologist to have it checked out. Since this occurred in June, during tanning time, I was very tan and burned in places when I went to my initial appointment. The nurse practitioner who I met with was not impressed with my tan. I received a lengthy lecture on skin damage as she examined my body and charted all the types of skin damage I presented with. She biopsied my nose, and told me someone would contact me with the results.

About a week later, I received a letter in the mail stating that the pathology results showed skin cancer, and I needed to call to arrange a surgery date. I was completely freaked out by this information. I saw the words skin cancer and surgery date, and felt a jolt of adrenaline and anxiety. I had always known that I was at high risk for skin cancer, but continued to live in a world of denial. I remember thinking to myself how ironic it would be, after so many times of being seriously suicidal, if it was my need to lay out in the sun that ended up killing me. This event was probably the first thing that caused me to face the reality of my own mortality, and realize that I could easily die of something I could not control. In the past, this would have definitely fed right into my negative life philosophy. In my mind it would have been a direct punishment for laying in the sun for all those years, or to put it another way, karma smacking me right in my suntanned face.

It was only after I contacted the dermatology office to arrange my surgery that I was told I did not have melanoma, the deadly form of skin cancer. I had basal cell carcinoma, which needs to be removed but is not fatal. Had the letter just informed me of this fact in the first place, I would have been saved a great deal of fear. Looking back, I've wondered if they kept the letter vague to give me a scare. I assume that was probably not the intent, but it was the result.

I went in a few weeks later for my surgery, accompanied by my mom. It went fine, except for the shots to the face to numb the area. It was the worst physical pain I've ever felt. Granted, I've been lucky not to have any major injuries, so I don't have much to compare it to. Suffice to say, shots in the face are very painful. When the procedure was over, I had a compression bandage on my face, on the right side of my nose, which I had to wear for twenty-four hours. Because of the location, my glasses sat crooked on my nose. I was quite a sight. Most people would likely avoid sunlight after an experience such as this. Unfortunately, my obsessive-compulsive tanning issue prevented this. I continued to regularly lay in the sun. As a result, I've repeated this experience four more times so far, with more skin cancer incidents likely to occur in the future. I don't know what will happen if or when I'm diagnosed with melanoma.

Sharon Discusses 2004 to 2007

The meltdown year was a nightmare of epic proportions, for both Robin and I. But it was a necessary part of her healing process. The events of that year enabled Dr. Greene and me to accurately diagnose her, stabilize the biology of her brain, and get clearer about the issues we needed to address in treatment going forward. It was after the meltdown year when the real work of Robin's healing process began.

It was a rocky road between 2004 and 2007, and Robin was hospitalized three times following disappointments, losses or life stressors. As had become clear toward the end of 2003, even when she was biologically stable her brain would shift to thinking about suicide whenever she was experiencing emotions that were overwhelming and painful. The work we did in therapy following her meltdown year, helping her deal with painful feelings in healthier ways, allowed her to shift away from automatically thinking about suicide as the answer. I have no doubt that clearing up the misunderstanding leading to her fear of me "ditching" her made an enormous difference. It makes me sad to think about all the years when she thought she couldn't be honest about suicidal thoughts. Once she was able to talk openly about it, we could address this pattern directly. Suicide, for

Robin, over time, became less and less of a focus as she was able to tolerate pain with a new perspective.

Unfortunately, this process took a while. Even though she did not want to kill herself, it became apparent that once Robin's brain locked onto suicide rigidly enough, hospitalization was the only one way to get it unlocked. At some point, Dr. Greene and I had another "epiphany" about her treatment. Robin would get so stuck in terms of her obsessive focus on suicidal thinking, she needed to have any possibility of acting on those thoughts removed. Medication was not the answer. We realized that being in the hospital, where she no longer considered suicide an option, caused Robin's brain to shift quickly. Unfortunately, it usually shifted to obsessively focusing on getting out of the hospital, which was what happened in 2003 as well.

Once we figured this out, I was able to point it out to Robin. As long as she was obsessing intensely about getting out of the hospital, it meant she still needed to be there. Sure enough, if we could keep her there long enough for her brain to shift away from obsessing about anything intensely, she would eventually relax and be ready to return home. The hospital became simply the safe place for her to go and unlock her rigid brain.

Robin did not attend groups in the hospital. Dr. Greene mostly made no medication changes. She and I did nothing different when she was in the hospital than we would have if she were at home. The simple reality of being completely unable to carry out any suicide plan...to have an insurmountable barrier, allowed her rigid brain to relax and shift to thinking about other things. There was no battling with the staff, or arguing about whether she would attend programming like there had been in 2003. Everyone was now on the same page. Robin just needed a little time in the hospital to shift her brain.

In the midst of Robin working to rebuild her life and figure out what job situation would work for her, we continued to work in therapy on the two major issues I was sure were contributing to her ongoing depression…her very pessimistic world view and her complete feelings of isolation.

The music CDs with my notes suggesting spiritual interpretations of the lyrics, and the spiritual books Robin and I shared, were important interventions that helped shift Robin's belief system. Early in this process, I was choosing and supplying books to her. My goal was never to tell Robin what to believe. In fact, I purposely gave her books written by authors whose proposed framework I did not believe, in addition to the ones I most connected with. I simply wanted Robin to be exposed to different ways of thinking about how life works, so she could get clear for herself about what resonated for her. Eventually she began to buy and read books herself, in an effort to continue the process of getting clearer about her own beliefs.

Robin has documented well the impact this spiritual shift had on her life. I firmly believe this was crucial to making her much less likely to destabilize to the point of self-destructive behavior. With the view that there is a bigger plan for her life and the lives of others, she is able to maintain a different perspective even when she is having suicidal thoughts. Rather than "life sucks and then you die," in which suicide is simply an escape from unbearable psychic pain, she now understands that suicidal thoughts are a symptom of her illness, which is part of the plan of her life. It took a long time for her to get there, but the difference in terms of how her world view now impacts her symptoms in a positive way, is truly amazing.

There were very few clients during my long career as an outpatient therapist, for whom I purposely made shifting to a spiritual perspective an intervention. But with Robin I trusted my gut when it told me she needed to shift her world view. Thank God (pun intended) I did. It is now clear that to not have done so would have kept Robin from getting to the place she is today.

Throughout her attempts to get back to her "normal" life and her eventual failure to do so, I purposely talked extensively about staying focused on what is most important in life…loving the people we care about. We talked about how her job had always been her identity, and that she did not need to have a "career" in order to have a meaningful life. I was trying to prepare her for what I came to believe was inevitable...that Robin was going to have to give up on her dream of returning to her previous role as a full-time case manager. Although these conversations did not immediately cause Robin to believe any of what I was saying, I was planting seeds for the future. I wanted her to believe that what she did for a living was not the main determiner of her worth, or her identity. Eventually, she was actually able to make this shift, which made losing the job as a case manager after spending two years trying to get it, a more tolerable loss.

Although Robin was making significant progress in therapy in terms of tolerating painful feelings, accepting her illness and shifting her world view, she remained mostly socially isolated until January 2006. She lived alone and, although she was being open with me, she continued to completely minimize any symptoms or difficulties when talking with her family and friends.

We had decreased the frequency of our contact after the meltdown year, so she didn't feel as "dependent" on me. Phone calls became less necessary except during the infrequent times when she was suicidal. I wasn't feeling stressed by Robin's situation like I was during the crisis of 2003, because I knew Robin didn't want to kill herself and would be open with me if she had these thoughts. But, over time, I began to become more and more uncomfortable being her only confidante. It began to feel unhealthy to me...not for me necessarily, but for Robin.

My job as a therapist was supposed to be to help her get to the point where she didn't need me anymore. If I was her only confidante, she would always need me. In order to get to a healthy place, Robin needed to get past the excruciating anxiety she felt when talking openly about her feelings and experiences to others. I began to push her, more strongly, to consider attending a group. I purposely selected a small group of women from my caseload who I felt had enough in common that they would be good for each other. I made it as easy as I possibly could for Robin to take the next step in her evolution, which was to face her avoidant personality pattern and begin to open up to other people.

There is no question in my mind that convincing Robin in 2006 to attend that small group of smart, funny women who were also disabled by mental illness, was a crucial part of her healing process. For the first time in her life she was able to face and overcome her anxiety about opening up to people. It was the important next step, after she had initially gotten comfortable being open with me. It was a process, and it took time like everything else. But the group members helped Robin get to a place where she finally became able to be open with her family, employers and other friends about her illness, her disability and her experiences. I am not sure the members of the "Book Club" truly understand what a difference they made in Robin's life. I am grateful to Robin for being willing to face the overwhelming anxiety she experienced in order to make this transition. It has touched me deeply to witness her transformation from feeling completely alone and isolated, to being open about who she is and feeling accepted by her many friends and family. Today, she no longer needs me to be her only confidante!

• • •

The experiences I had as Robin's therapist in 2003 changed my life, positively and permanently. I never expected her to have such a dramatic meltdown. I certainly never expected it to take a year for her to become stabilized. It is difficult to verbalize how being a witness to her pain, knowing I was the only person on the planet who she could be honest with about her experiences, affected me.

Before 2003 I used to worry about many things related to my own security...finances, job security, my husband's job security, issues related to our house whenever repairs were needed (because it added stress both financially and in terms of disrupting my routine), and other things like that. I need to be clear...I was needlessly worried. We were doing okay financially, and our jobs were not in jeopardy. I was excessively and irrationally anxious and easily stressed, somewhat like Robin. There is a reason I could relate to some of Robin's issues. Anxiety clearly runs in my family, going back at least several generations, and I got a healthy dose of it. My spiritual framework was helpful, but it was an intellectual shift that required effort on my part. It didn't change my fundamental hard wiring as an anxious person who became stressed by change or uncertainty.

When I was immersed in the intense process of trying to figure out how to help Robin, my spiritual framework was tested on a level I had previously not experienced. I truly had to "go with the flow" and I absolutely had to trust my gut when it was telling me to extend the therapeutic boundaries with Robin in ways I never would have previously done with any client. The stakes were high. Her life was on the line and I needed to be there for her.

I knew deep down, almost from the beginning, that the experience was going to be as important for me as it was for Robin. There was no question in my mind that I was being spiritually guided throughout the process, and that this guidance helped me to figure out Robin's diagnosis, to know when to intervene and when to give her distance, and when to consult with colleagues. I was being guided to know what Robin actually needed at any given time in order to survive and heal. I learned to trust my gut at a level I never could have imagined.

During that year, I frequently thought about my spiritual beliefs. I knew what Robin and I were each going through was happening for some reason that had to do with our own evolution. I knew we had been put into each other's lives in order to live through that experience together. I never questioned that I needed to stay in it with her, and see it through no matter how stressful it was for me. But, I didn't know whether that meant she was supposed to live through it. I had no idea whether Robin's destiny was actually to kill herself.

Many times, I wondered whether this was the case. This scared me and made me very anxious, but I frequently tried to remind myself that what was happening was "bigger than me."

Mostly, I just tried to stay clear about what my gut was telling me to do, and then do it. I had to live in the present and try not to worry about what would happen. It was completely clear to me that I was not the one controlling the outcome.

About halfway through 2003, as Robin was hitting rock bottom, I began to notice some of the changes that were happening to me. I realized all the small things I had previously worried about no longer mattered to me. I was no longer as stressed by changes in my routine, or by uncertainty in minor areas of my life. There is nothing like being immersed in a life and death crisis for months to help one gain perspective about what is and is not important! I wrote about this realization in my journal, and wondered at the time whether the change in perspective would continue after Robin stabilized (or killed herself) and the crisis was over.

The amazing thing is, not only did I continue to worry less about things and to experience much less anxiety after 2003 was done, but there was an even more profound change that happened. The most succinct way I can explain it, is that I went from having to consciously shift my brain to think about my spiritual belief system (which often didn't work to make me feel better), to just automatically living it… free from much of the anxiety and fear that had previously run my life.

This transformation continues to this day and has become much more ingrained. I don't have to think about tuning into my gut. It's automatic. I don't have to remind myself to "go with the flow." It's just how I live. For the most part I stay focused on what is happening in the present, rather than the past or the future. I have no idea what the future will bring, and I am mostly okay with that. I am no longer stressed by change or ambiguity unless, of course, it is something major like the threat of losing someone I love…I am not saying I've turned into a Buddha or anything. I still have issues and times of irrational thinking like everyone else. But, anxiety and fear do not control my life or determine my decisions. I trust my guidance for that.

An outcome of the transformation I experienced involved developments in my career after the meltdown year with Robin. In 2003, I was settled into my career as a psychologist. I loved my work as an outpatient therapist. It was very rewarding to help my clients. After spending my days immersed in the worst of people's pain, I would usually go home to my relatively calm life feeling grateful. I had no regrets about my choice of careers. The problem was, being a full-time therapist was exhausting and stressful. I started to get to the point where something had to change, or I was going to completely burn out.

The administrators of the agency where I worked identified me as a leader early on, and had tried several times through the years to promote me to various management positions. But, the thought of this had previously made me too anxious. I was afraid doing administrative work and supervising others would be overwhelming. Part of me was intrigued by what it would be like to take on more responsibility, but my fear of change and my desire to keep my life as stress free as possible had always won out.

In July 2003, in the middle of the nightmare of Robin's meltdown year, I was summoned to a meeting with the President and CEO of the agency where I worked. In the eleven years I had worked there, I had never had a conversation with him before. I wasn't even sure he knew who I was, since the agency had over a thousand employees. I had no idea why he would want to talk to me.

This conversation was the beginning of what would become my new career path. I don't know if I would have said yes if I had not already experienced some of the changes that happened as a result of helping Robin through her nightmare, but my gut told me that if the CEO of the agency suddenly asked to talk, it was important to listen.

I was asked to lead the professional staff organization, and was then promoted several times over the next few years to increasing levels of responsibility. I fairly quickly became a member of the senior management team, and was involved in the decision making of running the agency. In 2007, I was asked to become the Senior Vice President of Clinical Services. In this position I was the administrator over all clinical programming for the agency including three psychiatric hospitals, residential programs for all ages, and many outpatient and day treatment programs. Needless to say, this was a stressful role. But, in the years following Robin's meltdown my increased stress tolerance and ability to handle change and keep perspective continued. It felt miraculous to me. I enjoyed being able to use my skills as a leader.

As I took on more management responsibility, I decreased my caseload of clients. I went from an active caseload of over 100 when I was a full-time therapist, to a caseload of fifteen clients who I felt I either wanted to or needed to continue to see. Robin was obviously one of those people. She was aware I was seeing fewer clients and had become a big administrator, as my office had changed several times over the years and I felt compelled explain why. Also, Robin was working at the agency in various capacities during parts of that time, and would hear about my administrative role from other employees.

I reassured Robin through all the changes that I had no plan to stop our work together. We got to a point where we were meeting in group (with the book club) every other week and individually on the opposite weeks, with very little phone contact in between sessions. She was stable and we both felt better with a bit of distance built into our connection after the intensity of 2003.

There was something, however, that Robin did not know during this time. As I was continuing to expand my management role at the agency, I was starting to imagine a time when I would stop being her therapist. Not just her therapist, but everyone's therapist. I was beginning to realize that many of the clients I was still seeing, all people I had worked with for a long time, were stable enough that they no longer needed me as their therapist. I realized there would be benefits for many of them to work with other therapists, and some probably did not need to be in therapy at all. At the same time, I was enjoying my new identity as a leader. People who I supervised responded well to me in that role. I began to imagine a point in time when I would end my time as a therapist, and that stage of my career. But Robin was not aware of any of this. I was not ready to tell anyone, especially not the few therapy clients I continued to treat, who would undoubtedly be upset by this news.

10
Robin Talks About Achieving Acceptance

IN SEPTEMBER 2007, I had finally (mostly) accepted the reality that I needed to stay on disability and work part-time. In order to find a part-time job, Sharon helped me get a job in housekeeping at her agency. She spoke with the manager of the department, telling him my situation, and he agreed to interview me. I accepted the position, figuring I may not be doing a mental health job, but at least I was working in a mental health agency. I worked every evening for several hours. Each night I started by doing general cleaning in the agency's newest building. I actually enjoyed this. The small building was easy to clean. I was alone in the building most of the time, able to work at my own pace. It was not at all stressful.

Then I had to clean the child/adolescent day treatment building. I hated this part of the job. The building had lots of kids in it during the day. They would miss the toilet. They did craft projects with glitter, which I learned was impossible to clean up. In this setting I had co-workers. Many of them didn't get along and they were constantly complaining and talking about each other. I worked very hard to remain a neutral party in all of it, and it was stressful trying to maintain my island of neutrality. But, the job was twenty hours per week, Monday through Friday, which worked well for me in terms of hours.

I was stable for about nine months, working and doing well overall. I experienced decreased suicidal thoughts, and was not drinking. Working a set schedule, five days a week, provided the structure I needed and I was making enough money to pay my bills without stress. I had finally not only accepted that I would need to be on disability and could only work part time, but living it turned out to be okay for me. I actually felt okay about myself, which I never could have imagined five years earlier.

It was May 2008. Because I was settled and doing so well, I thought it was a good time to try to decrease my Abilify dosage. I was worried that having a job would cause me to lose the "extra help" provided by Social Security to pay for my Medicare Part D premiums and which eliminated the "coverage gap." I knew if I lost this assistance I would not be able to afford Abilify. Sharon and Dr. Greene agreed that it was a good time to try decreasing it, since I was settled and had been stable for over a year.

I gradually decreased the dosage of Abilify in increments, first from 20 to 15 mg, then from 15 to 10 mg. The second change was too much, and resulted in the very fast emergence of an episode of mixed mania. Dr. Greene raised my Abilify dosage immediately, but it didn't help right away. I was very quickly right back to the familiar experience of a deep depression and obsessive suicidal thoughts. I felt crazy again. The fact that I decompensated quickly was clear evidence of how important Abilify was in terms of keeping me stable, but in the middle of my mixed mania I was unable to achieve any perspective about the fact that I would likely feel better quickly being back on the right dose.

Sharon and I were talking daily during the crisis, and discussing whether I needed to be in the hospital. I wanted, as usual, to avoid that. My life ended up taking a dramatic turn during that 4th of July weekend. July 6th was a beautiful day, with not a cloud in the sky and warm temperatures. I went to my mom's house and laid in the sun for four hours. During this time, I continued to have suicidal thoughts, and I decided that this was the day I would kill myself. There was no rational reason. I wasn't thinking clearly. It just seemed like the time. I thought about it all that day while lying in the sun.

I told my mom I loved her before leaving for home. I was supposed to go to Christi's house that night to watch TV at 5:30 pm. Sharon, who was staying in close contact as she always did when I was not stable, told me to call her when I got back to my apartment that night.

When I got home from laying in the sun at my mom's house I began to drink vodka and Hawaiian Punch, and at 5:00 pm I called to tell Christi I couldn't come over. She didn't answer, so I decided I would go, but just for an hour. Thus began a series of minor incidents that delayed my planned suicide attempt.

Once I arrived at Christi's, she asked if I minded going with her to check on a wounded dog she had passed earlier while walking her own dog, Leo. She had no idea how bad I was feeling or what I was planning to do that night, and I certainly wasn't going to tell her!

We drove around the corner from her home, where a wounded dog lay on the sidewalk. Christi checked with the neighbors, who weren't familiar with the dog, so she called Animal Control. It took another thirty minutes for them to arrive and pick up the dog. I then told Christi I needed to leave, but she asked if we could go get ice cream at Dairy Queen before I left, and with some cajoling, I finally agreed.

As time kept passing and delays kept happening, I was getting more and more anxious. I was supposed to call Sharon when I got home. My mind remained fixated on killing myself that day. I knew at some point, if she didn't hear from me, Sharon would call me and expect to talk to me. I knew I had limited time. I was starting to panic!

Most people would wonder why I didn't just wait to talk to Sharon, get that over with, and then kill myself. I lived alone. It would have been the next day before anyone would wonder where I was. But, I knew I would not be able to lie to Sharon if I talked to her. It was one of my compulsive things. I was, literally, unable to lie to her if she asked me a direct question. I knew I needed to get home and get enough medication in me to have it be too late for Sharon to figure out what was going on.

When I arrived home I quickly resumed drinking. But, because I had eaten the ice cream I quickly got full. It took two vodka and Hawaiian Punch drinks, which I drank with five Ativan pills each. By this point it was getting late, and I still hadn't called Sharon. As I was preparing another drink and more Ativan, Sharon called me. I debated whether to answer it, but was afraid she'd call the police if I didn't answer. We talked briefly about what happened at Christi's house, and then she asked me if I felt like drinking.

I had to admit that I was already drinking, and after further questioning I admitted to taking the Ativan as well. At that point I realized the jig was up and I was going to the hospital. After getting me to promise not to drink any more or take any more Ativan, Sharon called the on-call psychiatrist, and they decided I could go straight to the psychiatric hospital rather than the ER. I didn't want Sharon to call my mom, as it was late at night and she worked early in the morning.

For obvious reasons, Sharon wouldn't let me drive myself to the hospital. I agreed to let her call Christi to drive me, and Christi immediately got in the car to come and get me. Sharon stayed on the phone with me while I waited for Christi to arrive. Christi drove me to the hospital, where we met Sharon, who had gone to do the crisis admitting paperwork. I was drunk so I didn't contribute much substance to the conversation while the three of us waited for the nurse to come get me. The last thing I remember is the ride up in the elevator with the nurse. I blacked out the rest of the night.

Had Christi been home when I called at 5:00, had there not been a wounded dog, had the Animal Control officer not been late, had Christi not insisted on getting ice cream…had these minor incidents not delayed me, I likely would've already been dead or at least unconscious by the time Sharon called me that night. I really was clear in my own mind that it was my time to die. Only it wasn't. Now, I believe all those things happened so I would not die that day.

Before…I have no idea how I would have felt. By this time my spiritual beliefs were more integrated. The bottom line is that I was not the one in control of what happened that day. I was not thinking clearly, and my impulse control and judgment were severely impacted by my illness. I was depressed and manic all at once. And, that higher power I now believe in saved me from myself, with the help of Christi and a stray dog.

During my final hospital stay, Sharon asked me how I would feel about moving in with my mom, to alleviate the stress about finances and how I would pay for Abilify. I had mixed feelings about this. I knew it was the option of last resort. I was worried about taking Epiphany so I would never have brought it up. It would never have occurred to me to suggest it. But, once Sharon asked and I was able to think about it, I knew it would help stability wise. I was realizing that living alone was not working, and didn't have other options. I was finally, five years after my Meltdown, coming to terms with my illness.

Sharon then spoke to my mom about it, and she didn't hesitate to say yes. Since my dad's death from cancer in January of 2007, she had been alone. I think she was open to having my company and any financial help I could bring to her would also be welcome. So, I gave my thirty day notice to my apartment manager, and moved in with my mom in August 2008.

Part of me felt like it was a step backwards, and part of me was relieved. Mostly I just needed to do something different. I was surprised and happy to realize that my mom and I got along great, as we have many things in common. She was (and is) the best roommate I've ever had, and giving up my independence was made easier by this.

Living by myself obviously didn't work for me, financial concerns aside. I had too much alone time, which led to depressed thinking and drinking. My mom provided both companionship and accountability, as I was not comfortable drinking in front of her (she knew I wasn't supposed to drink). I had always said I would never kill myself in my mom's house, because I didn't want her to be the one to find me. It didn't take long before I began to feel closer to her again. Living away from home for so long had built up some distance between us, as had my need to hide my symptoms from her. But living together again rebuilt the lost intimacy, and I became more open with her. When I am becoming depressed, I'm now able to talk about it much more easily than before. I don't try to appear "normal" and hide my feelings as much as I did when I was struggling with accepting my illness.

The financial relief from moving in with my mom was considerable. While I help pay the house payment, our cell phone bills, and buy my own food, I don't have to pay the rest of the household expenses as I did while living alone. So if I have to leave my job for some reason, there's less pressure to just take the first job I can find. I can try to find the right job. Also, my Jeep, Chuck, was on his last legs in 2008. He turned fifteen that year, and was beginning to have more serious issues. Living with my mom allowed me to trade Chuck in for a 2000 VW Beetle, lime green, which I named Sally (another *Peanuts* character). I was sorry to see Chuck go, but he was going to cost me a fortune in repair bills soon.

I look back on that time in 2008 as the turning point, because attempting suicide in the context of a mixed manic episode after doing so well for so long erased any question in my own mind about how differently I think when I'm not stable. It scared me. Since then, I have taken my medication as prescribed and have never used alcohol to numb painful emotions. I take my illness very seriously now, and do everything I can to keep my brain stable. My life depends on it.

• • •

In early 2009, Sharon again helped me get another job at her agency, this time in an office position. It was a great job, mostly just doing data entry and scanning documents. It was a Monday through Friday, 8 a.m. until noon position, which was perfect for me. I was lucky enough to be able to take a week off of work in December, to go on a Caribbean cruise with my mom. We had stops in St. Thomas, Puerto Rico, and Grand Turk in the Turks and Caicos Islands. We laid in the sun while on the ship during the travel days, and laid on the beaches while in port. I had a great time and felt very fortunate to be able to go. I was only able to afford this because I had saved my tax return money, and we got a good deal. If I didn't live with my mom, I never could've afforded it.

Things became rocky for me in 2010 when both Sharon and my psychiatrist, Dr. Greene, left the agency where they had both worked for many years. I was lucky enough to get another experienced psychiatrist, (a female this time), Dr. Turner. When Sharon left her job it destabilized me. She had been my therapist for sixteen and a half years, and had saved my life. I had a mini-meltdown after she left, which didn't necessitate hospitalization but which did require that I miss a week of work.

Dr. Turner came through with the final piece of the medication formula...the key to treating my mixed mania episodes. The early signs of mixed mania for me are intractable insomnia and depression. Dr. Turner prescribed high doses of Seroquel to treat the insomnia and depression, which alleviated the mixed mania before it got bad enough to require psychiatric hospitalization. There have been a couple of other instances of mixed mania since then in which this medication intervention has worked. I'm not going to say I will never need to be in the hospital again, but I am very grateful to Dr. Turner for understanding what I needed to quickly stabilize my mixed mania episodes. I keep a supply of Seroquel on hand at all times, and am always able to taper back off it within a few months of experiencing a relapse.

My life was abruptly changed again in April 2011, when the agency where I worked and received treatment, closed for good. It had been having financial problems for years and had been gradually closing specific treatment programs, but it finally went under in 2011. I was not only out of a job that worked really well for me, but it also meant that I no longer had a treatment facility. After receiving treatment there from 1993-2011, I would have to start over with a totally new agency.

Ironically, the agency from the neighboring county where I had worked as a case manager so many years earlier, took over the psychiatric care in my county. I became a patient of the agency where I had tried to get back to my beloved job. Luckily enough, Dr. Turner was hired by that agency in the transition, so I did not have to lose my psychiatrist.

For a while after Sharon left, I didn't have a therapist. I felt like I was doing well enough and had been in therapy long enough that it wasn't necessary. Sharon had set the bar very high and I knew I wouldn't ever meet that level of care again. She had stretched boundaries to save my life, and I knew this wasn't the norm. I didn't expect that. But it is really hard in general to find a therapist to click with when I have such difficulty talking about my issues. I did eventually find a new therapist who is "good enough." I see him on an as needed basis, to have support and backup in case I have another meltdown or need to be hospitalized in the future.

In 2011, with the loss of my job that worked so well for me, I found myself in the familiar place of not knowing what the hell I was going to do. I had been stable since I moved in with my mom, and had done well at the office job. But, I didn't have the necessary computer skills to go find another office job.

I decided to get back in touch with Vocational Rehabilitation, thinking they may be able to help me to finance some computer classes or something. I was shocked to find, after they put me through psychological testing, that Voc Rehab would pay for me to go back to school in a different career, so I could attempt to go back to work full-time and stop collecting disability benefits! I had a renewed period of motivation and optimism that I might be able to get back to a "normal" life.

I applied at the local campus of Indiana University, in a Paralegal Certificate program. It was a year round program that lasted one year. I did very well in my classes, earning A's in every class. Doing well in school helped me regain confidence that had been lost over the past ten years, and it provided some structure to my days. It also provided socialization, as it was the same group of students in every class. I didn't end up making friends that I hung out with, but it was comforting to go to class with familiar faces. While I was taking classes, in January 2012, I got an opportunity to do an internship at the Prosecutor's Office of the adjoining county, which lasted for six months. I learned about the opening from one of my former case management coworkers. I enjoyed the work, as criminal law was the area of paralegal work I was interested in. I could see this as a replacement for my mental health career. I was back in a professional environment, and continued to have renewed hope for the future.

As I was working on stabilizing my life, Epiphany remained a constant. I don't think I consciously thought about the fact that she was getting older, right along with me. She was just always there, part of my life. I had to finally face her mortality early in 2012, when I noticed she was losing weight. A trip to the vet revealed a thyroid problem, and I began a long journey of trying to medicate a cat. It began with little pills, which I dutifully shoved down her throat once a day. I thought everything was dandy, until about a month later, when I found a small pile of partially dissolved pills hidden under my bed. It seemed that Epiphany learned the art of "cheeking" her meds, and hadn't ingested any in quite some time. The vet came up with plan B, which was having the pills compounded into a lotion-type of substance, which I then rubbed into the skin on the inside of her ear. Epiphany didn't care for this method either, but at least she couldn't sabotage it. Unfortunately, she continued to lose weight in spite of the medication, and the vet brought up the issue of quality of life.

Epiphany was 19 by this point, and I didn't want her to suffer in any way. I made the difficult decision to put her down. My mom drove us, as I knew I wasn't capable of doing it alone. Anyone who has ever had to put down a pet knows what a painful experience it is. I coped with Epiphany's loss much better than anyone (even I) expected. I had a typical mourning experience rather than a depressive episode, suicidal thoughts and most likely a hospitalization, which would have been my response in the past.

In January 2013 after finishing school, I was hired in my first paralegal type job at a title research company. It was only part time, but it didn't take long for me to feel overwhelmed and stressed. It involved mainly computer research in various programs, doing research on real property titles. There was a lot of money involved if you made a mistake, so I felt a lot of pressure. I didn't feel competent, although I was told I was doing fine. There were three other people in the office, and the owner came in occasionally in the afternoons. The other workers were younger than me and weren't very sociable. Everyone pretty much worked in their cubicle. I had someone training me, but I wasn't comfortable asking him questions, because it made me feel stupid.

I had been hired in anticipation of an increase in business which didn't occur. Instead, it actually slowed down. I was laid off after three months, which was a relief to me. I had been wondering how much longer I could last and was getting the familiar depression and insomnia. It hadn't taken long to realize that if I couldn't handle a "real" job on a part time basis, I wasn't going to make it full time.

I thought this would be a devastating realization for me, but it actually wasn't as bad as I expected. While I was saddened at the failure, I didn't have to be hospitalized, which would have been a given in the past. I had finally come to accept the fact that I can't work full time due to the stress, and will need to be on disability for the rest of my life. I had tried again and failed, but this time I was surprisingly okay with it.

I began looking for a part time job, and was hired at Target in August 2013. I didn't want to be a cashier but accepted an early morning stocking position. There was minimal customer contact because of it being an early morning shift, and it wasn't stressful work. It gave me some structure and extra income, as well as providing some social contact with coworkers. I liked working at Target, but the early morning hours became a problem with my sleep schedule. The regular start time was four a.m., and during peak times like back to school and Christmas, I had to start at 2:30 a.m. I managed these hours for some time, but in January 2015 it caught up with me.

I began to have insomnia regularly, and started to have a mixed episode. Dr. Turner prescribed Seroquel again, as this is what has helped when I have mixed episodes. Unfortunately, I had to take a very high dose of Seroquel in order to go to sleep, which then prevented me from waking up in the middle of the night to go to work. I took a medical leave from my job to try to get my sleep back on schedule. I missed several weeks of work, during which my supervisors were very supportive. Eventually though, I realized that working early morning hours wasn't going to work for me, and I quit my job at Target. I was unemployed again, but I was okay. I didn't do anything self-destructive throughout the time I was experiencing mixed mania, and I avoided hospitalization.

After quitting the Target job, it was back to job search mode again. I had no idea what I wanted to do, but there were several criteria to consider. It obviously needed to be part-time, preferable 20 to 25 hours per week. The hours needed to be during the day, so that I didn't disrupt my sleep again. It couldn't be too stressful, or require a ton of people contact (or I could've just taken a cashier job at Target). I was hoping it would not be too far from my home, so I wouldn't have to drive far in the winter.

I really was befuddled, because I wasn't sure what type of job I was qualified for that met my criteria. There are only so many part-time jobs, and I wasn't interested in food service or retail. I searched on-line job sites and checked the classifieds. I had been out of work for over a month when I came upon a listing for a fingerprint technician at the local Goodwill. It was a part-time position, only twenty hours per week, and was located about ten minutes from my home. I immediately applied, and received a call to arrange an interview a week later.

I interviewed twice for the job, which involved fingerprinting clients using digital technology in order to perform background checks. Goodwill contracts with a security company to perform the fingerprinting of the clients, and the security company takes care of the rest. It sounded like a great job for me, somewhat interesting with just the right amount of people contact. Best of all, the hours were Monday through Friday, 8:30 am to 12:30 pm. Perfect for me! It would even allow me to get home to lie in the sun by 1:00 pm in the summer...

I was offered the job after the second interview, and thus began the slowest hiring process I've ever experienced. I had to do a drug screen, a criminal background check, and a credit check on top of the usual reference checks. For some reason, it took the security company over a month to clear me to be a finger printer. I handled this slow transition pretty well, with only a slight amount of anxiety and minimal sleep loss.

This job, which I continue to work to this day, is the right job for me. After years of trying different part-time jobs and learning what does and does not work for me, I have a good balance. The job requires people contact, but not in a stressful way. My role with them is limited, and clear. The interactions are friendly and superficial, and I'm not expected to help them resolve any of their stressful mental health issues, or talk to them on the phone. I feel challenged enough, but not overwhelmed. I like my co-workers, and the hours are great.

I have evenings, weekends and holidays off, and most importantly I am able to maintain a consistent sleep schedule which is important for my brain chemistry. I don't get paid as much as I would at other jobs, but it doesn't matter. All the other factors are more important than the pay.

In addition to an improved job situation, my social interaction has dramatically increased. In early 2015 someone I went to high school with moved back to town from Oklahoma. We were not friends in high school, more like acquaintances. However, with some assistance from Facebook, we got reconnected after she returned to the area and started to hang out. She's an extrovert, and a very social person who is always doing something fun. She organized a woman's only social group in the area, which I joined.

Joining a social group was a huge step for me, with my social anxiety, but I did it. I have done more socially in the past year than I had since a couple years prior to the Meltdown. I've taken bus trips to two Chicago Cubs games, took the train to Chicago for "Taste of Chicago," and I took a bus trip to an Indianapolis Colts football game. I participated in a Canvas and Cocktails party (I have no artistic talent, so this was painful for me, even with the cocktails.)

By the way, I am now able to drink socially like a normal person. In the past, my relationship with alcohol was obviously unhealthy. I was not an alcoholic, but I was a binge drinker. During periods of depression I drank when I was alone at home to numb myself. I also drank when I was lonely or bored. As I've become healthier, my drinking habits have changed. I no longer drink alone, even if I'm unhappy for some reason. I drink socially, but don't drink to excess or drive while I'm drunk. In fact, I rarely get intoxicated. It's probably partly the combination of alcohol with the meds I take and partly just maturity, but being drunk isn't as pleasurable as it used to be.

Members of my social group have football watching parties, in which we go to local bars to watch Notre Dame or pro football games. These are just some of the events in which I've participated;

there have also been pool parties, movies, and dining out. In 2003 I was completely isolated. Now I have plenty of friends, and a job situation that works for me. I am open with people about my illness. I am stable, and having fun.

To this day, stressful situations still arise, but my ability to cope with them remains better than I ever would have expected. For example, in February 2014 my mom and I adopted a cat from a local rescue organization. Joylene, or Joyjoy as we call her, is a Siamese/manx mix. She is beautiful, with blue eyes. She looks like a Siamese, except she doesn't have a tail (like a manx). Unfortunately, Joyjoy is prone to urinary tract infections. In October 2015 she got a double infection, requiring two different antibiotics which had to be given consecutively. So we had to give her oral antibiotics for two straight weeks. Let's just say that Joyjoy is not thrilled with taking meds. Giving her the antibiotic with a dropper is a traumatic experience for all involved. I hold her while my mom gives her the meds. We also have to give her a pill to help cope with the repeated infections. Apparently, fluoxetine (or Prozac) is commonly prescribed to cats to help in these situations. So even my cat is on antidepressants!

Following the first week of antibiotics Joyjoy stopped eating, then she stopped pooping. She started to hide all day, and looked terrible. She cried pitifully when we talked to her or picked her up. The antibiotic was stopped, and a new one prescribed. We also had to give her an appetite stimulant, and an oral laxative. She had to have an enema. She started to eat once she took the appetite stimulant, but then had to have another enema before the laxative took effect. I'm telling you, this cat went through hell! It's very difficult for me to watch someone in pain or suffering, especially an animal I love, so this time with Joyjoy was a real trial. It was very stressful for me.

About halfway through this experience with Joyjoy, my grandma became very ill. She had fallen and broke her femur and arm. She moved to a rehab facility, where she was beginning to heal. Unfortunately, her kidneys suddenly stopped functioning and she went downhill very fast. She passed away in about a week in October 2015.

In the past, these stressors, especially because they were happening simultaneously, would've led to a crisis for me. I would've been deeply depressed, leading to sleep disruption then suicidal thinking. This time, however, I managed the stress amazingly well. I was understandably stressed and unhappy, but nothing extreme. My sleep was only minimally impacted, I was able to continue working consistently, and I had no suicidal thoughts. How I made it through this stressful time was the most recent example of the huge progress I have made in the last twelve years.

• • •

For people to understand how far I have come, I believe it is important to talk about my symptoms, past and present. I think depression is an individual thing, feeling different to different people. There are common themes like the obvious sadness and hopelessness, and also varying degrees of depression. When I was in therapy with Sharon, she would always have me rate my depression on a scale of 1 to 10. I think everyone gets depressed at a low level sometime, usually for situational reasons, but I'm going to focus on how it has felt for me to be a 10 on the depression scale.

What I call straight depression, without the mixed mania component, has not happened to me at a 10 on the scale in quite a few years. When it did happen, the sadness and hopelessness that are characteristic of depression were completely overwhelming. There was no light at the end of the tunnel, just a train waiting to run me over. I would feel really sad, but I couldn't usually cry unless I'd had a lot to drink. It sounds contradictory, but while I felt crushing psychic pain, I also felt numbness. This is often when self-harm behaviors occurred. I would cut or punch something to counteract the numbness. It would reassure me to see the blood or the swelling. It didn't hurt at the time

I cut or bruised myself, but it helped me ground myself. When the depression was especially bad, my tendency to dissociate would surface. Hurting myself physically helped bring me back to the present, even though I didn't want to be there. I didn't want to be anywhere.

When depressed at a 10, I would feel self-hatred. I loathed myself and felt like I needed to punish myself in some way. I hated my life and wanted to be dead. If I could've just willed myself to stop breathing, I would have. This is when the obsessive suicidal thoughts would enter the picture. All I could think about was the pain and hopelessness, and how I wished I were dead to escape it. Being depressed at a 10 was a selfish time. I would not think about my friends and family, or how they would be affected by my suicide. I was not thinking rationally. Thoughts of death and suicide would run through my head over and over and over and over.

Thankfully, with all the years of treatment, I am now able to refrain from being self-destructive when I am depressed. I am able to maintain more of a perspective that things will get better, and I am now much more aware of how my death would affect the people who love me. I never thought about those people in the past. I am much closer to people now, and even if I am very depressed and having suicidal thoughts, I am able to stay clear within myself that people would be devastated if I kill myself.

If I am having a full-blown mixed bipolar episode, I feel all of the above depression symptoms and then some. This is when I truly feel "crazy." During mixed episodes I continue to obsess about death and suicide, but the thoughts race quickly through my mind. It is impossible to distract myself from them. I'm completely unable to sleep, which means I have no way to escape the overwhelming feeling of despair. Insomnia happened to me during straight depression too, but is much worse during a mixed episode. I'm impulsive during these times, which makes the possibility of suicide higher. I feel unable to control myself. I become irritable, which isn't normal to my personality. I'm very agitated and will often just pace around. I still experience mixed bipolar episodes, but the early signs are now unmistakable to me. Usually I just become really anxious and completely unable to sleep. I know that when this starts happening, I need to get help before it gets worse.

I have to say I don't care for the fact that people get diagnosed with "personality disorders." I don't like describing someone's personality, especially my own, as a "disorder." As a mental health patient who has been diagnosed with two personality disorders, I find it rather insulting. However, I understand that labeling a cluster of symptoms makes it easier for treatment providers to communicate with each other about patients.

I've been diagnosed in the past with both Avoidant Personality Disorder and Obsessive-Compulsive Personality Disorder. The fact that I was not open about my symptoms with anyone was the most obvious sign of Avoidant Personality Disorder in 2003. I faked "normalcy" to hide my symptoms from friends and family, not wanting to be negatively evaluated by them if they knew the truth about how I felt. Being at all vulnerable with people caused severe anxiety, so I avoided it. Even while I was in the hospital the first time, and immediately afterward when my people knew I wasn't doing well, I continued to fake it. I don't think I consciously made a decision to fake it, I think it was just natural for me to do so. I was obviously very aware of the stigma associated with chronic mental illness and I think this may have unconsciously influenced my behavior. My family dynamic of minimizing difficulties also contributed. But, I don't remember thinking to myself "Ok, I have to act normal now so people don't think I'm crazy."

Sharon being more open with me during my Meltdown year in 2003 caused a great deal of anxiety and discomfort for me. I'm not a touchy feely person who talks a lot about my feelings in general. I get uncomfortable when anyone compliments me. For someone to say they care about me (other than a family member) causes a lot of anxiety. I've come a long way in resolving the issues described as Avoidant Personality Disorder. I'm much more open now with everyone about my symptoms and my situation. I'm much more comfortable with feeling close to people. I continue to have some social anxiety, but I don't think it's enough to get me diagnosed with Avoidant Personality Disorder any more. Obviously broadcasting my story to the world, in detail, with this book, is evidence of the progress I've made.

My other personality disorder diagnosis, Obsessive-Compulsive Personality Disorder, is sometimes helpful. It makes me more organized and efficient. I'm a responsible person. I'm very reliable and predictable. My OCPD symptoms generally revolve around the way in which I organize my life, in what I call my routines or rituals and the rules in my head that I follow. I do certain things either in a certain way or on certain days. For instance, I do laundry and tan in the tanning bed every Sunday and Wednesday. I tan, then take a shower, then start my laundry. My morning and evening routines do not vary at all either. I make a lot of lists and like to cross things off the list when I complete them. An example of a typical rule relates to shaving my legs. For about a fifteen-year period, it was a rule that I had to shave my legs every day. Never mind that they didn't need it, I had to do it.

Not following a rule or a routine causes anxiety for me. I can consciously change some rules, but it's not easy. It takes a lot of self-talk and reassurance from myself. When I'm depressed the rules become self-destructive, for example not eating while I was in the hospital in 2003, or needing to kill myself if I didn't move out of my parents' house in 1995. When I'm depressed it becomes much harder for me to change the rules for myself.

A rule that causes a great deal of anxiety, which I have never been able to change, is the rule about not being late. I show up everywhere at least ten minutes early as a result. I just sit in my car until it's appropriate to go in to the appointment. Everyone now knows this about me, and it is a source of much good-natured teasing and joking.

Having OCPD means I'm a fairly rigid person. Any type of significant change causes enormous stress and anxiety for me, even good changes. I like things to stay the same, which feels safe and comfortable. I don't even change my furniture around, for God's sake! I realize that change is a necessary and natural part of life, but it remains very stressful for me. OCPD continues to contribute to my stress tolerance being low in general.

Obsessive-Compulsive Disorder (OCD) means feeling compelled to do something irrational, not functional. In my case, my OCD symptoms are also dangerous. My OCD revolves around tanning. I've been laying in the sun since high school in the 1980s.

Despite the work Sharon and I did to try to address this issue, my obsession with tanning has continued. I enjoy tanning (except on those really hot and humid days), and I like the way I look when I have a tan. Whether it is healthy or not, being tan is part of my identity. I receive positive attention from others when I'm tan which reinforces my tanning habit. Unfortunately, these factors only make it harder to address the obsessive-compulsive issue.

Tanning is more than a hobby or a habit for me, it is OCD. It is not rational or functional. If I'm unable to lay in the sun on a sunny day, I obsess about it and become anxious. I obsessively check weather forecasts so that I can plan my tanning time. I check the UV index daily on a weather website to track how much sun I'm getting. If I have control over appointments or social engagements, I plan them in the morning or evening so as to leave prime tanning time open. I have re-scheduled appointments on sunny days, just so I could lay in the sun.

There is a large grassy area at my house where I lay out, that I call the Beach. I go out at five minutes to the hour to lay in the sun. There is a power outlet on the shed near the Beach where I plug in my radio/CD player. Until I got my current job, I'd lay out from 10:00 a.m. to 3:00 p.m., except early in the season when it's still cold in the morning. Then, I wouldn't go out until 11:00 a.m. When it's hot out,

I take a five minute break every thirty minutes. If it isn't hot, I take a ten minute break every hour. I have a specific beach towel I use, along with my tanning chair. It's all very regimented. One concession I have made since I worked with Sharon on my tanning OCD in therapy is that I now put sunscreen on my nose and eyelids. These are the areas that burn the quickest. With my current job, I'm limited to tanning only from about 1:00 pm until 3:00 pm. The rational part of me knows this is another benefit of what feels like the right job for me. But, it causes some anxiety to feel like I'm not getting enough "fresh color."

My outdoor tanning season usually lasts from sometime in April until sometime in September. I use a tanning bed the rest of the year, at least once per week. I understand that tanning is dangerous. It damages my skin and causes skin cancer. I've had basal cell carcinoma removed four times since June of 2007. I now have three scars on my face and one on my chest. I undoubtedly will continue to have to have cancer removed in the future. I go to my dermatologist every six months to get checked. I've been lucky enough not to have melanoma, the skin cancer which can kill me. People ask me what it's going to take to get me to stop tanning. It would probably take a diagnosis of melanoma before my brain would be able to stop compelling me to do this. I just hope it doesn't come to that.

• • •

In the few years leading up to the Meltdown I thought my life was pretty good. I was generally content, as long as I wasn't biologically depressed. I'd made a lot of progress in therapy and had gotten to a reasonably good place. In spite of it being stressful, I liked my job. I felt I was doing what I was meant to do, and my identity was strong. I liked my coworkers and was making fairly good money. I had a ton of debt, admittedly, but I paid my bills on time and lived a comfortable existence, independently. I didn't have a busy social life but I got enough social time to satisfy me. I was used to living with periodic episodes of depression. They had always been a part of my life.

As Sharon identified, I felt alone in my illness as a result of my tendency to put on a façade to the world, hiding how I really felt. But, I'd never known anything different. I did this automatically, and unconsciously. I didn't know what I was missing by being so disconnected from people. Although I felt generally content with my life, my negative world view and sense of isolation, in hindsight, were certainly contributing to my tendency to become easily depressed. Alcohol and suicidal thinking continued to be the result when the depression surfaced, but always resolved when the depression went away.

The Meltdown in 2003 took away any sense of contentment I felt. I was utterly and completely devastated, having lost everything. In Dante's terms, I had "abandoned all hope." I was stuck in suicidal thinking because I felt I had nothing left to live for. My life, as I had always known it, was over. I lost my job, my friends, and my identity. That year was full of despair, grief, loss and isolation. Just when I would begin to feel some hope that things would improve, something else would happen to knock me back down. It was a very dark and painful time that I wouldn't wish on anyone. I truly felt like I had entered and was descending through the circles of hell. The subsequent years included lots of ups, downs, successes and failures as I tried to navigate my way to a new identity. It felt like, with the help of Sharon (my Virgil), I was slowly climbing up through the circles of hell and finally escaped, just like Dante.

I now understand and accept that I have a severe and chronic mental illness. I'm unable to live independently, either financially or emotionally. I experience significant symptoms of anxiety on a regular basis, and I'll always go through periods of mixed mania when I'm overly stressed over a long enough period of time. I'm guessing I'll always struggle with my tanning compulsion and will always be stressed by too much change. But, I've come a long way, in many areas of my life and have healed beyond what I ever thought possible. I have come full circle and am back to feeling content with my life.

I'm more mentally stable than I've ever been. I rarely experience depression any more. I know what I need to do to minimize the likelihood of a bipolar episode, and I do it. I have completely stopped the self-destructive patterns of the past, as I know the consequences of this behavior are just not worth it. I have a network of supportive people who understand my illness and can help me. I have friends who I have fun with, and family members who I love dearly. My life is full and meaningful, despite my illness. I have actually reached a point where I am happy.

Sharon's Conclusions

Robin's depression always had both psychological and biological components. She continues to take four medications on an ongoing basis...a mood stabilizer, an antipsychotic and two antidepressants. This was the combination of medications that finally stabilized her in 2003 after her meltdown.

After she finally accepted the loss of her ability to work full-time and was settled into a part-time job that was working for her, in 2008 she and Dr. Greene made the decision to gradually decrease her Abilify. I have to admit, after the nightmare we went through to get her stabilized and knowing that Abilify was a crucial piece of the puzzle, I was nervous about her decision to try tapering off of it. I was not surprised when she destabilized as a result, but it really was amazing how fast and how severely she crashed. The familiar signs of mixed mania returned with a vengeance and suddenly, for the first time in quite a while, I was back to the familiar role of being her life line.

Robin has fully documented the events that took place after she quickly destabilized, leading to her suicide attempt and subsequent hospitalization. I don't know what would have happened if I had not been staying in close contact, and if I had not felt clear I needed to talk to Robin on the phone that night. I don't know what would have happened if I had waited longer to call, since it quickly became clear she had already begun the process of taking what she had planned to be a lethal overdose. Quite possibly, after all the work we did in therapy and all the progress Robin made in terms of accepting her illness and finding a job that worked well for her, she could have ended up dead simply because she chose to try decreasing one medication.

This experience highlighted the importance of making sure the biology of one's brain chemistry is paid attention to. Robin's suicide attempt happened because she was just not thinking clearly at all, and was experiencing the full blown ramifications of her bipolar illness. Mixed mania is a dangerous state, even for someone who usually feels completely clear that she does not want to die. I am thankful to Robin for being honest with me that night when I called, and for agreeing to go to the hospital, yet again, in order to stay alive.

The final piece of the biological puzzle was later discovered by Robin's current psychiatrist, Dr. Turner. Robin now knows when she feels depressed, anxious and stops sleeping, it is time to take Seroquel. Within a week, it usually helps. Ever since 2008, when she has begun to recognize that she is experiencing mixed mania she has been able to intervene early enough to avoid needing the hospital. She still gets depressed, and still experiences urges to drink when she feels overwhelmed. But, she is able to avoid doing so. She still experiences anxiety and racing thoughts, and still obsesses about suicide when her mixed mania starts. But now she knows what to do to get back on track, and she does it. The biological picture in terms of what her brain needs is now completely clear.

The final piece of the psychological puzzle for Robin, without a doubt, was the decision to move in with her mother. In the span of five years Robin went from not wanting her parents to know she was in the hospital, to embracing her mom and letting her in. They are so good for each other!

Unlike prior to 2008 when the hospital was the only way for Robin to experience a complete barrier to attempting suicide, thus allowing her brain to shift, she now has different barriers which have enabled her to avoid hospitalization for many years. Now that she has let her people in and feels close to her family and friends, thank God, Robin is now clear that suicide is not an option...not just when she is in the hospital, but all the time. She has become close enough to her mom and the other people she loves, that she will stay alive and avoid self-destructive behavior even when she is feeling overwhelming pain, because she does not want to devastate them. She has gone from hating herself, hating her life and wanting to die, to loving herself and her people enough to take care of her brain chemistry and avoid self-destructiveness completely.

Robin knows she may need to go to the hospital sometime to stay safe, if she is too biologically unstable. But, suicide is no longer where her brain automatically goes when she is stressed and upset. Suicidal thoughts are now an early sign of mixed mania. They are a sign that intervention is needed. It is the absence of feeling alone in her illness, or alone in general, that has helped Robin to actually change her avoidant personality traits. She has many friends, socializes regularly, and is having fun.

Living with her mom has had the added benefit of removing the pressure for Robin to support herself financially. She has been through various job changes, gone to school, made another attempt to resume working full-time, and failed. She did all of that without destabilizing enough to need to be hospitalized. When I think about where we were in 2003, I continue to be amazed by all the changes she has made.

• • •

After 2003, as I began to realize how I had been transformed by the experience with Robin, I began to think it was significant enough that it warranted writing a book about it. Of course, at that time I was still Robin's therapist. I was still very focused on helping her to recover from the devastation that had happened to her as a result of her meltdown.

But, being a writer, I kept feeling compelled to try to write a book about the significant events Robin and I had gone through. At some point, several years after things stabilized for her, I actually began to try to write the book on my own. I wrote probably twenty pages. But I was trying to disguise Robin's identity and write the book from my own perspective without Robin being aware of it. It wasn't appropriate for me, as her therapist, to talk to her about writing a book about her. At that time I was more focused on how the experience had impacted me, and I wanted to tell that story.

The problem was, it was mostly Robin's story. And, as I wrote I realized that it would be impossible to tell the story in enough detail for people to truly understand what happened, without violating Robin's confidentiality. Her issues are very significant and very specific. I couldn't reconcile a way to tell the story and honor Robin's privacy at the same time. I quickly abandoned the whole idea.

In 2008, years after I had given up on the idea of writing a book, a truly amazing thing happened. Robin, shortly after her suicide attempt and before she moved in with her mother, was still trying to come to terms with her identity as a person with a severe mental illness. She was reading various memoirs of people with bipolar disorder or severe depression. Imagine my surprise when one day, Robin came into my office and said, "I was reading a book by someone who has bipolar disorder. I think my story is as interesting as hers. I've been thinking about writing a book about my life."

Wait. What? I was shocked to hear these words come out of Robin's mouth. It is important to understand that in the fifteen years I had known Robin at that time, I had suggested about a million times that she journal as a way to process her emotions. She had, not once, made an attempt. It had become a kind of inside joke between us. I would say "Gee, journaling might help," and she would say, "yeah,

I'll get right on that." And then we would just laugh, knowing it was never going to happen.

So, I was well aware that Robin was not a writer. But, suddenly she was serious about writing a book. It didn't make sense. I asked her to explain her thinking...while inside I was already debating with myself about whether I should tell her I had also thought about writing a book.

"I have lots of time. I need more to do. I just thought it would be a good way for me to do something productive," said Robin. She said she had gotten a new computer, and thought writing a book would be a good way to use it. I couldn't believe she was serious! She had no idea how compelled I had felt to write about her story and how she impacted me, or that I had actually started trying to write about it.

During the five years following her meltdown year, I had given Robin some information about the positive changes that had occurred for me as a result of being so closely involved with her throughout the crisis. I wanted her to know that what still felt to her like a terrible experience, ultimately had a positive impact. I wanted her to know she had actually helped me by letting me in.

My gut told me in 2008 that it would be okay to let Robin know I had also thought about writing a book about our stressful year in 2003 and how it had impacted me. At that time, I wasn't yet ready to tell her I could envision a time when I would not be a therapist any more, even though I was getting clear that at some point this would likely happen. I didn't want to freak her out, and I had no particular time frame in mind. I wanted to support her in writing her own book. But, I also jokingly said something about the idea of us writing a book together "someday." Robin jumped right on it, and we talked about what a unique idea it was to have the story told by both the therapist and the client. Neither of us could remember reading a similar kind of book...probably for the same reason we could not have written the book at that time. I was still Robin's therapist. Boundary issues and all, it wasn't appropriate.

So we went on, and would joke with each other at times about "that book we'll write someday." Robin actually did spend some time writing her version of it but ended up abandoning the idea eventually. She was not a natural writer.

Meanwhile, my job was starting to get very stressful. I was in a top leadership position within the large mental health agency where I had worked throughout my entire career. In 2008, after a large sum of money had been borrowed in the form of a bond issue to build several new buildings on campus…and then the state government had made cuts to funding for mental health services, it all caught up and the agency lost a lot of money.

The bondholders were not happy with the turn the agency had taken financially and, in 2009 sent in a group of consultants to turn the business around. I was in the wrong position at the time they arrived. While I was one of the last of the executive management team to go, I knew my days were numbered. I still had the same fifteen clients I was continuing to treat, Robin included, when I was asked to pack my office and resign in January 2010.

I'll never forget having to call Robin and my other clients to let them know I would no longer be working there. I was devastated, and had to pace myself in terms of making the phone calls so as to not start crying on the phone. I was traumatized by having lost my job so suddenly, especially after working so hard to try to turn the agency around and dedicating so many years of my life to the place.

In order to be able to transition things appropriately and not feel like I was just abandoning my long-term clients, I rented a "virtual office" in a downtown office building and was able to see people within a couple of weeks. I did not ultimately stay in private practice, though, as this had never been my goal. I was able to help people get connected with new therapists and psychiatrists (Dr. Greene also ended up leaving the agency), and then I ended up taking a new administrative job, supervising social workers at a small inpatient and residential facility. Like Robin, I was not ready to give up my new identity as a mental health administrator. My days as an outpatient therapist, though, were over. And, after almost twenty years I was ready for them to be.

When we therapists are trained, nobody talks about what to do when you are ending your career. When therapists work together, it is never a topic of conversation. As I've stated, I was always quick to consult with other professionals when I was unsure about what to do in a situation with a client. But in 2010, as I was planning the end of my career as an outpatient therapist, I had no one to consult who had been through this. All the therapists I knew were still happily practicing. We could talk theoretically about what was healthy for me to do, but each client's situation was different. So, as usual I trusted my gut about how to end my work with each of my remaining clients.

For most of the fifteen clients I was still seeing, it was a somewhat painful transition in which we talked about the work we had done in therapy over a long period of time, and then we ended our relationships. For a handful of them, I decided it would be in their best interests if I offered to stay in touch, at least at a minimal level, so as not to completely trigger abandonment issues. I made it clear in these cases that I could not do anything that would be unhealthy for them, and that we would continue to talk through any issues that came up in the transition to me no longer being the therapist.

In Robin's case, I felt clear that we needed to stay in touch, and that she was in a healthy enough place that we could successfully transition our roles. I insisted she have a new therapist, at least who she could see when she was in crisis. It was important for me to know I would not have to, by default, be in the role of being her therapist if things got rough for her. She was able to get connected with a good psychiatrist and eventually a good therapist, although it was a difficult transition for her.

After a period of time during which I focused on getting settled into my new life, it was 2011 and Robin was doing much, much better than ever before. By then she had not needed to be hospitalized for several years, had a stable job, and was content with her life. We decided to have our first outside of an office meeting in our new roles as "ex-therapist" and "ex-client" at Barnes and Noble's café, as this was a place where Robin felt comfortable. After a few awkward meetings in which I told her more about myself, we became more comfortable and began to spend time together here and there mostly watching sports (a common interest). We continued to joke about "writing that book" someday. Finally, in February 2014, we actually began the process.

My new job lasted two years. I was commuting an hour each way, while also caring for my then 91-year-old mother-in-law who had moved in with my husband and I in 2003, right in the middle of Robin's meltdown year. The job itself, I found to be very stressful. All the reasons I had originally wanted to avoid middle management were happening...corporate pressure on the leadership of the agency led to me being in the impossible position of trying to please my boss and meet the corporate expectations for productivity, and keep the people I supervised happy. It became apparent to me, over time, that this job and caring for my mother-in-law at the same time, were just too much. I was stressed and exhausted. And, after the transformation that had happened in 2003, I completely trusted that things would work when I left that job. I needed to take care of myself!

I quit my stressful administrative job in 2012 and opened another private practice office, this time to do disability evaluations in order to make some income flexibly while spending more of my time caring for Peaches as her dementia progressed. Being her caretaker became my focus and was probably the most meaningful "work" I've ever done in my lifetime.

Peaches died peacefully at the age of 93 in August 2014. I had begun part-time work in long-term care facilities (nursing homes) in 2013 with the expectation, or more accurately the gut feeling, that she would eventually need to be in one. I wanted to know which places in town were the stable ones, where she would be well cared for by the staff. This strategy was successful, as we were able to get Peaches into a great facility with good care.

It is December 2015 and I continue to work, now full-time, providing diagnostic assessments, neuropsychological testing, and some psychotherapy in long-term care facilities. I love the fact that this job uses my clinical experience and skills, but is not at all stressful for me. I love working with the patients and the employees at each of the five facilities I visit each week. I am in charge of no one, and nothing. Unlike when I was an outpatient therapist, the patients I see now are cared for and supervised by 24-hour staff when I am not there. I don't have to worry about them killing themselves. I have come full circle in my career, back to the place where I am happy just seeing my clients and doing my paperwork.

I cannot finish telling the story of Robin and how she impacted my life, without pointing out the irony that has come from our respective life experiences since the meltdown year of 2003. In 2010, I knew losing my job happened for some reason, but could not imagine what good could come from such a painful experience. Being asked to pack my office and resign was a big blow to my self-esteem and my identity, similar to Robin's feelings in 2003. I was stuck for a while in my own career identity crisis, similar to hers. I now know losing that job was one of the best things that ever happened to me, as it allowed me to ultimately find a much better sense of balance in my life...just like Robin.

Also like Robin, I now have a low stress job that works for me, and I am much more focused on spending time with and caring about the people I love. I have much more time and energy to take better care of myself and my health. The spiritual lesson I worked so hard to teach Robin for so many years...that we are not defined by our careers, and our identities do not need to involve a particular type of job, seems to have now become clear in my life too. It was very easy for me to say all of this to Robin back then, when I was settled into my career and had no threats to my security or my identity. Now, having lived my own version of this lesson, I can say the same thing but with more conviction.

As Robin does, I now live my life consistently with what I believe our spiritual purpose is, which is to learn to love ourselves and others. When I was working so hard to teach Robin these spiritual beliefs, ironically, in many ways I was not living them myself. The transformations that happened for us both during 2003, and then during the subsequent years of ups and downs, have led to us now living similar meaningful and balanced lives.

Robin, like me, has truly gotten better at dealing with ambiguity and change. While she still has significant issues with obsessive-compulsive anxiety and has to make sure to minimize stress in order to avoid destabilizing, she has created a life for herself that allows her to deal with change within the context of support and awareness of herself and her illness. She really is, finally, happy. Her illness does not define her identity. She is living a life of stability, balance and meaning.

I will forever be grateful to Robin for allowing me to be her therapist for so long, which enabled me to be transformed by her strength, her courage and especially her willingness to stay alive in the face of such overwhelming and unimaginable pain. When I think back to all the stress, worry and anguish Robin and I experienced throughout 2003 and the subsequent years, I am so glad we have both come to a point in our lives where we each feel a sense of peace. There are no words to fully describe what an honor it has been for me to be a part of her journey from despair to deliverance.

Acknowledgments

ANYONE WHO HAS ever written a book knows it is not a solo process. Many people were involved and should be acknowledged. Robin and Sharon would like to thank all the friends and family who encouraged us to pursue this project and see it through to the end. Daniel DeVinney, our editor, was instrumental in helping us get out of our own heads and look at our writing from the perspective of the reader. We are grateful to him for his honesty, his sensitivity and his attention to detail.

For all the people who read various drafts of the manuscript and gave us feedback, we thank you for your time and your thoughts. David Wolf, Elaine Barlin, Lin Hoppel, Giselle Urruti, Christi Carr, Terri Huegel, Ellen Wildman, Dawn Bontrager, Susan Burton, Joseph DeVinney, Andree Wolf, Marion DeVinney, Julie Simmons and Chris Schoeninger all read the book at various points and were very helpful and encouraging with their words. If we left anyone out of the list, please forgive us. We are especially grateful to Jamie DeVinney, Rhoda Massanari and Jessica Maich for their willingness to give very thoughtful and brutally honest feedback, which led to a complete re-write after the first draft. Thank you all for caring enough to tell us the truth.

We will be eternally thankful to Bill O'Hanlon and the members of his on-line class on how to write and publish a book, which took place during the winter of 2014. It was this class, where we received feedback from others on-line and on the phone, that got the project started and focused. During this class we became inspired to start our blog. The blog was instrumental in keeping us motivated to continue writing the story even as life got in the way. Thanks to everyone within the WordPress community who read the blog, "liked" it, commented, supported us and continue to be interested in our story.

Finally, thanks and much love to Charlene Personette and David Groff...the two people in the Universe who support Robin and I the most. Without their unconditional love and encouragement, this story would not likely have had such a happy ending.

About the Authors

ROBIN PERSONETTE HOLDS a bachelor's degree in psychology from Indiana University. Over the years of working in the mental health field, Personette has been a psychiatric technician, a supervisor at a group home, and a case manager at a community mental health center. Personette enjoys reading, watching sports, and spending time with family. She recently successfully navigated a major life change by moving to Florida with her mother.

Sharon DeVinney, PhD, earned her doctoral degree in clinical psychology from Purdue University. With ten years' clinical practice at a mental health center and eight years' experience as an administrator at the same center, DeVinney has led a life serving the mental health community. Currently she provides clinical service in long-term care facilities. In her free time, she enjoys writing, reading, and spending time with friends and family. DeVinney lives in South Bend, Indiana, with her husband, David.

Read more about their story at www.despairtodeliverance.com.

www.ingramcontent.com/pod-product-compliance
Lightning Source LLC
Chambersburg PA
CBHW060239290526
45789CB00001B/118